# HUMAN RIGHTS ON DUTY

## Principles for better policing: International lessons for Northern Ireland

**Mary O'Rawe**
**Dr. Linda Moore**

# Foreword

This report is presented in the hope that it will contribute to a constructive and creative dialogue around policing in Northern Ireland. It does not give easy answers but highlights principles and practice which should inform and shape new policing arrangements.

Many people have helped and advised us on a number of levels. We thank them all, in particular a great debt of gratitude is owed to Maggie Beirne for her tireless efforts in keeping the process on track.

Finally we would like to acknowledge the enormous support given by our respective partners and sons, especially Jack who undertook a number of field visits before he was born.

Mary O'Rawe
Linda Moore

# Contents

# *Preface*

The Committee on the Administration of Justice (CAJ) is an independent cross-community organisation dedicated to the protection and promotion of human rights in Northern Ireland. CAJ has been active in researching, publishing and campaigning around issues of policing since its inception. Our list of publications (see Appendices) shows that many of our reports to date have been devoted to specific policing issues such as accountability, complaints against the police, public order or harassment. The goal of this current report is to look at policing from a much broader perspective.

The origins of this research project lie in the fact that there was a burgeoning of public interest in policing issues in the immediate wake of the loyalist and republican cease-fires in 1994. CAJ, seeking to make a constructive contribution to this debate, and thanks to the generosity of charitable trusts such as the Ford Foundation, commissioned two expert researchers to carry out a detailed comparative study of policing across a number of jurisdictions.

> *Mary O'Rawe, a barrister and lecturer-in-law at the University of Ulster, has had extensive knowledge of policing in Northern Ireland as a legal practitioner, academic, and in her volunteer work in the peace movement and on justice issues.*

> *Dr Linda Moore, lectured from 1993-1996 in criminology at Edge Hill University College and is co-author of several publications on policing in Northern Ireland. She is now working in NIACRO's youth justice unit.*

This report is the result of eighteen months' work carried out by these two researchers. CAJ's executive would like to thank them warmly for the highly professional and expert way in which they approached the enormous task they were given. We would also like to take the opportunity to thank the hundreds of others who contributed, many of whom are leading experts in the field, and often senior figures in policing in their countries, and whose names are all listed in the acknowledgement pages (Appendix 1). The end-result we believe provides an exciting, constructive, and important contribution to the debate on policing in Northern Ireland.

CAJ Executive
November 1997

# *Introduction*

## Policing: its centrality to the pursuit of peace

The Committee on the Administration of Justice (CAJ) believes that abuses of human rights are wrong in themselves but also that they have fuelled the conflict in Northern Ireland. This report starts from the premise that only by addressing issues of justice, equity and equality before the law, can the conflict be resolved. Effective and impartial policing is one of the most central components in any debate on justice and the rule of law.

The origins of this report lay with the extensive public and official debates which were initiated around policing in the wake of the paramilitary cease-fires at the end of 1994. The issues raised included: whether there was any need for change at all; what significance, if any, should be accorded to the symbols of policing (uniform, name, flying of the flag); how could the force become more representative; were mechanisms for accountability sufficient; how could the police take on a more normal policing function than previously. It was clear to CAJ that an important component in any fundamental review of policing ought to be an assessment of good and bad practice in other jurisdictions. Although the subsequent breakdown in the IRA cease-fire stalled the public discussions around policing, we persevered with the research since it was clear to us that the powers and nature of the police service would remain matters requiring serious public attention.

The completion of our basic research was followed in quick succession by a number of extraneous factors which will hopefully resurrect the intense public interest in policing witnessed a few years ago. First, there was a change of government. After some 18 years of Conservatism, a new UK government was elected with a clear mandate to effect radical social change. Second, there are now cease-fires in place by the major loyalist and republican groups in Northern Ireland, which at the very least allow people to envisage the possibility of peace in the future. Third, historic political negotiations have begun, involving most of the major political parties. CAJ would argue that issues of policing need to be addressed whether there are cease-fires or not, and whether there are political negotiations underway or not. However, the window of opportunity provided at this time means that whereas we had always hoped that this report would make a constructive contribution to the debate on policing, we now can also hope that it will be a particularly timely contribution.

# Policing: the context for this project

This research is founded on the fact that policing is a function carried out in the name of society as a whole. Accordingly, it is not merely desirable for people to discuss and critique policing - it is a civic responsibility to monitor closely how policing is carried out, and to ensure that it is discharged in accordance with international principles, and with respect for all. Criticism, if fair, cannot and should not be dismissed. It is in the interests of the police and society as a whole that policing be subjected to regular and intense scrutiny.

Much of the debate in Northern Ireland so far has focused on the "disband" versus "reform" argument. Our report makes no simple choice between these options, both because they create a somewhat false dichotomy and because this does not facilitate constructive debate. We do, however, give some important pointers about police change; we highlight the principles which should permeate policing; and we indicate how other societies have introduced radical change sometimes by disbanding, and sometimes by reforming, their current policing structures.

Our research would indicate that there are certain key values for policing in a democracy. Jones et al (1996: 190) for example, identified these to be: *equity; delivery of service; responsiveness; distribution of power; information; redress; and participation.* It is not our intent in this report to provide a detailed critique of the RUC against each of these measures in turn. While this could be a valuable exercise in its own right, and CAJ has explored many of these issues in other publications, our experience of policing in Northern Ireland suggested that something more fundamental would be required. Accordingly, we sought instead to explore how these values are being pursued, and what good practice exists, outside Northern Ireland, and whether this might have any application to the situation here.

While we discuss a broad range of policing issues, we believe, and this is confirmed by our research into international comparisons, that policing cannot be viewed in a vacuum. Policing is not only about how individual officers respond to pressure on the streets but it is about a whole array of factors which influence the reality and perception of policing. The Royal Ulster Constabulary (RUC) itself has acknowledged that it has had to work in extraordinary circumstances. The toll of 297 deaths and 8,168 injuries to police officers between 1969 and 1996 is poignant testimony to this fact. The existence of such a serious threat from paramilitaries, a framework of constant and all-pervasive emergency legislation, the origins and history of policing in the state, the authority and reliance invested in the police by government, the serious communal and class divisions within society and their differential experience of policing, have all had their effect. This report cannot hope to address all of these issues in any detail, but the commentary and recommendations are made with due cognisance of this context.

Our research took as a starting point that policing by consent is a natural objective in any liberal democracy, but also recognised the special problem the concept poses in divided societies like Northern Ireland. It is harder here for the police to win consent for several reasons. With society deeply divided about the legitimacy of the state, there is a real risk that people will also be divided about the legitimacy of the police institutions established by that state. There is also the problem that serious armed conflict, much of it directed at the security forces as emblematic of the state, has meant that the police have to protect themselves against attack. The methods used to do this can result in the police distancing themselves from communities (by the building of fortress type stations and joint police-army patrols in some areas). The RUC has had to deal with more difficult (and often violent) conflicts than their colleagues in more peaceful societies. However, despite the violence waged against the police and the more militarised style of policing in Northern Ireland, the RUC remains in principle a civilian police institution (and describes itself as a police service). Policing by consent must be at the heart of this philosophy, however difficult it may prove in practice.

While policing by consent remains an ideal, at its core policing everywhere, and not just in Northern Ireland, is about the management of conflict. If there was no conflict between individuals, or between groups, policing would be unnecessary. Clearly, it is impossible for even the best police service to please all the people all the time. As Robert Reiner argues, policing by consent cannot imply complete and universal approval(1992: 5). However, the philosophy of policing by consent implies that the role of the police is to manage conflict in the interests of society as a whole. The police must act as neutral arbiters between opposing sides. By acting fairly and impartially they can hope to win support for their right to police.

In Reiner's words, for the police to be accepted as legitimate it is crucial that "*the broad mass of the population, and possibly even some of those who are policed against, accept the authority, the lawful right of the police to act as they do, even if disagreeing with or regretting some specific actions.*"(Reiner, 1992). However, in policing the conflict in Northern Ireland, the RUC as an institution has failed to win the support of important sections of the community - especially within working class areas (O'Mahony et al, 1997). Given this, police are not simply managing the conflict, they have become part of the conflict. We would argue strongly that the project of building peace cannot be effectively addressed without an informed debate around the creation of effective, accountable policing.

## Research Methodology

This research project began from the long-held CAJ contention that basic minimum international human rights standards must be adhered to in any society committed to the rule of law. These standards have, furthermore been endorsed by the government. The report will highlight at appropriate places in the text the international law which is relevant to policing. However, key elements in the research were to go beyond a simple reiteration of principles and to comment on how these principles have been put into practice in other jurisdictions. Given the centrality of policing to the conflict in Northern Ireland, it was thought particularly useful to examine and analyse a number of key jurisdictions which were themselves emerging from violent conflict or which had engaged upon a process of major transition and change. It was, therefore, considered important to look at policing in long-established democracies such as Canada, Belgium, Netherlands and Australia, as well as societies attempting to totally restructure policing arrangements, such as Spain, El Salvador, and South Africa.

In pursuing this comparative approach there was no intention to look for an ideal model for policing, or to suggest that any model could be imported wholesale to Northern Ireland. We are indeed sure that no single ideal model exists, since policing must be responsive to local needs and realities. Equally, in a short research project, we cannot claim to have become experts on policing in any or all of the countries studied. However, by meeting and corresponding with those in each jurisdiction who are experts in their field, much insight has been gained. This report seeks to convey what has been learned from both the successes and the mistakes made elsewhere.

Drawing on the debates already in the public arena, and after consultation with a number of independent academic and professional experts, we identified a number of issues for study, for example: securing a representative police service; ensuring that policing respects the rights of all and that a culture of rights is inculcated in police officers of all ranks; how to ensure effective accountability; the pre-requisites for a credible and effective complaints system; the functions of policing in a divided society; the relevance of international standards for policing in Northern Ireland; policing structures and the role of community policing; and the conditions for introducing change or ensuring that transition is effectively managed.

The research methodology included a literature survey, the preparation of written questionnaires, the appointment of local researchers in each of the core jurisdictions, an extensive gathering of written resource material, and a series of field visits to the core jurisdictions.

**1.    *Questionnaires:***    A wide-ranging questionnaire was developed and adapted for use in key jurisdictions - with academics, police personnel, government ministers, civil servants, civilian oversight bodies, community activists, human rights lawyers, complaints investigators, members of police service boards and police authorities, people in community fora, police trainers etc.    The questionnaire raised a complex and extensive number of issues ranging from the structure of police forces and accountability arrangements in a given jurisdiction, to issues of representation and management of change in times of transition. The questionnaire was piloted, translated into French and Spanish, and distributed widely to relevant individuals. The purpose of the questionnaire was not to secure quantitative data, but to gain detailed information prior to fieldwork. Accordingly, the questionnaire was long and required a great commitment of time and energy on the part of respondents. We were fortunate enough to receive forty detailed responses.

2. *Local Researchers:* Initial exploratory work regarding the chosen jurisdictions resulted in the identification and employment of well qualified local researchers. The local researchers, all with particular expertise in their field (for details see Appendix 1) assisted with the identification of local issues, prepared literature surveys, provided and gathered extensive resource materials, identified key stakeholders in the areas of interest, helped in the development and distribution of the questionnaire, and advised upon and facilitated all the practical arrangements around the field visits to the jurisdiction.

3. *Written resources/literature surveys:* A review of primary and secondary sources was undertaken. This survey, even if non-exhaustive, was very helpful in confirming that the issues relating to policing in other jurisdictions mirrored the concerns identified at an early stage in the research project in relation to Northern Ireland. As the project developed, an immense collection of written material was brought together and was drawn upon for the preparation of this report. A select bibliography is attached in Appendix. The project has gathered together a unique compilation of key texts on policing in a variety of jurisdictions around the world. The very size and diversity of the collection has meant that it has not proved possible fully to exploit it all in a single report; we hope to make the material more widely available in due course. In the interim

we have produced separately from this report, an annotated bibliography, covering over 800 documents, which is available upon request.

**4.    *Field visits:*** Field visits to a number of jurisdictions – Australia (New South Wales and Queensland), Belgium, Canada, El Salvador, Netherlands, South Africa, and Spain – the Basque Country and Catalonia - were undertaken between September 1996 and April 1997. The field visits comprised work with the local researchers in building up the written research base, interviews and informal contacts with key stakeholders, and detailed discussions around the topics raised in the questionnaires previously distributed. Sometimes the brief for the field visit was very wide and touched on all the various issues under review; on occasion, specific issues of interest were the main focus. Personal interviews in relevant jurisdictions with government ministers, police officers, administrators, academics, and civil liberties activists, were invaluable in developing a sense of both good and bad practice which might have some relevance to the situation in Northern Ireland. We had anticipated that there might be problems of access to government ministers and high-ranking police officers, given the busy nature of their lives.  In every country visited, however, we were delighted with the access given and the time taken to explain to the researchers the intricacies of the different situations. The openness of the process was only matched by its frankness: whether talking of successes or failures, the vast majority of those interviewed were honest and self-critical.

# Report Structure

The report which follows brings together the mass of material collected under certain specific themes of particular relevance to Northern Ireland.

- **representation:** how, particularly in a divided society, and one where the legitimacy of policing is challenged, can a police service which is genuinely representative of the whole society which it is meant to serve be established?

- **training:** having tried to secure a representative body of officers, how do we ensure that their training inculcates in them important principles of human rights, equality, impartiality, and service?

- **legal accountability:** what legal mechanisms for accountability are required to ensure that the police provide a proper service to the whole community without fear or favour?

- **democratic accountability:** what are the mechanisms by which society can play an active role in designing and monitoring the kind of police service it wants?

- **structures:** what should we be looking for in any proposals regarding the structure of policing?

- **transition:** the above changes, if they are to occur, are dependent on those responsible consciously determining to leave behind the legacy of the past and to bring about fundamental change. This chapter will explore how transition and change has been introduced elsewhere and what lessons are of interest to Northern Ireland.

At the end of every chapter there are a number of conclusions and recommendations, and these are all reproduced in an executive summary. Some of the conclusions run like a thread through the whole report since they are relevant to each topic in turn. As such they can be usefully highlighted here:

1. Changes to policing are both necessary and feasible. The key component for successful change is sufficient political will to bring such change about, though change of any kind is more easily managed with the active participation of those most directly affected. While change is nearly always initially feared and obstructed, it is very often embraced in due course by its stoutest critics.

2. There is no single ideal model of policing but there are many interesting lessons to be learnt from other jurisdictions.

3. Issues of policing are frequently inter-related, so that concerns, for example, about the under-representation of certain social groups cannot be dealt with in isolation from training, or accountability, or structures, or powers. Accordingly, the issues have to be addressed in a holistic fashion and cannot be dealt with in a piecemeal or tokenistic way.

4. Some aspects of policing cannot be resolved outside of the framework of a broad consensus about society's needs and are therefore dependent on reaching political or constitutional settlements. At the same time, it may be difficult if not impossible to reach such settlements without progress on policing, given the centrality of justice issues to the conflict. Progress on some aspects of policing might pave the way for dealing with other issues.

Perhaps the main problem facing any debate in Northern Ireland about policing at the current time is the fact that people do not experience policing in the same way, and do not share a common perception of policing. Given this, the need for change, still less the form it should take, is not a matter of consensus. While recognising this, the report attempts to go beyond what divides people and look at what could unite them in terms of what every society has the right to expect from its police. No-one would argue against the need to have a police service that is representative, responsive, accountable and respectful of the rights of all. The objective of this report is that, in showing how these goals are achieved elsewhere, a growing consensus could evolve here about policing objectives and the standards by which policing should be measured.

# Chapter One

# *A representative police service – diversity and cultural awareness*

## Introduction

Policing within society takes many forms and formal state policing is only one facet of a much wider spectrum. Family, individual support networks, and communities are all important in preventing crime, both by their very presence, and by running specific projects and schemes. Building upon and working alongside such initiatives allows state policing to carry out its functions by consent.

As Lord Scarman has argued: *"The success of policing operations depends in the last resort not upon questions of technique or professional expertise, but upon the degree of confidence felt by society in its police"* (Scarman in Roach & Thomaneck, 1985: 7). Securing the consent of those policed is the goal of every police force we studied, including the Royal Ulster Constabulary (RUC).[1] Policing by consent, however, can take place only if those being policed believe that policing is being carried out impartially and on behalf of the whole community, rather than on behalf of particular groups within it. A representative police force is not a panacea, but it contributes both to the reality and the perception of impartiality. Our research has shown that coercion tends to be felt most keenly by those who do not feel they have any direct stake in the organisation of policing. Broadening ownership of the police agency to as wide a spectrum of society as possible helps to build the trust

---

[1] "The watchwords are consent and service" (NIO, 1996: section 1.7).

necessary for police and community to work in tandem, and to create a model of policing by consent.

Frequent reference is made by the RUC to its commitment to creating an inclusive representative force. Yet in spite of this stated commitment, and the demands of international law in this regard,[2] Northern Ireland provides clear evidence of how the under-representation of certain groups can seriously damage relationships between the police and a large section of the society they police[3]. The RUC is by no means alone in this regard. Every jurisdiction visited exhibited some degree of alienation between its police force and certain of its people, for example the Aboriginal community in Australia, or the black and first nation communities in Canada. In many countries, women and gays provide examples of often less vocal, but no less real, marginalisation. Our research further concluded that police organisations unable to command respect will feel compelled to rely more heavily on coercion, in turn provoking increased opposition.[4]

The RUC recognises that, with only 10.5% regular female officers, and 7.5% Catholic officers, it is an unrepresentative force and that something must be done to rectify this situation

---

[2] In 1979, the United Nations General Assembly resolved that *"... like all agencies of the criminal justice system, every law enforcement agency should be representative of and responsive to the community as a whole."* UN General Assembly Resolution 34/169 of 17 December 1979.

[3] See Northern Ireland synopsis.

[4] This was most evident in the pre-transition phases in the countries visited. In states where the police completely lacked legitimacy (e.g. South Africa and El Salvador) they relied on brute force. However, in those countries where police relations with the broader society were better (e.g. Australia) their poor relationship with some communities – e.g. Aboriginals - has contributed to resistance and a cycle of violence. This 'vicious circle' of lack of co-operation leading to increased repression, leading to increased alienation, and therefore a lack of co-operation, has been well described in relation to black communities in England by Lea and Young (1984). They observe that it is not only the individual or group directly affected by repressive policing that becomes alienated but that there is a spiral effect throughout the community.

(HMIC, 1996: 22-23). Yet despite this recognition of the problem, the number of Catholics, nationalists, and women remains woefully inadequate. In other jurisdictions, the pressure to become a more representative force has often come about as a result of a crisis in policing, whether caused either directly by community unrest or, on occasion, by media exposure of serious individual instances of racist or other unacceptable behaviour.[5] Many of the police organisations studied for this research project have struggled with somewhat similar issues of representation, and it is clear that some have fared better than others in establishing good practice. In the final analysis, effective change requires a commitment to change coming from inside as well as outside the police service concerned.

In each of the different jurisdictions visited, three areas of concern were raised in any discussion of representation - the under-representation of particular groups within the police, relationships with minority communities, and the ethos and culture of the force. This chapter will first summarise some of the problems facing the RUC, and consequently society, in relation to these issues. We will then suggest some strategies for change in the light of international experience.

## The RUC - a service for all the community?

> *"The object of policing must be that the composition of the police fully reflects that of the society the police serve. Nothing less will suffice."* Lord Scarman ( in Roach & Thomaneck, 1985: 9)

---

[5] See chapter 6 and footnote 4. In Australia for example public disquiet over the findings of the Royal Commission into Aboriginal Deaths in Custody in the 1980s created demands for change. A fly-on-the-wall documentary *Cop it Sweet* in 1992 further fuelled public concerns (Chan, 1997).

There are difficulties for the police in achieving the goal of diverse representation. Some individuals and communities may feel that, for their own personal, cultural, political, or religious reasons, the police service is an inappropriate career for them. Nevertheless, it is in the interests of society, and of policing, that police membership be as much a mirror-image of society as possible, so that the police is perceived to be and in fact is representative and knowledgeable about the whole community. This is not just an argument about individual officers from minority communities understanding the population of 'policed' communities better. It would be too simplistic to suggest that, for example, black officers will necessarily relate better to black individuals or black communities than white officers - black officers can obviously behave as insensitively as white officers, or more so.[6] It is, more fundamentally, about the commitment of the organisation as a whole to understanding and working with all sections of society.

## 1. Under-Representation of Women within the RUC

The RUC, like many police forces, is a largely male institution. After a successful case of sexual discrimination was taken against the force in 1987, a working group was set up by the Equal Opportunities Commission (EOC) and the police authorities.[7] The working group made a large number of recommendations, and yet despite great progress being made in terms of new policies and procedures, little appears to have been achieved in terms of increasing women's representation.

---

[6] Brogden & Shearing (1993) cite reports of black police officers enthusiastically adopting brutal tactics against their fellow black citizens. *"African police... taking their cue from their European superiors, are especially inclined to assault Africans before and after arrest".*

[7] See Johnston –v- Chief Constable of the RUC and follow up outlined in EOC press release 11 August 1993.

The RUC faces problems in at least three areas: recruiting and retaining women, a male-dominated working environment, and the policing of women.

## *Representation*

Women are poorly represented in the RUC, making up just over 10 per cent of the total force. While this percentage is not unusual in comparison to other forces, it is clearly not a satisfactory situation. HMIC says of female representation in the RUC that *"Representation in the regulars and full time reserve remains disappointingly low, at an overall 9.1% in comparison with England and Wales at 14.5%"*. Moreover, female officers are over-represented in certain occupational groups and in lower ranks.[8]

## *Working environment*

Women within policing organisations face all the usual problems of working women, but also have the increased stress of working within what are essentially male-dominated institutions. Although there is no typical sexual harasser and no typical harassment site, research has identified certain organisational features which indicate a greater likelihood that harassment will occur (Brown, 1993: 16). Several of these factors are present within the RUC. The characteristics are:

-   the organisation has less than 20% of women in the workplace (the RUC has about 10%);
-   there are lone women present in organisational locations (anecdotal evidence would suggest that this happens in the RUC);

---

[8] Women make up 17.2% of police constables, 6.2% of sergeants, 4.1% of inspectors, 3.9% of Chief Inspectors, 2.5% of superintendents, and none at higher levels (HMIC, 1996: 22-23).

- the percentage of women managers/supervisors is lower than the proportional representations in the workplace (women in the RUC tend to be under-represented at higher ranks);
- uneven distribution of women in different departments/specialisms (within the RUC, women tend to be over-represented in particular areas and under-represented in others eg 5.3% within traffic, 7.3% in training and 56.2% in abuse - HMIC, 1996).
- there are sexually explicit materials present in the workplace (the RUC has anti-harassment procedures in place which are intended to prohibit the display of sexually explicit material).
- the organisation tolerates obscene/profane language in the workplace ('profane' language appears to be common within RUC 'canteen culture' – Brewer & Magee, 1991; Ellison, 1997).

*Police treatment of women*

The macho occupational culture of policing also has an effect on the police's treatment of female civilians. Brewer and Magee (1991: 52-53) talk of the ambiguous attitudes to rape in the police, and a study of the RUC response to domestic violence shows that this crime is inadequately and often insensitively policed (McWilliams & McKiernan, 1993). Robbie McVeigh (1994: chapter 8) found that police harassment of young women was experienced in a specifically gender-based context.

## 2. Under-Representation of Catholics and Nationalists within the RUC

Her Majesty's Inspector of Constabulary, in the course of his regular inspections of the RUC, has commented on the particular importance of balanced representation in a divided society (HMIC, 1996: 23). He also recently concluded that, despite efforts by the RUC to try and encourage Catholic recruitment, *"little has so far been achieved."* (HMIC, 1996: 2). Current figures show that only 7.5% of RUC members are Catholics (and yet Catholics make up over 40% of the population of Northern Ireland). Recent research has suggested that even these stark figures may be misleading since they appear to include Catholic officers of non-Northern Ireland origin (a group not normally counted by the Fair Employment Commission when assessing the religious composition of a workforce) (Ellison, 1997a).

Many reasons have been offered in explanation of this under-representation of Catholics. People will hesitate to join a force which has been specifically targeted by paramilitary violence. Between 1969 and 1996, 196 RUC officers and 101 RUC Reserve officers have been killed, and 8,168 officers in total have been injured.[9] In and of itself, this does not however explain the discrepancy between Catholic and Protestant recruitment. More relevant to this disparity is the charge that intimidation is deployed particularly by paramilitaries, or others in the nationalist community, to deter Catholics from joining the force. While, official police and government comments on under-representation often emphasise this reason for low levels of Catholic recruitment, there has been little academic research done on the issue.[10]

The possibility of indirect intimidation, though equally under-researched, must also be considered. For example, given the highly segregated nature of residential patterns in Northern Ireland, the perceived threat of violence in some communities

---

[9] Statistics on deaths from Chief Constable's report (RUC, 1996: 85), and injuries (RUC Press Office November 1997.

[10] Among the few studies which have been done are NISRA regular Community Attitude Surveys which ask respondents for their reasons as to why they would or would not join the police.

could well mean that RUC recruits would feel the need to relocate. The suggestion that officers could face difficulties in safely returning home for visits to family or friends would clearly be a further important deterrent to recruitment (Ellison, 1997: 257-258). Although police recruits face somewhat similar problems if they want to continue residing in certain unionist communities (Ryder, 1997), there is little disagreement that this kind of deterrent would disproportionately affect potential recruits from nationalist areas.

However, experiences from other jurisdictions suggest that the causes of serious under-representation are often more complex still. Any analysis of the under-representation of Catholics and nationalists in the RUC must not ignore or downplay the alienation of many in those communities. International comparisons highlight, for example, that people from communities which have experienced violence and harassment at the hands of the security forces, or in which the legitimacy and impartiality of policing is seriously challenged, are less eager than others to want to play a part in a policing institution.[11] It is, therefore, only in exploring such questions in depth that one can hope to develop a series of effective measures which will bring about genuine change.

Concerns about the use of lethal force, allegations of collusion with loyalist groups, the use of plastic bullets and the weakness of accountability structures, all attested to by leading international human rights groups,[12] contribute to a legitimacy-gap between the RUC and civilians – particularly Catholics and nationalists (NISRA, 1996; Ellison, 1997; PANI, 1997). While RUC officers justify quasi-military style policing and saturation

---

[11] See Hamilton et al, 1995:45-48; Pollak, 1993:61. A report of the New South Wales Police Service (1994) found that a complete transformation of perceptions about policing in Aboriginal communities would be necessary before Aboriginals would consider joining the police.

[12] Amnesty International annual reports (1995-1997); Human Rights Watch 1991, 1992, 1997; Lawyers Committee for Human Rights (1993, 1996).

policing within nationalist areas by reference to the existence of a "terrorist campaign" against the state, many residents of these areas feel that they are being treated as potential criminals by this 'over-policing'. There is concern about how the RUC treat Catholics both as suspects and as victims of crime (particularly politically motivated crime) (Brewer in Stringer & Robinson, 1992; Breen in Breen et al, 1995).

## 3. RUC relationships with working class communities and young people

The issue of the composition of the force is both influenced by relationships with the civilian population, and will in its turn influence those relationships. Research by Brewer and Magee (1991) and Ellison (1997) found, for example, that RUC officers tend to stereotype the Catholic population as 'decent' Catholics or 'bad' Catholics.[13] The actions of 'bad' Catholics are seen to justify the heavy policing tactics used in working class Catholic areas. Yet Brewer warns against generalising about 'Catholic' attitudes and suggests that intra-communal divisions are evident, for example between 'Catholics' and 'nationalists' (the latter being less supportive of the RUC). Brewer also notes that Catholics in higher socio-economic groups tend to be more supportive of the RUC than those lower down the socio-economic scale (Brewer in Stringer and Robinson, 1992).

In a major study about community attitudes to policing, carried out before the public order disturbances around Drumcree in 1996, the findings suggest that there is a considerably worse relationship between working class urban Catholics and the

---

[13]According to this theory 'good' Catholics secretly welcome the RUC in their areas but are too intimidated to display their support; 'bad' Catholics (i.e. republicans?political activists) are hostile to the RUC. The latter category can also include the unemployed, who are seen as scroungers.

police than that experienced by their middle-class or rural co-religionists (O'Mahony et al, 1997). There has however been some speculation as to whether this class division is so marked in the wake of Drumcree.

Similarly, the Protestant and unionist community should not be seen as monolithic. Although surveys suggest that satisfaction with the RUC is higher amongst Protestants, at times tensions have emerged between the force and some within that community. After the signing of the Anglo-Irish Agreement in 1985, some loyalists felt that the police were 'selling them out' (Paisley in Kennedy, 1995). Certainly by the time of the public debate around policing which mushroomed in the wake of the cease-fires in 1994, it was clear that there was much dissatisfaction with policing to be found also in loyalist working class areas.[14] More recently still, tensions between the RUC and unionists have risen sharply in the context of the marching disputes, which led to many police officers being intimidated out of their homes,[15] and in June 1997 to a policeman being killed in Ballymoney.[16]

It is inevitable that in a politically complex society the police will find themselves being criticised by one group or another, and often by several groups at different times. In some instances this can be presented as a positive sign of police independence and impartiality.[17] However, given the particular divisions in Northern Ireland, sometimes independence from unionist domination is exemplified by the fact that the police

[14] McVeigh (1994) and Hamilton et al (1995) provide evidence of a tense relationship between some young, working-class Protestants and the police. See also *the New Ulster Defender*, December 1995:5; the Progressive Unionist Party submission to NIO on policing, 1995; and Ulster Democratic Party policy statement carried in *New Ulster Defender*, April 1995.
[15] CAJ (1996: 85).
[16] *The Newsletter*, 2 June 1997.
[17] Brewer (1993) argues that the RUC's refusal to associate itself with unionist opposition to the Anglo Irish Agreement is an indication of the force's impartiality and professionalism.

have lost support in Protestant areas. In fact, a focus on the different attitudes held by Catholic and Protestant communities can obscure the fact that these communities have many shared experiences. Some of the resentment towards the RUC in working class Protestant areas has little to do with police attempts to distance themselves from unionism, and more to do with the police using the same methods of harassment and violence against Protestants as against Catholics (McVeigh, 1994: chapter 7).

Young people (especially men) in working class communities often report serious problems with the police. This problem is obviously not peculiar to the RUC, but is experienced by many police forces around the world. The Police Authority for Northern Ireland, recognising this problem, has established a special committee to look into how the police service can be made more responsive to young people and youth culture.[18] Many of the issues raised in this chapter, and others, about making and presenting the police service as less authoritarian and less state-representative, could help in this regard.

## 4. Ethos and Culture of the RUC

Nor are the disincentives to Catholic, female and ethnic minority recruits all external. Potential recruits will be concerned about allegations of harassment within the force, and they will be aware of the institutional and political culture which is seen to predominate. In many instances, this culture is one that they may consider unattractive or even antipathetic.

All organisations have a working culture which is peculiar to them. International research suggests that the organisational

---

[18] PANI press release and press launch, 30 June 1997.

culture within police forces tends to be particularly strong.[19] Loyalty to one's colleagues and to the institution are obviously important in relatively dangerous occupations like policing, where trust can be vital to survival. This is especially true of the RUC, where many officers and their families have paid a heavy cost in terms of injury or death. However, given the special powers held by police officers, and the discretion which they have in enforcing those powers, it is particularly important that police officers should not hold stereotyped views of individuals or whole communities.

The culture of the RUC remains predominantly British and unionist. The name of the force, the oath of allegiance to the Queen (which is currently more fulsome than in other UK jurisdictions), and the flying of the union flag at police stations, can all be viewed as partisan in the context of Northern Ireland's divided society.[20] Events around Drumcree in 1996 (CAJ, 1996; HRW, 1997), and again in 1997 (CAJ, 1997), seriously undermined the rule of law and reinforced for many in society their concerns about the force's impartiality. The Police Authority, in commenting on the events of Drumcree in 1996, recognised that:

> "Both the Authority and the Chief Constable of the RUC have acknowledged that the events of the past summer have undermined the confidence of people both in the police and the rule of law. The Chief Constable said recently that the damage to relationships with the RUC had been particularly marked within the Catholic community" (PANI, 1997).

---

[19] Studies of police occupational culture originated in the USA with the work, of Skolnick (1966), Wiley, Manning & Van Maanen (eds) (1978), etc. Brewer & Magee (1991) provide research on the occupational culture of the RUC.

[20] While Sir John Wheeler, former NI Security Minister saw these issues as "of marginal interest, largely irrelevant to most people"(Irish Times, 2 May 1996), others would argue that cultural symbols are a reflection of the ethos of the force as a whole.

The view of the RUC as a unionist force is supported by interviews with serving police officers (Ellison, 1997). As one RUC constable explained to Ellison: *"What nationalists and Catholics don't understand is that the RUC is a British police force. We live and work in Northern Ireland which is part of Britain ... that's why we have the title 'Royal', that's why we play the National Anthem, that's why we fly the Union Jack ... those are all symbols of my country."*(Ellison, 1997: 261).

In the course of Ellison's research, he discovered that sectarian banter, to the detriment of Catholic officers, was prevalent and the resentment of some Protestant officers towards their Catholic colleagues was clear. Ellison was told on "numerous occasions" that the force was "bending over backwards" to recruit Catholics. (Ellison, 1997: 254-256). This was linked to the strongly held opinion that Catholic officers "get a better deal" within the force through their ability to "play the Green Card"(Ellison, 1997). While some officers described to Ellison a positive working relationship with Catholics, noting that "we're all policemen(sic)" (ibid. 257), some Catholic officers explained how they adapted their behaviour to suit working in an overwhelmingly Protestant environment: *"Certainly I would never mention going to Mass or maybe going to see a Gaelic match on a Sunday when I'm off. There would be no point in talking about the [Gaelic] match anyway because nobody knows anything about the game. But it's not something I would mention"* (Ellison, 1997: 259).

Confirmation of the deep-seated sectarianism highlighted in Ellison's findings is said to be available in a recent internal RUC survey carried out by consultants (*Sunday Times*, 26 October 1997). In his study of the social attitudes of part-time members of the RUC, Richard Mapstone found that Catholic officers tended to display views more typical of the wider occupational culture of the RUC than the Catholic community in general. Indeed, Mapstone argues that *"... the organisational culture of the part-time RUC means that Catholic recruitment is limited to those who are prepared to subscribe to a set of values often apparently irreconcilable with those of the Catholic community at large."* (Mapstone, 1992:192).

## 5. Living in a diverse society

This section on the RUC's relationship with the community served should not conclude without noting how most studies on policing in Northern Ireland have tended to concentrate on the traditional communal divisions. Yet McVeigh's study (1994) also documented allegations of harassment against gay people and against ethnic minority groups, particularly Travellers. A focus on the divisions in society that have produced the most visible and violent conflict sometimes obscures other important issues. Northern Irish society is not made up only of Protestants and Catholics, nationalists and unionists. Issues concerning class, gender, sexual orientation, ethnic and religious background, and disability must also be addressed if policing is to meet the needs of the *whole* community. International parallels hold several examples of attempts to address some of the serious social divisions which ignored – and thereby sometimes exacerbated – other problems.[21]

---

[21] In El Salvador much attention was paid to the relative percentages of guerrillas and former security force members in the new police, but much less has been done to encourage women and other minority indigenous groups to become involved. In South Africa, Duxita Mistry of the Centre for the Study of Violence and Reconciliation in Johannesburg, noted the absence of information on other minority groups within the police: *"Apart from observing that the composition of the South African Police Service reflects the legacy of apartheid, we have limited information on ethnic composition"* (Questionnaire response).

# Changing police culture: International lessons

Experience from elsewhere shows that a representative police service will never be achieved by a piece-meal approach. The ethos, culture and composition of policing can only be effectively changed as part of a holistic process aimed at overhauling the philosophy, policies and practices of policing. No one would suggest that the process of institutional change is easy. The following commentary provides ideas as to how this change could be managed and has been managed in other jurisdictions. In addition to citing a number of practical proposals for action, this chapter provides a measuring stick against which the authorities can be judged. If there is a genuine commitment to change, and to making police institutions in Northern Ireland truly representative, there are many international lessons to be used in drawing up good practice models.

## 1.    Recognising the problem: political will to change

A central theme emerging from our international research is the need for an acknowledgement of the necessity of change. To develop effective partnerships with the community served, policing organisations also need to recognise that there may be historical legacies of mistrust. As noted by an Australian police sergeant, this can be a challenge and an opportunity:

> *"Police should take the opportunity to come to terms with history (much of it very recent) and realise just how serious a legacy they have been left, and be assured that much can be done to bridge this gap by developing an empathy with the Aboriginal culture and history. Because of past history, Aboriginal people have great difficulty in accepting that the law is there to assist them. It is*

*up to the Police Service to do everything possible to change this view"* (Queensland Police Academy, 1993).

This is not easy, especially in a society which has been riven by political violence and where the police have been under physical attack. Furthermore, the police may not like all that they hear from communities or researchers. The chapter on transition comments in more detail on the management of change and it is clear that crucial to such change is a willingness on the part of the police to deal with unpleasant truths. In Tottenham, England, a project has been established which encourages young black men to express their views to the police. As the local community and police consultative group note *"this process is likely to be painful and angry"*. However it is also useful for the police to hear their views (NACRO, 1997). In Australia, Janet Chan, who carried out an evaluation of attempts by the New South Wales (NSW) police to build bridges with minority communities, praised the NSW police for giving her wide access and for their response to her final document:

> *"In reality ... the findings of the study were not what the organisation would have been eager to put out in press releases. The final report contained many criticisms, but there was not a single attempt by anyone to ask me to change any part of the report. In fact that report was widely circulated, both formally and informally, within the organisation"* (Chan, 1997: 8-9).

An example from the Netherlands demonstrates that the impetus to change can sometimes come from government itself. In 1993, a report based on two years' research on sexual harassment in the Dutch police was published, and a female government minister attended a conference on the research. Anita Hazenberg, who was at the time working for the

European Network for Policewomen, said of the minister's impact on the conference:

> *"I will never forget. She walked to the stage, she looked at the audience and she looked at the chief constable and she said 'gentlemen, this is ridiculous and you should do something about it!' And she walked away. It caused so much bad publicity for the police in the Netherlands that every chief constable realised that they had to do something about it."*[22]

In all our research, great emphasis was placed on the importance of political will at the highest levels of police and government. Without this, effective strategies and policies geared at more equal representation are extremely unlikely to be achieved.

## 2. Symbols and cultural diversity

The experience of other jurisdictions is that when policing organisations break from an unpopular past, when new policing institutions are created, or when important new changes are introduced, different symbols and name-changes are often designed to reflect the spirit of the reforms. For example, in winning popular support for the Autonomous Police in the Basque country it was crucial that the new organisation be seen to be civilian in character, in contrast to the highly militarised policing of the past.[23] The name of the new police, the 'Ertzaintza' means 'shepherd of the people', and historically was the name of local Basque police. Rather than

---

[22] Interview Anita Hazenberg, European Network for Policewomen, Netherlands, 11 November 1996.

[23] See synopsis and chapters 5 and 6.

the traditional dark, military style uniform, the Ertzaintza wear bright red uniforms with red Basque-style berets.[24]

Nor is it only in countries emerging from conflict that names and symbols need to be considered. It is also important that well-established police organisations are sensitive to the way in which their symbols and culture will be interpreted by under-represented or marginalised groups within society. This was recognised by the federal police in Canada who stress the importance of ensuring that symbols are *"changeable over time to meet modern needs."*[25] It is important that the symbols chosen are inclusive, not exclusive. For example, permission can be given to accommodate symbolic requirements for different religions: turbans for uniformed Sikhs, braids for Aboriginals.

Language diversity is also important. In several of the countries visited, local languages (even those spoken by the majority of people in some cases) were an important symbol of changing police attitudes. For example, in both the Basque Country and Catalonia, use of local languages had been forbidden under General Franco's dictatorship. In Catalonia, members of the Autonomous Police now have to be able to understand, speak and write Catalan. In the Basque Country, the language (Euskera) is quite unlike other European languages and can prove difficult for Spanish speakers to learn. Hence, police recruits do not have to speak Euskera, although it is considered an advantage if they do.[26] Australia has more than 100 ethnic groups, speaking 80 immigrant languages and 150 Aboriginal languages, and historically a major problem has

---

[24] Unfortunately, the Ertzaintza response to the continuing conflict and violence in the Basque Country has been to become increasing militarised (see chapters 5 and 6 for more detail).

[25] Questionnaire response S/Sergeant Dave Wojcik, RCMP HQ, Ottawa. S/Sergeant Wojcik noted that *"As Canada becomes a more ethnically diverse society the response of the police must mirror that diversity"*.

[26] Interview, Ertzaintza Training Academy, Arkaute, Basque Country, February 1997.

been police insensitivity to language barriers. Interpreters are now more often used than previously but more effort is thought necessary (Chan, 1997: 19). In Belgium, police officers are, in principle, required to speak both French and Flemish. In Quebec, although it is a bi-lingual society, French is the official language of the province and all police officers must speak French. Interestingly, in both Belgium and Canada, the special linguistic problems created for potential recruits from ethnic minorities were noted. Given the linguistic divide, it is difficult for people from minority groups to be appointed to the police since, to pass the language requirements, they will often have to speak three languages.[27]

From this starting point, if the police are genuine about their commitment to serve all the people in Northern Ireland this can be demonstrated by -

-       a willingness to adopt symbols which reflect the culture and aspirations of different communities. To reflect fundamental changes introduced - and not as a tokenistic gesture that is meant to compensate for the lack of other change - consideration should be given to the creation of new symbols reflecting the diversity of cultures and the commitment to the impartial upholding of the law in Northern Ireland.

-       a commitment which encompasses a recognition of language rights. Northern Ireland is not a monolingual society, and its police service should take steps to show that it recognises this. The decision of the Police Authority to create a working group to look at the needs of minority ethnic communities[28] is very welcome in this regard, and is likely to lead to proposals regarding the special language problems of certain minority ethnic

[27] Interview with Ligue des Droits de l'Homme, 15 November 1996.
[28] PANI press release and press launch, 30 June 1997.

groups. The Irish language also is of particular importance. There are people within both the unionist and nationalist communities (and beyond) who see Irish as part of their identity, and who favour increased support for the language (Ulster People's College & Ultach Trust, 1994; CAJ, 1992).

## 3. Strategies for cultural change

Policing scholars have identified two types of strategies used to make changes within policing organisations: 'rule-tightening' and 'changing police culture' (Brogden et al, 1988: 164-172). The first advocates tightening police rules to control police discretion and, for example, can include measures such as changes to legislation, administrative rules, codes of practice, accountability mechanisms. The second type of strategy - changing police culture – involves measures such as recruitment strategies, changes to the working environment, and training, all intended to increase the representation of minority groups or women.

It should be emphasised, however, that it is clear from our own and other research, that neither 'rule tightening' nor 'cultural change' will be effective on its own. Cultural change will be effective only if systems of accountability are there as a back-up to discipline those who continue to infringe people's rights. Conversely, changing the rules without working to ensure cultural change within the organisation is only likely to increase resentment amongst the rank-and-file about those rules. An example of this inter-play can be found in the issue of police membership in the Loyal Orders.

The RUC has publicly stated its commitment to impartiality and non-sectarianism, yet recent estimates suggest that some

15% of police officers are members of the Orange Order,[29] an institution which is perceived by many as being hostile to Catholicism.[30] Clearly all police organisations need to counter any institutional damage which might arise from the private activities of serving police officers. This could be done in part by rule-tightening. A former chairperson of the Police Authority, David Cook, has called for a registry of names of RUC officers involved in organisations such as the Orange Order, but his proposal was rejected by the Authority.[31] Though the situations are not entirely analogous, it is interesting to note that, in response to the public concern about senior police being members of the Masonic Order in England and Wales, the Association of Chief Police Officers has proposed a registration scheme. Indeed in its testimony to parliament they *"went further and stated that membership of organisations such as freemasonry was undesirable because of the impact on public confidence and staff morale"*(House of Commons, 1997: para ll). The Home Office in the same parliamentary hearings said: *"it is not enough for police officers to be impartial, they must also be seen to be impartial"* and stressed the value of openness in reducing the risk of damage to public confidence (House of Commons, 1997: para 20). This suggests that there is a strong case for a "register of outside interests", since such a move would protect the civil liberties of individual police officers, while giving practical expression to the organisational commitment to impartiality and accountability.

However, in isolation, a purely procedural approach might only succeed in alienating police and community alike, since it

---

[29] See Ellison, 1997: 282. The RUC have neither confirmed nor denied this estimate, and do not require officers to declare membership. During the summer of 1996 seven RUC officers were suspended on full pay for their involvement in Orange Order protests (*Irish News*, 5 September 1996).

[30] For fuller discussion of police membership of the Loyal Orders see Pat Finucane Centre (1997), and Topping (1997).

[31] *Irish Times*, 11 November 1996. Cook was later sacked by the Secretary of State after PANI passed a vote of no confidence.

might fail to address either the reality or perception of sectarianism within policing. Therefore, a combination of measures consisting of rule-tightening and changes to the organisational culture will be required if such an issue is to be tackled to everyone's satisfaction. Later chapters (on legal and democratic accountability) put forward specific proposals in the area of rule-tightening, but this chapter (and that on training) tend to concentrate more directly on strategies which could contribute to 'changing police culture'.

Many strategies have been evolved internationally to bring about cultural change through a more representative police service; the following analysis proposes a range of measures which should be examined closely for their relevance to Northern Ireland.

## (a) Recruitment and promotion measures

Clearly, if one is to ensure a more representative force, a natural focus for attention will be on the recruitment methods to be used, and on the methods whereby people from under-represented groups, once recruited, are retained. A variety of useful ideas relating to recruitment, selection, and equal opportunities, were gathered in the course of the research.

**Outreach** was seen as important by most of those interviewed and some imaginative strategies have been adopted:

■ placing advertisements in a wide range of community magazines and informing ethnic media outlets of vacancies (e.g. Toronto)
■ wide range of recruitment material in different languages (e.g. Netherlands, New South Wales)

■ leafleting gay marches to attract gay recruits (e.g. The Hague, Netherlands)[32]

**Bridging schemes** have been established, for example in New South Wales, to help people from Aboriginal communities reach the academic standards required for police training.

**Targets** were set for the recruitment of under-represented groups. For example in the Netherlands, the Ministry of Interior sets targets for the police for recruitment of women.[33] In New South Wales, all government departments and statutory authorities were requested by the Prime Minister to prepare an ethnic affairs policy statement and submit an annual report to the Ethnic Affairs Commission regarding their progress in achieving previously set objectives. This ensures that the police and others have to set goals, design performance indicators, and establish schedules (Chan, 1997: 52-53).

**Lateral entry schemes** are in operation in South Africa so that qualified recruits from under-represented groups can enter higher up the occupational ladder.

**Mentoring schemes**: in South Africa, for example, such schemes have been used to identify potential recruits from under-represented groups who then work with a 'mentor' to achieve the standard needed for recruitment at different levels.

**Fast-tracking** for promotion of candidates identified as having high potential from under-represented groups has taken place in South Africa, Australia and Canada. In the Netherlands

---

[32] One such leaflet sought to draw the reader's attention by stating *"The police are also fond of young men in uniforms"* (Klerks, 1993: 86).

[33] The Ministry of the Interior had set a target for police organisations to have 25% females by 1995. This target has proved hard to reach: by 1994, the percentage of women in the Netherlands police had only risen to 12% (and only 2.5% of these were in managerial positions). [European Network of Policewomen, 1995).

under a policy of positive discrimination ten or twelve officers from ethnic minorities (primarily Turkish and Moroccan) are admitted to the officers' training school every year to undertake senior officer training. These officers follow the standard course, but if necessary are given individual tuition and the chance to attend supplementary courses.[34]

**Selection processes:** in El Salvador the selection procedure is not controlled by the police but by a separate training institution. This separation of authority ensured that the training school was able to reject numerous candidates suggested by the police authorities or others because of their failure to meet the entrance criteria (Call, 1996). Elsewhere, recruitment panels are deliberately constructed to reflect the diversity of society and best management practice is drawn upon to develop objective, measurable and appropriate selection criteria.

**Changes in the testing process:** these include in the main changes to height and fitness requirements. In the Gendarmerie in Belgium for example, *potential* physical fitness is measured rather than actual fitness levels. Sometimes, for example in the Netherlands, academic requirements are lowered for particular ethnic groups. Also in the Netherlands, the psychological tests were changed when it was discovered that women, who tended to be more honest about their fears, were consequently being judged to be more nervous and unfairly disqualified.[35]

**Tie-breaks:** in some countries, for example the Netherlands, a *'tie break'* can be used if two candidates are equal after the

---

[34]Information from National Police Institute, undated, The Police in the Netherlands.

[35] Spiegel van de Tijd, 40 jaar vrouwen bij de politie, 195-3-93, Utrecht 1993.

selection process.  All else being equal, the candidate from the under-represented group will be chosen.[36]

**Screening:**  Many police forces studied have been anxious to ensure that recruits have appropriate character traits (e.g. cultural sensitivity, maturity) before expending energy on their training.  Some forces have used psychometric testing (though note problems above with such testing), others give preference to those with further education, or to older candidates who will bring with them a wider life experience.

**Quotas:**  In Canada it is the practice of the RCMP to select a proportion of qualified candidates from each of the following groups: visible minorities, Aboriginal peoples, women and caucasian males.   This is done to ensure a more equitable representation of candidates within designated groups and "falls within the spirit of employment equity legislation".[37]  In El Salvador, as part of the peace agreement, it was agreed to create an entirely new force and, as a way of balancing the different constituencies of interest, it was agreed to fix quotas of former guerrillas, former police, and ordinary civilians.

The above examples are merely some of the options which have been used by other forces to ensure that their recruitment and promotion strategies actively seek out members from under-represented groups.  The implementation of each of these risks its own problems, and needs to be carefully considered so that further inequalities are not created.  They also need to be used as part of a much wider process of reassessment and change and will not be successful in isolation.

---

[36] Recent decisions on Marschall and Kalanke at the European Court of Justice have created important European jurisprudence on the issue of positive discrimination.  The full implications of these rulings for different affirmative action measures still have to be assessed, but suggest that positive discrimination of this kind is likely to be found acceptable (also SACHR, 1997:162-165; Marschall , ECJ, C-409/95; Kalanke, ECJ, C-450/93).

[37] Questionnaire response S/Sgt. Dave Wojcik, RCMP HQ, Ottawa.

In response to a recommendation from HMIC, a working group, involving respected members of the community, will consider under-representation of different groups within the police (HMIC, 1996: 23). It is inconceivable in our opinion that such a working group will be able to resolve the many problems of policing which are given practical expression in the debate around composition. Nevertheless, even a relatively limited measure of this kind must be welcomed if the group is given a wide remit, is able to commission research, and can make recommendations on a broad range of issues including employment practices, working environment, structures of accountability etc. The various ideas cited above should all be examined by such a group, with a view to drawing on best practice elsewhere.

When looking at the different ideas for pro-active recruitment evolved elsewhere, the police must of course comply with current fair employment and equal opportunities legislation in Northern Ireland. This sets limits as to what can lawfully be done to increase representation. CAJ has already carried out a substantial body of work on the fair employment legislation and we highlight below a couple of areas where the inadequacies of the current law may affect the efforts of the police to increase Catholic representation.

■ Fair employment monitoring to date has focused almost exclusively on the procedures surrounding recruitment and appointment. There needs to be more attention given to issues around training, promotion and working environment - all areas where discrimination can take place.

■ Fair employment legislation, since its aim is to encourage the achievement of a balanced and representative workforce, should not focus on *procedures* to the exclusion of *outcomes*. As discussed above, targets and quotas are two ways of encouraging outcomes. In the present circumstances, CAJ would not support the setting of fixed quotas, since experience elsewhere suggests that it increases resentment, and encourages the recruitment of candidates unsuited to the job. However, the interesting example of El Salvador suggests that quotas can play a positive role in a transition process. As an immediate step, we call for the official setting of targets to encourage greater representation of Catholics, women and ethnic minorities within the police and a timetable for implementation. The Chief Constable should be made responsible for ensuring that the targets are met, or accounting for his or her failure to meet them.

■ If properly managed, the tie break mechanism might play a positive role. In submissions to the Employment Equality Review,[38] CAJ contended that the tie break mechanism did not necessarily undermine the rigorous application of objective job selection criteria, and might in some senses strengthen the important concept of merit. The Standing Advisory Commission on Human Rights (SACHR) in its report at the end of its major review of employment equality spoke specifically of the situation in the security occupations. The Commission talked of the need to examine *"whether special measures should be permitted under the fair employment legislation to bring about a more representative and acceptable police service"*.

Earlier, the point of principle was made that political will is critical to bringing about any real change. It is worth again emphasising at this point that practical strategies for increasing levels of recruits from under-represented groups as outlined above will fail unless they are part of a whole package of measures which has clear support from the highest levels within and outside the police.

---

[38] A review carried out by the Standing Advisory Commission on Human Rights into the operation of NI's fair employment legislation (SACHR, 1997).

For example, in Ottawa, Toronto, and in the Netherlands, fast-tracking of minorities has led to problems of resentment by other officers. In Toronto, it was reported that one police chief had fast tracked minorities and women (including appointing a civilian leader of a gay rights group as his executive assistant) but this had caused alienation between him and his officers.[39] In the Netherlands, a scheme under which less qualified candidates from ethnic minority groups were recruited was abandoned following hostility from white officers. The scheme seemed to actually increase racism within the force.[40] This problem was emphasised in research carried out in England in the 1980s where it was found that training was actually confirming prejudices rather than increasing tolerance (Southgate, 1984). There seems to be some confirmation of this in the suggestion that the RUC's Community Awareness Programme has been nicknamed the "Campaign against Prods" (*Sunday Times*, 26 October 1997).

Part of this reported resentment presumably derives in part from a fear that jobs will be lost if there is an active drive to recruit from the under-represented communities at a time of reduced recruitment. Indeed, as the peace holds, there will be intense pressure to reduce the current size of the force and the Chief Constable has spoken of the possibility of needing to halve the force in coming years (*Belfast Telegraph*, 1 November 1997). So the process of change in the overall composition of the force is likely to be painfully slow, unless very radical measures are considered. Ellison (1997a) calculates that, without any change to current recruitment practices, it will take approximately fifty years to increase Catholic representation to even 20%.

---

[39] Interview with Marian Dewar, Ottawa, Canada, October 1996.
[40] Interview with Dr Sandra Wykhuys at Police Training Academy, Amersfoort, Netherlands, 14 November 1996.

Economist Paul Teague, however, talks of a two-stage process which seeks to change the composition and size of the force and suggests that this might be done over a period of some seven years (Bew, Patterson & Teague, 1997: 98-103). This would entail a series of measures including generous redundancy packages as happened in South Africa (see transition chapter). In the case of Northern Ireland, whether or not to introduce large-scale redundancy packages, or to extend and strengthen fair employment legislation, or have a combination thereof, are all issues which need to be considered.

## (b) Changing concepts of the job of policing

Despite our recommendations on fair employment legislation, we must emphasise again that merely changing the rules is not enough. It is important to challenge the ethos and outreach ideas of the organisation. For example in order to recruit women it may be necessary to change the central emphasis placed on physical tests. Anita Hazenberg, formerly of the European Network of Policewomen (ENP), notes that the emphasis put on physical/sporting tests is off-putting to many women who might otherwise be keen to join the police. As a former police woman she felt that most police work does not involve running around:

> *"First they say we want to have women because of their social skills, we want to have them for this extra value, for the reflection of society. So women please with your social skills come in. First thing they do is the sporting test! And that's a mixed message. If you want to have them for their social skills, why are the sporting tests so important?"*[41]

---

[41] Interview, Anita Hazenberg, European Network of Policewomen, Netherlands, 11 November 1996.

Martin and Jurik (1996) say:

> *"Instead of viewing women's performance as negative deviations from the norm of street cop culture that emphasises crime fighting, variations in policing styles might be viewed as potential sources of alternative definitions of social control. The insistence on assessing women's performance by the standard of masculinity obscures the fact that the crime-fighting model embraced by 'a predominantly male-oriented police system has failed to prevent, deter or resolve crimes that have been brought to its attention'".*

Similarly, police organisations need to be creative in considering ways in which people with disabilities could play an effective role in policing (and not only those officers who become disabled during employment). A serious debate on this would naturally challenge traditional concepts of the police, and could pave the way for the creation of a police service truly responsive to and representative of all in the community.

## (c)     Working environment

Improved outreach and recruitment measures are of relatively little use in isolation – the working environment and occupational culture within the force also need transforming. It is clearly unwise to invest extensively (in human and financial resource terms) to ensure that under-represented groups join the service, if they then leave shortly thereafter because they find the working environment hostile or alien.

For example, when addressing the issue of women in the police service, we need to consider issues such as -

**creating a women-friendly environment:**     Male-dominated workplaces, and problems associated with working conditions (e.g. lack of child-care, job-stereotyping or difficulty in gaining promotion) can result in many women looking for careers outside the police. Even those organisations which have made substantial efforts to recruit and promote women have had problems in this area. For example, in certain regions in the Netherlands,[42] some forces have established 24 hour child-care centres (e.g. Rotterdam and the Hague), and in others, the force will pay for child-minding (though this is not an arrangement offered for the children of male officers). Part-time work has also been introduced (since 1985) and it is possible for women at all ranks to work part-time. However, it was noted that, while part-time work is completely accepted at lower levels, there is still a tendency to frown on it at management levels. This reinforces our central thesis that changing rules makes little difference if attitudes within police organisations remain unchallenged.

**dealing with sexual harassment**: Sexual harassment of female officers in the workplace has often made the news in England. While there has been less publicity given to the issue in Northern Ireland, the RUC recognise that the problem exists at some level and have taken steps to deal with this (HMIC, 1996: 33). The European Network for Policewomen (ENP) has carried out extensive research on sexual harassment of women officers and how best to tackle it. Along with a confidential and effective grievance procedure, the following strategies are key:

-       making employees conscious of the problem e.g. through training, meetings, newsletters;
-       creating a safe working environment: women should not be assigned to groups or teams without other women;

---

[42] This and the following information on child-care and part-time work comes from interviews with policing organisations in the Netherlands, November 1996.

- creating a supportive occupational culture where all officers feel free from discrimination or harassment;
- creating a gender balance in the personnel at all ranks;
- setting up networks of women to provide mutual support.[43]

The European Network for Policewomen which is very active, and has substantial experience of working with and for female officers, has reported little interest in their work from the RUC.[44] Membership in the Network is, however, apparently under consideration by the force.

These recommendations are also instructive in relation to other under-represented groups. For example, it is important to be clear that harassment - whether sexual, racial or sectarian - is not just about individual cases. Rather it is about behaviour which is part of the daily pattern of relations in the workplace. While it is difficult to challenge offensive behaviour in any work environment, the difficulties are even greater in policing organisations, where a high value is placed on loyalty to the organisation.

## (d)  Training for diversity and justice

One way of tackling prejudicial attitudes within police organisations is through training in cultural awareness. All of the countries researched have adopted training strategies to encourage respect for different cultures in society. Since 1993 initial training for RUC recruits has included a Community Awareness Programme which aims to help officers understand different cultures within our society. It is planned to extend this training to the whole force in the near future.

---

[43] For a more detailed discussion of these issues see ENP, 1993.
[44] Interview Anita Hazenberg, ENP, Netherlands, 11 November 1996.

The issue of training is dealt with more fully in the following chapter. However, there are two important lessons of immediate relevance to the issue of representation and cultural diversity. Firstly, training on cultural diversity must be a thread which runs throughout the whole curriculum; secondly such training must not be abstract but must be relevant to the job police are expected to do on the streets.

In the course of our research, the training programmes in the Netherlands were particularly impressive in the way the theme of cultural diversity and respect for others was woven as a common theme throughout every module of officer training. Thus, this element was not 'tagged on', but integral to every part of training. The same was true of training in Catalonia,[45] and elsewhere. There is clearly a role for specialist courses in human rights and cultural awareness, but these themes must also be incorporated into the curriculum as a whole. For example, firearms training in the Netherlands deals with issues of prejudice and human rights. The 'virtual reality' training in which officers are placed in a simulated, potentially dangerous, situation and have to decide whether and when to use force, does not only deal with how the officer can protect their own safety (although this is of course fundamental to the training). It also helps them to see how they may have been prejudiced against a particular individual and thus been more ready to use force, and encourages them to match their actions against international human rights legislation on the use of firearms.

## (e) Police culture - encompassing the whole process

On their own, or even as a package, the above measures in recruitment, promotion, working environment or training are unlikely to have a significant impact on either the make-up or

---

[45] The police training in Catalonia was influenced by Dutch and Canadian (RCMP) practices.

the ethos of the force.    Policing does not take place in a vacuum.    The outside world with its social and political institutions has a strong influence.  The police themselves are formally bound by the laws of the jurisdiction.    If the legislation which the police enforce is biased or ineffective, then no amount of training or recruitment strategies will overcome problems between themselves and minority communities. Legal and social reforms must form part of an overall package of change.

The need to change the environment in which policing takes place is clear from a review of some of the countries visited. In Catalonia and the Basque Country, the unpopularity of the state police made the creation of new autonomous police organisations an essential prerequisite to change.  That process could only occur alongside the creation of agreed democratic structures (see chapters 5 and 6). In South Africa    it is inconceivable that more representative police services could have been created without changes in the political structures. The appointment of a black South African Minister of Safety and Security would have been unthinkable before the transfer of power. However, even once the political situation is transformed there can still be problems of representation.  In the Western Cape (South Africa) for example in 1994, out of 14,000 police, approximately 60% were black or coloured but the maximum rank of a black officer was an inspector and there was only one of these.[46]

In El Salvador new policing structures could only be created because of the ending of the bloody civil war.  The setting of quotas determining the relative levels of former guerrillas, former security forces, and civilians had a very profound impact on ensuring representation within the new police.  Less

---

[46] Details from questionnaire response from Peter Stevens, adviser on community policing to the Minister of Safety and Security, Province of the Western Cape.

positively, as discussed in the chapter on transition, in El Salvador the failure to transform legal structures along with policing had a negative impact on the ethos and practice of the new police. In both South Africa and El Salvador, a failure to tackle discrimination against smaller minority groups meant that their needs are still unmet. In El Salvador, the predominant masculine environment in the outside world means that the new policing organisation has made only small steps in addressing the needs of women, either inside or outside the force.[47] Furthermore, in both countries continuing economic crisis and massive crime waves have meant serious problems for the new police. In El Salvador this has led to the re-introduction of emergency legislation and of joint police/army patrols.

Janet Chan found that in New South Wales, despite the substantial efforts of the police to introduce programmes designed to improve the force's relationship with minorities, these had failed to undermine the predominant discriminatory culture. She noted that racism has been historically embedded in the wider social and political institutions of Australian society: consequently, changes in policing must be reinforced by changes in the broader social and political institutions (Chan, 1997: chapter 9).

Thus, in the case of Northern Ireland, a significant improvement in the relationship between, say, Catholic communities and the police can only come about through a combination of change. For example, to encourage greater acceptance of policing in working class Catholic areas, there would need to be a change in the police occupational culture in relation to attitudes to Catholics, and in the overall philosophy of policing, and the police role in these communities. Structures

---

[47] Although it has to be recognised that the newly established police force (PNC) is the first police force in El Salvador's history to include women in anything other than administrative positions.

of local police accountability will need to be put in place to ensure that local people have a role in saying how their area should be policed. This would need to be accompanied by external changes such as the ending of emergency legislation which encourages over-heavy policing tactics, for example the regular stopping and searching of young Catholic residents, and the blanket searches of houses in nationalist areas. The current political negotiations may provide the climate necessary to facilitate such changes.

A similarly holistic approach has to be taken when looking at how the police can recruit more women, more gays, more officers of working class origin, if they wish to diversify their organisational base. Research from several countries, however, shows that the police will face problems in some of their outreach work because they are more likely to treat as delinquents certain groups within society (i.e. the young, the unemployed, and men from minority backgrounds) (Reiner, 1985; Brogden et al, 1988). While this is in part connected with police prejudice, this behaviour also has its basis in the problems of 'anti-social behaviour' which develop in local areas where young people have nothing to do and no real prospects. Hence, broader strategies aimed at reducing unemployment and community regeneration are also essential in reducing the possibilities for this negative police-community contact. John Alderson, former Chief Constable of Devon and Cornwall, aptly describes the effect of poor social conditions on police-community relations:

> *"Where social conditions are good, insensitive use of the police will result in complaints through formal channels provided for such constituencies; where they are bad, they will result in riot"* (Alderson in Roach & Thomaneck, 1985: 25-26).

As Chan concludes, if police culture is viewed in the light of all of the points of the process then:

*"Changing police culture now has a new meaning: cultural change is no longer restricted to efforts such as improving police training or the adoption of community policing; it can encompass changing the field, that is, the social, economic, legal and political sites in which policing takes place"* (Chan, 1997: 92).

## Summary of conclusions

1. It is vital that membership of the police service be as representative as possible of the diversity in society.

2. The achievement of a broadly representative police service is complex and will have to be addressed in a variety of ways. It cannot be achieved through a piece-meal approach since the ethos and culture of policing can only be effectively changed as part of a holistic process aimed at overhauling the philosophy, policies and practices of policing.

3. The importance of political will at the highest levels of police and government in bringing about effective change cannot be over-emphasised. Without this, CAJ was assured by all policing experts that strategies and policies geared at more equal representation are extremely unlikely to be achieved.

4. To address the issue effectively, serious independent research will need to be commissioned into the obstacles which currently exist. This CAJ report will be a contribution to such an analysis, though its focus is on practical measures for change rather than a detailed critique of the current arrangements.

5.  The experience of other jurisdictions is that when policing organisations want to break from an unpopular past, create new police structures or introduce important new changes, they have found it useful to design different symbols and name-changes to reflect the spirit of the change. Moves towards inclusive symbolism have also been made by well-established police organisations sensitive to the need to reach out to marginalised or under-represented groups.

6.  Though the religious and political dimension of under-representation is particularly marked in Northern Ireland, there are many groups which are under-represented. In examining the obstacles to women, ethnic minorities, people with disabilities and others to joining the police service, one is obliged to challenge traditional concepts of policing.

7.  Most importantly of all, perhaps, is the need for changes in policing to be seen in the wider context of institutional, and even social, change. Measures addressing recruitment, promotion, working environment or training will not on their own have a significant impact on either the make-up or ethos of the police. There is a need to challenge outmoded views as to what policing is, should, and could be, so that legal and social reforms can form part of an overall package of change. The cease-fires allow society to discuss what kind of policing it wants in the new political – and hopefully peaceful – situation.

## Summary of recommendations

1.  Practical expression of police commitment to recruit widely and serve all the people in Northern Ireland is needed and several recommendations figure in the text. This commitment can be expressed in a number of ways, for example:

- by a willingness to adopt symbols which reflect the culture and aspirations of different communities;
- by giving recognition to minority language rights, especially Irish;
- by developing guidelines to regulate situations where there may be a conflict of interest for serving police officers, and establishing a register of outside interests.

2. There are a large number of recruitment and promotion strategies being used effectively by police in other parts of the world to ensure a representative service:

- outreach measures (advertising, leafleting, targeted translations and distribution of promotional material);
- bridging schemes;
- target setting;
- lateral entry schemes;
- mentoring schemes;
- fast-tracking;
- changes to selection processes;
- changes to testing processes;
- tie-break schemes.

We recommend that all these options be carefully examined with a view to seeing which would be appropriate for Northern Ireland.

3. The recommendation of HMIC that a working group be established to monitor religious representation in the police will only have value if it has a broad membership, is given a wide remit, can commission research, and can make recommendations on a broad range of issues including employment practices, working environment, structures of accountability etc. The work of the group should include studying under-representation of different groups.

4.  SACHR's recommendations regarding fair employment and the special situation of the security services should be pursued actively. In particular, CAJ recommends that monitoring efforts focus more effectively on issues around training, promotion and the working environment.

5.  It is particularly important that official targets be set for the level of Catholic representation within the police, and similarly for women and other under-represented groups. The Chief Constable should be responsible for ensuring that these targets are met, or accounting for his or her failure to do so.

6.  Clearly attempting to change the composition of any police service at a time of reduced recruitment is particularly difficult. Moreover, the authorities have signalled that they intend, as a response to a negotiated long-term peace settlement, to reduce the number of police officers. CAJ recommends that consideration be given to the practices in other countries in this regard. It is open to the authorities to introduce large-scale redundancy packages and/or extend the fair employment legislation and we recommend that both options be considered.

7.  A basic requirement of any institution wishing to attract from a wide spectrum of society is the creation of a neutral working environment, the positive promotion of an environment in which under-represented groups will feel comfortable, and the establishment of good management practice to deal effectively with sexual, racial and sectarian harassment. Many good-practice models from other jurisdictions are enumerated in the text; it is recommended that these are all studied closely and changes introduced as appropriate.

8.  A police service wanting to promote inclusiveness will ensure that the concept of cultural diversity is a thread

running throughout the whole training curriculum. It is recommended that issues of racism, sexism, sectarianism, and prejudice reduction need to be addressed in initial and refresher training, as well as in standard managerial terms. Concrete examples of good training practice are discussed more fully in chapter 2.

9. Selection criteria and training practices should be regularly re-assessed; international experience shows that it is in these areas that, often quite unwittingly, barriers are placed ensuring the continued exclusion of people of different gender, ethnicity, religious denomination, etc.

# Chapter Two

# Training and Organisational Culture

## Introduction

Training alone can clearly not provide the answer to the creation of a totally impartial and accountable police service. It is, however, an important component in the 'shaping' of the constable, and of the organisation.

The importance of training lies particularly in its potential and actual impact on the organisational culture[48] within the police. Militaristic and/or security-driven forms of policing lead to particular forms of training that do not equip an officer for community policing. Yet effective policing is largely dependent on co-operation with the community policed, so a focus on security-led policing, and training, can be entirely counter-productive. The decision about the forms of policing needed is clearly one for the wider society to take, and this decision must then determine the nature of the training that is to be given. A number of our police inverviewees stressed the inappropriateness of the quasi-military model of police training in circumstances when policing draws its responsibility and legitimacy from the actions and authority of individual officers.

---

[48] "Organizations live two lives; there is the structural life - and then there is the culture. The structure is formal and represents the reality of what is *supposed* to happen. Culture is informal and represents the reality of what *actually* does happen. Make no mistake about it, it is the culture that runs things.... The culture is at the root of the worst problems in policing. That culture is at odds with the mandate of consent policing "(Braiden, 1994: 312-313).

Training needs to be shaped with a view to its vital role in developing a positive organisational culture, protective of people's rights. As one former English Chief Constable argued: *"it cannot be stressed too emphatically that the education and training of police officials to understand and employ the principles of human rights is of the utmost importance"*(Alderson, 1992: 15). The link between policing and the protection of civil liberties needs to be regularly revisited and strengthened, and changes to training are clearly part of that process.

This is particularly true of Northern Ireland, where the existence of emergency legislation since the foundation of the Royal Ulster Constabulary (RUC), poses a serious threat to human rights and gives even greater discretion to individual police officers than normal. Tackling the problems created by such a situation means that good human rights oriented training is all the more vital. Our research indicates that the priority which training should have in creating an organisational culture that respects and promotes the rights of all without distinction is heightened, not lessened, in conflict-ridden societies. As Ralph Crawshaw, himself a former senior British police officer, and currently an adviser to the Council of Europe, has stated:

> *"In the event of a serious breakdown of public order, perhaps even involving armed insurgency or acts of terrorism, police and members of other security agencies are faced with great personal danger and formidable challenges to their professional expertise. For these, and other, reasons they almost invariably feel justified in breaching legal and ethical standards which would constrain them under other, less daunting, circumstances. When they do so they risk undermining the democratic and legal principles on which the legitimacy of the state they are defending and their own legitimacy are based"* (Crawshaw, 1995).

The impact of (formal and informal) training on the culture of a policing organisation is all the more significant because a sizeable body of literature attests to the fact that the policing milieu actually lends itself to an extreme form of subculture. Relevant factors include a uniquely stressful work environment, and the similarity of police officers economically, racially and culturally. *"Police are further set apart by the stress, danger, working hours, social stigmatism and unpleasant experiences which their occupation entails and this often results in closed viewpoint and the legitimization of subcultural values".*[49] Training in police work cannot afford to ignore or deny the organisation's tendency to develop a subculture which creates solidarity and looks to protect itself in ways that do not necessarily conform to best practice.

It was very marked in all of the jurisdictions visited that police training is moving away from more traditional methods. Although the extent of the change varied, the need for change and a commitment to introducing new approaches seemed widespread. Despite the introduction of some degree of change (for example, the introduction of a Community Awareness Programme), in essence training is still confined to the closed and militaristic police-designed and police-led model which is now so criticised by senior police managers in other forces. The principles distilled in this chapter make it clear that a complete overhaul of training is required: minor changes will be insufficient. We do not seek to propose a detailed alternative training programme, since there is no single ideal training model. Indeed, few forces would claim to have done more than recognise the problems with their traditional training methods, and begin to introduce some improvements.

Having visited training centres in all the countries studied, we found it instructive to see how police elsewhere are both eager

---

[49] Scheingold, S. The Politics of Law and Order, Longman New York 1984 cited in Project Honour Report (1996).

to share their good and bad experiences, and to learn from practice in other places. Despite the special problems posed to policing in Northern Ireland, many of these vary only in degree from problems that face policing around the world. It is therefore to be hoped that in the course of a thorough overhaul of policing, serious consideration can be given to good training practice elsewhere.

The chapter will therefore start with a brief examination of the problems which experts suggest arise from traditional police training methods. The problems derive from the closed nature of policing institutions and their training programmes, the lack of community involvement in training design and delivery, the discrepancy between the theory taught to a new recruit and the practice on the street, the failure to integrate human rights and cultural awareness training across all courses, and the lack of external scrutiny. The chapter will then go on to examine the solutions that have been or are being explored by police in other countries.

# Problems with traditional training methods

## 1. Closed institutional training settings

The 'shaping of a constable', and the creation of an appropriate organisational culture, traditionally have been achieved through removing the recruit from the community, and 'disembedding' other loyalties in favour of loyalty to the police and state.[50] This continues to be the case in many training models today.

---

[50] Training based on instilling discipline through the use of drill, regulations and fear and respect for authority, was prefaced by a need to remove officers from partisan politics to ensure impartial policing. Unfortunately, where the organisation itself is perceived to be partisan, "total institutional" control is actually harmful. (Niederhoffer, 1967: 51-57; Goffman,1961).

The particular danger this creates is that, where a police force is trained in an almost 'total institution', human rights may suffer at the expense of internal loyalty. Total institutions tend to demand total loyalty, whether to the organisation or to individual colleagues. Officers who do not conform and fail to preserve a code of silence have in many cases been ostracised by their colleagues - something which is particularly dangerous in a situation where officers' lives could come under threat at any time. Professor John Kleinig posits this code of silence as operating within a false dichotomy so often accepted by many police officers - that one is either loyal or disloyal, and there is no third alternative. He sees a code of silence as justified by loyalty to colleagues, and normalised by fear and peer pressure which ensures the silence of many would-be whistleblowers (Kleinig, 1996). Training in a closed academy contributes to this dynamic.

This is not the only danger however. In arguing against the closed academy model, where police train police in relative isolation, Chief Superintendent Cioccarelli of the New South Wales (NSW) police,[51] asserts that the insularity of the model is problematic because:

-        it tends to encourage a siege mentality and inhibits the development of alternative or critical views;
-        it denies student police officers the opportunity to forge enduring relationships with members of other occupations and professions;
-        it may be the nursery of many of the dysfunctional aspects of police culture;
-        it is an integral part of the closed organisational structure which encourages an organisational orientation rather than a community and practice orientation;

[51] Interview, Sydney, November 1996.

-        it cannot provide novice police officers with a real sense of their personal legal responsibilities because of the importance given to professional loyalty and obedience to orders from higher authority.

## 2. Inadequate or non-existent community involvement in police training

Policing impacts differentially on the police and on the community it serves. Yet the community is often not involved in questions of police training. Traditional police training was seen as something best carried out by the experts alone, ie the police themselves. More latterly, the drawbacks of this approach have been recognised. If policing itself is too important to be left to the police (RUC, 1996: Foreword), then so is police training. Many forces, including the RUC, have attempted to involve people from outside the police in training. In the case of the RUC, this has principally been done by inviting groups in to give presentations to police recruits (CPLC, 1997). Yet community involvement must be at the *core* of designing, implementing and evaluating training courses.

## 3. Discrepancies between the theory and practice of policing

There is widespread recognition that, even if initial training succeeds in imbuing an awareness and respect for ethical issues, this can be quickly forgotten, unlearned or actively discouraged when 'real' police work begins.[52] There is always the danger that time spent at a police college is seen as formal rather than real. Many recruits are frequently told by

---

[52] Shearing and Ericson (1991) have argued that while the academy shapes the 'doing of accounts' the street shapes the 'doing of policing'.

experienced colleagues that academy training is something to be 'unlearned' in carrying out real police work (Brewer & Magee, 1991: 71-75).

The RUC has recognised the difficulty of ensuring that what is taught to new recruits is not unlearned once they leave the training programme: *"To impact on the culture of this organisation, there can be no better place to start than the Training Centre because the recruits are fresh, open, receptive to new ideas and keen to contribute to the building of a better future...".*[53] However, much of what is learnt can be undermined, as Superintendent McCune further says: *"Certainly mixing new wine with old can revitalise and stimulate but only to a degree, as much will be lost to peer group pressure which should not be under-estimated".*

Partly however the problem can lie with training itself if what is taught at the academy does not conform to the recruit's experiences once they go into the stations. Throughout this report we are arguing for the need for human rights and cultural awareness training for police. It is crucial, however, that this training relates to real police work. Mission statements and codes of practice are effective tools for ensuring police accountability and it is crucial that recruits are given an understanding of these. However, unless they are related to practice on the streets, they can be viewed as little more than presentation or window-dressing. As Francesc Guillen of the Police Academy in Catalonia said:

> *"You can have police officers who can say the whole contents of the Convention of Rome about freedom and liberties, but they do not know what to do, for instance, about a violent group that is attacking people. In that case, they have to know how to apply human rights in the operational field".*[54]

---

[53] Superintendent Roy McCune, RUC, speaking at 1996 CPLC conference.
[54] Questionnaire response.

One consequence of any discrepancy between the language of presentation (taught in the academy) and the language of action (learnt on the street), is that recruits quickly become cynical and learn the value of image management (de Lint, 1989: 189).

## 4. Marginalisation of human rights and cultural awareness training

Many commentators believe that the teaching of human rights issues and of conflict resolution techniques *"must be understood because they are essential to effective and humane policing."* (Himmelfarb, 1991: 55). Clearly, given that a key responsibility of the police is to ensure the protection of everyone's rights, it is insufficient that issues of rights, equality before the law, and cultural diversity are seen as 'add-ons'. However, this often appears to be the case in traditional police training. A constant message from those interviewed was that these fundamental objectives of policing must pervade the whole training programme, permeate the mission statement of the organisation, and inform the strategic objectives and every aspect of the initial and subsequent training modules. Anything else risks being mere tokenism.

## 5. Limited evaluation and external scrutiny

A further problem of the insularity and closed nature of traditional police training is that it does not lend itself to external scrutiny or to effective evaluation by the community the police serve. This sits uncomfortably with the recognised principle of good management that evaluation should be built into any process to ensure adaptation to changing circumstances. It is also good practice that such evaluation and oversight not be restricted solely to people from within the institution being monitored.

# International responses to the problems of traditional police training

## 1. The location of, and responsibility for, police training

A key problem in traditional police training is the existence of dedicated police training centres, where police alone do the training, and recruits live and largely socialise with other police. Some forces appear to assume that only the police can train police[55] and that the old ways are the best.[56] Yet in most of the countries visited, serious reservations were expressed about these traditional methods of training, and reference was made to complementary and/or alternative approaches being considered and introduced.

For example, in El Salvador, further to the complete disbandment of the former police and in its attempts to create a totally different police service, it was decided that new training processes should be established within a specialist police academy. This academy was established as a separate institution from the National Civilian Police (PNC) and has power to select and train police agents and officers. The idea

---

[55] For example, in the United States, the editorial of the debut issue of the *National Police Magazine* complained that *"one of the heaviest crosses that the policeman (sic) has to bear...is the interference of the so-called league of reformers--the short-haired woman and the long-haired man who want to tell the police just how to run their business, how to do police work, and how to conduct the city."*
[56] Traditionalists strongly defend as a rite of passage rituals such as highly militaristic 'passing out' parades" (Cioccarelli, 1996: 15).

behind the formal separation of the two institutions was that a focus on operational training should not dilute the emphasis on human rights. Power was therefore spread over different parts of the policing process and not concentrated in one single police institution. The Peace Accords spelt out the mechanisms of training oversight including the establishment of a pluralistic academic advisory council. This clearly allows for more independence in training, more external input, and less danger of an all-pervasive police 'occupational culture' swamping ideas. However, one criticism voiced by a number of our interviewees (both within and outside the police organisation) was that training has been too abstract and not entirely suited to the needs of the institution. It is crucial therefore that, if for the reasons mentioned above, it is decided that training should take place in an institution separate from the police, the training must be relevant to policing needs.

In South Africa, the National Peace Accord signed in September 1991 set the pace for policing change in many ways. The top management of the South African police responded with a Strategic Plan in 1992 which included, among other proposals, reform of the existing training system. Further legislation followed in terms of the Interim Constitution of 1994 and South African Police Service Act 1995. Crucial to the reform of training practices were the Police Board (a civilian/police advisory structure),[57] and its offshoots - the International Training Committee (ITC)[58] and the Multinational Implementation Team. The latter both had substantial international input and *"in no small way contributed to a widening*

---

[57] Established by the National Peace Accord 1991 as a transitional structure, the Board agreed to end its existence in December 1994 when its function had been fulfilled, and replacement structures created.

[58] A committee of respected academics and experts created by Minister for Law and Order in October 1992, with the explicit function of reviewing and overseeing all reform in the field of police training, including evaluating the role of the South African Police Academy and studying community needs and international standards.

*of vision in the face of the tight inward looking culture of the police institution"* (Scharf & Van der Spuy, 1996). Training in the formal academy setting, and in the field, were both targeted for reform. "Post-Apartheid" South Africa has only had one intake of new police recruits (in 1995) but international and academic input into the creation and implementation of the pilot basic level training programme was enormous. It will be undoubtedly important to assess how much this new style training contributes to the *"mutation of police into socially aware and self-critical officials"* (Scharf & Van der Spuy, 1996).

In Catalonia, the police training school is an autonomous organisation under the authority of the Catalan Home Office. The Director of the School, a civilian, is appointed by the Catalan Home Office with the approval of the Conseil de Direccio (a collegiate organ which takes important decisions about the life of the school). Similarly, the police training institute at Arkaute in the Basque country is an autonomous institution with a civilian director who is a political appointee of the Basque government. The majority of training staff is civilian, although police trainers are brought in as necessary.

The challenge to the principle of specialist police training institutes run by and for the police is not restricted however to those countries having undergone major political transition. Cioccarelli[59] of the NSW force in Australia, and several of his colleagues, were very critical of the traditional approach. The force has long trained its recruits in a dedicated police academy. However, the force has recently been exposed for corruption at the highest levels, and investigators commented specifically on the process by which corrupt officers were trained together and then moved through the ranks together as they built an empire of corruption around them (Wood, 1996a).

---

[59] Interview, Sydney, Australia, November 1996.

Cioccarelli concludes, with others,[60] that dedicated police training should not take place in an academy which *"in its exclusiveness and remoteness...represents the very antithesis of community-based policing and a substantial repudiation of the conception of a civil, civilian and democratic people's police"* (Cioccarelli, 1996: 15).

In the Netherlands, while it is still mostly police officers who are employed to do the training, civilians are also used and teaching staff get professional teacher training. LSOP (the National Police Selection and Training Institute) claims that students respect the non-police trainers, because the institute has integrated the social science and the operational training parts of the course, rather than there being seen as an "add on". At first students were suspicious of the 'outside' trainers but now they are an accepted element of the course.[61] Amnesty International, the international human rights organisation, is involved in the training of police, particularly in the development of training material.

In Canada (Ontario), the authorities have introduced a model of police training and education called the Police Learning System (PLS). The process is based on the idea of the need for 'lifelong learning' (i.e. continuous in-service training) within the police. It involves co-workers, supervisors, and managers as well as teachers and trainers in and outside the service. To qualify for police service, a cadet must complete at least two semesters at an accredited community college or university. Following this, a person is hired and trained in police procedures at the Ontario Police College. This is followed by a local placement and 'directed work assignment' consisting of not less than forty hours in a

---

[60] For example, see: Closing the Gap: Policing and Community, Final Report of the Commission of Inquiry into Policing in British Columbia Volume 1 (1994: xvii-xviii) - *"rigid paramilitary structure has outlived its usefulness...such a rigid structure does not lend itself to the needs of the organisation, the best interests of the officers involved, or the community at large"*.
[61] Interview with Dr Sandra Wyhjuys, LSOP, Netherlands, 14 November 1996.

community agency in an effort to understand the agency and the people it serves. Finally, 'learners' are required to perform a second ten-day academy course within twenty four months of their initial academy training, and this course is to be individualized with respect to their unique performance assessments.

From the above examples, it is clear that although there is no international consensus about where training should take place. There is agreement, however, that the focus to date in traditional training on the need for separate, closed, insular, training institutes has been widely criticised. There is an increasing tendency to, at the very least, open up dedicated training institutes to civilians. In some instances, civilians engage directly in the work of the institute, whether as trainers, managers or both. In other instances, the training provided at the institute is actively complemented with more community-based learning initiatives.

## 2. Community involvement in police training

A big problem in Northern Ireland is the lack of community involvement in the design and delivery of police training. External involvement in training was strongly resisted for very many years by the RUC, with an internal Training Committee having only one external (academic) representative. The Committee's remit has essentially been limited to making suggestions to the Assistant Chief Constable responsible for training, and it has had no authority to consider issues deemed sensitive, such as the activities and training of Special Branch. The Committee used to meet three times a year and there is now at the time of writing some speculation that it may well be disbanded altogether. In terms of 'outside' input in the delivery of training, there has been very little, apart from occasional selected guest speakers, and the provision for a period of a short Community Awareness package to new recruits by Mediation Network.[62]

The issue of community involvement was addressed in 1990 by the federal Royal Canadian Mounted Police (RCMP) when it undertook a fundamental review of its training. It soon identified the fact that *"a multicultural strategy and training programme must be created in consultation with the... communities served by the police"* (Himmelfarb, 1991). Dr Frum Himmelfarb, Chief Research Officer of the RCMP Training Division affirms that *"training is most likely to be successful if the community is fully and effectively involved in its development and design"* (1991: 55).

The Police Learning Centre at Durham College, Canada, actively builds partnerships with non-police organisations such as education boards and businesses to *"examine where they can share in professional development of senior managers and learning in general"*.[63] The Police Learning Centre at Oshawa, Ontario has centred round the continuous improvement of the individual officer, through the ability of members of the public to scrutinise actual training as it occurs. One of the unique innovations of this program is that, at specified times, the public can attend the Centre in order to see first hand the training that officers receive. Even training sessions relating to the use of force are subject to this form of public observation. Any concerns or comments can then be directly communicated, based on actual knowledge of what takes place. This permits a high level of transparency without interfering with the training as it happens.

---

[62] See CPLC 1997 for details of Mediation Network's work. In the wake of the public disquiet which followed the policing of a series of public order events in 1996, the organisation withdrew from the training programme to consider its implications for their work.

[63] Durham Regional Police Service; Police Learning Activities, 20 June 1996.

Similarly, the phenomenon of 'ride-alongs',[64] permits members of the public in various cities throughout the US and Canada to accompany police on patrol and see street training and practice at first hand. There are obviously security issues to be considered - ride-alongs in the States and Canada have involved excursions into deeply dangerous gangland territories.

Community involvement in police training is not, however, a one-way process. It requires that the police be open to external involvement and scrutiny, but it also requires the ready co-operation of the community. When, for whatever reason, there is distrust or suspicion between the police and parts of the community served, such co-operation may be difficult to establish. Many individuals or groups would hesitate to become actively involved in training programmes if their involvement was thought to be peripheral or tokenistic. Even if, after careful bridge building, and clear signals of a genuine commitment to change on the part of the authorities, such co-operation is secured, it can be quite fragile. What has been very clear from our research is the impact of police operational tactics on police/community relations. The resort to the use of force, for example, cannot be simply seen as an operational question of tactics and techniques, nor can the consequences be measured in individual incidents alone. Such incidents will have an impact on community attitudes to policing over the longer term, and the ethical issues underlying any resort to force need therefore to be fully explored and aired in training, and beyond.

---

[64] An established practice in many US and Canadian cities, (e.g. Detroit, Toronto) whereby members of the public can voluntarily accompany police officers on patrol day or night - to get an idea of what the police face and a better understanding of how police operate on the streets.

## 3. Training and policing - the link between the theory and the practice

The problem that the initial basic training can all too easily appear irrelevant when the new recruit goes onto the street is being addressed in several places by radically re-formulating the objectives of police training.

Training in the Netherlands, for example, relies extensively on the philosophy of 'action-learning'. This means that trainers talk to the students about problems and encourage them to develop skills of problem solving: the new recruits learn to develop ideas for themselves and to be more self-reliant. This approach is reinforced with the creation of a post-qualifying training for police once they start working. Officers attend training for a day a week and, just as importantly, trainers go out and visit police on the job and talk to them in the stations. This refresher training is said to be vital, since experience shows that it is when recruits start work that they are most likely to encounter problems. The further training gives new officers the necessary help in developing the confidence and skills to deal with practical problems.[65]

In South Africa, the concern about equipping the new recruit for effective policing on the streets led to a decision to extend the basic training period from six to twelve months, by including a six month probationary field training period. During the implementation phase, the Multi-National Team's work revolved around *"the introduction of a human rights perspective into the basic training environment, devising a style which was student centred, developing [appropriate] methods of assessment, addressing trainer skills and devising new management structures"* (Scharf & Van der Spuy, 1996: 18-19). The success of this team lay in its providing not only a radical visionary

---

[65] Details from interviews at the police training academy, Netherlands, 14 November 1996.

construct, but in translating the implications of this into managerial policy and organisational infrastructure - and constantly monitoring how this was done. This involved the use of a Field Training Work team within the training college, to monitor and assess how the formal training would and should blend with practice on the ground. Internal evaluation also formed a key part of the programme as it progressed.

There are, of course, problems to be expected in any process of change. For example, in South Africa:

> *"Initiatives often lacked synchronisation resulting in uneven training, and trainers in many instances could have been better trained, particularly during the field work element of the programme. The attitude of officers in the stations posed problems as none of these had received the same type of training as the new recruits. Furthermore, as the idea and practice had not yet taken shape throughout the country, there was no common understanding about how to implement the principles learned in college."*(Scharf & Van der Spuy, 1996: 137).

These problems and others have now been identified and discussed. A number of recommendations have been made, ranging from recruitment to the need to give greater prestige to training within the organisation. However, most agree that it will be some years before the new philosophy and practice becomes an institutional reality *"and even longer before a really significant body of graduates in new style policing has taken its place in the SAPS rank and file"* (Scharf & Van der Spuy, 1996: 24).

In Canada (specifically, in connection with the RCMP's CAPRA[66] programme) various consultations were carried out and a new model for training developed, based on problem-

---

[66] CAPRA is the term given to the RCMP's model for cadet training.

solving initiatives initially introduced in medical training.[67] The key to this process is not to have learners rely on the opinion of existing experts or authorities, but to have them develop expertise by using analytical, research and assessment skills and by forging networks and alliances to help them respond to each individual situation in the most appropriate way (de Lint, 1996). The emphasis in the six month basic recruit program is now not on drills and presentation, but on team problem-solving, negotiation, consensus building, and moral reasoning through case analysis. Although only in existence since 1994, initial feedback seems to indicate an important measure of success since anecdotal evidence suggests that cadets are now starting with an equivalent of 2-5 years experience on the job.[68]

Whereas in the past, people had been hired as RCMP officers and then trained, this was changed to allow people to be taken on as cadets on a contract basis until the completion of their training. The cadet is expected to come to the organisation with competencies already developed in first aid, driving, and computer skills, for example. This is deemed to be evidence that the recruit is self-motivated and has already taken on a degree of responsibility for his/her own training. Only when formal training is completed, is it decided if the recruits are suitable candidates to be offered employment. Not only does this save money in terms of a full pro rata salary for the training period, it also gives further time to trainers and recruiters to assess the extent to which prospective candidates display and develop a number of essential core competencies over the six month training period. The disadvantage, however, of this

---

[67] For example, the conference held in May 1992 by Police Educators' Conference Board of Canada *"brought together police trainers, administrators and operational personnel, outside experts and community and private sector representatives to define priorities and develop recommendations for the future of police training"* and *"Public consultations through conferences and advisory committees were instrumental in shaping these directions"* (RCMP, 1992: 5, 9).

[68] Interview with Dr Himmelfarb, Training Research Section RCMP, Ottawa, October 1996.

approach is that, since pre-job training costs the trainees money, there is a potential disincentive to certain socio-economic groups which would need to be addressed.

Both this RCMP's 'problem-solving' model for cadet training, and Ontario's 'Police Learning System'[69] appear to have been motivated by major constitutional reform, especially the Charter of Rights and Freedoms.  In particular, the Charter has created a demand for more sensitivity to Canada's multicultural reality. Both approaches are based on extensive research which has indicated that the disciplinarian quasi-military approach, which was formerly favoured, rendered trainees insufficiently capable of exercising responsibility when not under direct supervision. The new style training takes into account the fact that police officers on the job have an enormous amount of discretion. Rather than ignore this, or treat officers as infantile by imposing command/control measures, they argue that training processes should instead seek to shape this discretion, and render the trainees more responsible for their actions.

In trying to address the specific and special problems associated with the police's use of force, for example, the RCMP have changed their training package to focus on safety rather than force. The importance of such a change was highlighted during the football disaster at Hillsborough in 1989, when 96 people died in the crush.  Chief Justice Taylor found the main cause to be over-crowding and the main reason for that to be *"failure in police control"* (cited in Scraton et al, 1995: 115). Experts have argued that the South Yorkshire police were unable to cope with the unfolding disaster because they were specifically

---

[69] See Final Report of the Strategic Planning Committee (Ontario, 1992), developed by the Strategic Planning Committee on Police Training and Education set up by the Ontario authorities: *"[t]he police learning system is the product of the most exhaustive review of the state of police training ever undertaken in Canada. The RCMP's 'problem-solving' police training, under which the first batch of recruits was being trained in Regina in 1994, has been called the most major training reform in the RCMP's 120 year history."* (de Lint, 1996: 253).

briefed and trained to think in terms of crowd control and hooliganism rather than crowd safety. As Scraton et al (1995) conclude: *"Police officers were looking through a lens of hooliganism and failed to recognise a tragedy in the making"*.

Again, there is no single model provided internationally to ensure that the police recruit manages to translate his/her training into effective action on the streets for the protection of all. A problem, confirmed in many interviews and of particular relevance to Northern Ireland, is the difficulty police face in moving away from the traditional command/control structure. The response lies in part in changing the focus of the training as the examples above show. Nevertheless, the obstacles to change should not be under-estimated - police forces in many countries have found that elements of the old model remain,[70] and need to be challenged regularly and continuously.

## 4. Training in human rights and ethics

Few police forces in democratic societies fail to address issues of human rights in their formal training programmes. This is only proper since a fundamental objective of policing is to protect and defend the rights of all, to ensure equality before the law, and to do this by having as a primary goal the maintenance of the rule of law. Article 20 of the UN Basic Principles[71] specifically states that:

> *"In the training of law enforcement officials, governments and law enforcement agencies shall give special attention to issues of police ethics and*

---

[70] For example, in South Africa, *"Senior managers were virtually unanimous about the value of maintaining the troop structure of training"* leading to, among other things *"the development of pride [and] unity"*. (Scharf & Van der Spuy, 1996: 19).
[71] UN Basic Principles on the Use of Force and Firearms by Law Enforcement Officials (1990).

> *human rights, especially in the investigative*
> *process, to alternatives to the use of force and*
> *firearms, including the peaceful settlement of*
> *conflicts, the understanding of crowd behaviour,*
> *and the methods of persuasion, negotiation and*
> *mediation, as well as to technical means, with a*
> *view to limiting the use of force and firearms. Law*
> *enforcement agencies should review their training*
> *programmes and operational procedures in the light*
> *of particular incidents"*.

As a civil liberties organisation, CAJ was particularly interested to learn how this issue is being dealt with in different jurisdictions, and what lessons could be learnt from elsewhere about effective human rights training for the police.

Given the history of policing in El Salvador,[72] human rights were seen as a major concern to be addressed in the new dispensation. The United Nations Human Rights Division for El Salvador (known by its Spanish acronym of ONUSAL), conducted human rights seminars for the new police. The disastrous human rights record of the past meant that it would have been politically unacceptable and damaging in practice to the new police to have instructors from the old National Police or the army's Public Security Academy. Accordingly there was a great reliance placed on foreign instructors, and foreign police advisers (especially from Spain) were heavily involved in developing and delivering training courses.[73]      Problems remain, however, and riot training has currently had to be reorganised following excessive use of force by riot police.

---

[72] See El Salvador synopsis.

[73] US Justice Department's International Criminal Investigations Training Assistance Program (ICITAP), run by FBI agents and other civilian US police, provided support for training as did the UN Development Program which supported foreign instructors at the police academy.

In the Netherlands, all those interviewed talked of the importance of not treating human rights as some kind of add-on, or as a series of abstract international legal principles. Instead, human rights are principles that must inform many different policing situations. In practical terms, role playing is frequently used to address issues of community awareness, and actors from ethnic minority backgrounds are often hired to help with this. At the officers' training school, it is particularly noteworthy that the role playing of situations involving use of firearms includes a discussion of the human rights aspects. It is explained to students whether their actions fell within the bounds of the international human rights legislation governing the use of lethal force by police officers. Training institute personnel argue that human rights are most at risk when police officers are involved in a stressful situation. Accordingly, they think that it is important to put recruits in stressful situations and discuss how they react, and how they should react in such situations.

In Catalonia, considerable attention has been paid to ideas of diversity and how the police can work with very different groups in a pluralist society. Role plays, the use of professional actors, presentations from particular groups (such as gay and lesbian groups), and the use of foreign lecturers is also encouraged - both to introduce ideas of multiculturalism but also to talk about police in other countries[74]. The Academy has also started to work closely with the European Network of Policewomen with a view to developing its training around gender and equality issues. However, Francesc Guillen, research director, argues that it is difficult in basic training to go beyond ideas about avoiding stereotypes. He advocated continuing training during officers' careers as a crucial way of ensuring that concepts acquired in training are continually reinforced. The risk of relying alone on basic training to get across these important principles for policing was highlighted

---

[74] Questionnaire from research director of Academy.

in the Basque Country where, although new police recruits are all trained in the use of plastic bullets, police interviewed on the street were vague about situations when the bullets could be used: *"we were told to use our common sense."*[75]

In commenting on policing before the major political changes in South Africa, Janine Rauch found the training of the police to be *"still military in character [with] disproportionate attention on the use of firearms, military discipline and the socialisation of recruits into the police culture. Neither basic training nor in-service training adequately cover police-community relations, ethical problems in policing, police accountability and assessment of policing services and strategies."* (Marais & Rauch, 1992; Rauch, 1992). These problems have since been addressed by the Change Management Team within SAPS, drawing on international expertise. However, as only one intake of recruits had completed basic training at the time of writing it is difficult to assess the advantages and disadvantages of the new training programme. The evaluation process is to be carried out by respected academics and will be very interesting.

The Canadian federal police (RCMP) and others have been looking at new methods for dealing with the especially controversial area of the police use of force. They concluded that often training around issues of force has focused on the 'escalator model', whereby an approach to a confrontational situation is viewed in steps, with the use of lethal force at the top of the steps. In the escalator model, an officer is at the bottom of an escalator and a verbal warning may or may not produce the desired result. The officer would then proceed to the next step – that is, the consideration of whether to use physical force. There is a steady progression through a series of steps towards a decision to resort to the use of deadly force. The escalator approach is inappropriate in many ways, since it becomes almost impossible to de-escalate the situation. The

---

[75] Interview with police on streets of San Sebastian, April 1997.

natural trajectory is constantly looking to the possibility of deadly force. The alternative model now being favoured, is a circular approach which allows an officer, in the middle of a situation, to consider options as and when appropriate, and not necessarily as steps that need to be gone through. A major advantage of the circular approach is that disengagement is a real option. Even if a baton has been drawn - it can be replaced (de Lint, 1996: 235).

There are also lessons to be learned from much closer to home. In England the memorandum Human Rights and the Police, produced by Training Support Harrogate,[76] states that: "*The role of the Police in determining human rights and freedoms is a central policy thrust...and the provision of effective training is seen as making an essential contribution to ensure that these principles permeate from police policy to day-to-day contact between police and citizens.*" To this end, minimum training levels have been established for constables, sergeants, inspectors and police trainers, and human rights issues have been integrated across the curriculum of most courses.

Human rights training, if it is to be effective, requires organisational support at a policy, managerial and supervision level. According to Dr Robin Oakley (a training and research consultant), the Council of Europe Practical Guidelines for Police Training concerning Migrants and Ethnic Relations "*reflect how the need to address ethnic issues is an organisational need and not just a matter of training some individual officers.*"[77] The

---

[76] An integral part of National Police Training which develops and provides training for the police; it supports the ACPO (Association of Chief Police Officers) statement of common purpose and values and is in accordance with the strategy of the Police Training Council. Its remit does not extend to NI.

[77] See Police Training Concerning Migrants and National Minorities paper delivered at Council of Europe seminar, Strasbourg, 6-8[h] December 1995. See also the Lewis Report (198() Canada, which positioned race relations training at the heart of the reform agenda, arguing that systemic causes of discrimination require systemic solutions, including a training agenda "*to change the various attitudes which produce racism in all of us*" (cited in de Lint, 1996: 218).

guidelines, endorsed by experts from 32 countries in Europe, articulate the need for a clear training strategy drawn up in consultation with non-governmental organisations as partners, and the need for such training to permeate the organisation from the most senior levels.

This challenge to integrate human rights concerns into the management of policing was taken up in Queensland, Australia, when a specific programme was introduced to address the question of police ethics. Inspired by research from the National Police Research Unit and the Criminal Justice Commission, the programme highlighted the tendency of police recruits to place less importance on the ethical implications of their decisions, once exposed to operational policing. The Commissioner established a team to survey and conduct interviews into ethical standards within the service, to overview existing ethics training and education, and to develop and enhance systems for corruption prevention. The Project Honour report (October 1996) recommended comprehensive ethics training for sworn and unsworn officers - with managers demonstrating their own commitment by undertaking such courses themselves.

Professor Kleinig (1996) has looked at the ethical issues around professional loyalty within the police. While recognising the potential risks, he attempted to extract what is good from loyalty as a virtue, since it is clearly important in fuelling police heroism and solidarity. Loyalty to others can, however, mean giving up one's independence of judgement. Kleinig examined how an institution can actually foster a situation where an officer will always choose loyalty to a colleague over loyalty to an authoritarian, disciplinarian and bureaucratic organisation, and concluded that *"police must be enabled to see that the code of silence is based on a false dichotomy and is fundamentally at odds with any pretence of professionalism"*(Kleinig, 1996: 12). Historically, the training arena has fostered a particular set of ethics or perceptions. Therefore, it is not unthinkable that training can be shaped to more critically examine various competing loyalties in a way that allows for the formation and development of strong individual integrity and judgement.

The over-riding lesson from international experience is that human rights and ethical principles cannot be an afterthought to any training programme. Human rights are an integral concern to all aspects of policing and as such cannot be taught in isolation but must imbue all aspects of a police officer's training. Human rights principles need not merely to be taught but to shape the nature of a police officer's training and his/her formative process. There are many good-practice models which can be emulated in this regard. Similarly, a concern for ethical policing and for human rights protection needs to permeate all levels of policing, and therefore be an integral part of in-service and management training.

## 5. Evaluation of police training

It is clear that the quality, nature and content of training needs to be kept under constant and systematic review. Many of those interviewed within police forces, particularly in Canada and Australia, have developed or are in the process of establishing some type of research or policy body.[78] Such policy units allow ongoing analysis of the ethical questions which are relevant to police work. They can also draw on a broad range of people to develop police awareness of issues and to discuss policy issues. A similar function is performed in some jurisdictions by a representative Police Board/Authority. Such an authority frequently has responsibility for designing and monitoring the effectiveness of training, both in financial and policy terms. Whether the power this bestows on the group

---

[78] Interview with Chief Inspector Letendre, Montreal, October 1996; see also Project Honour, Queensland.

concerned is utilised to its full extent often depends on the political will and interest of those involved. The extent to which police insist on guarding what has historically been seen as their responsibility is also very important. External oversight and participation, however, was often seen to be largely beneficial by the police themselves.

Project Honour in Queensland, referred to earlier, has been an important impetus to the process of continuous evaluation. The programme was originally established to survey and conduct interviews in relation to the ethical standards within the service, to overview existing ethics training and education, and to develop and enhance systems for corruption prevention. Its report was delivered in October 1996, and it concluded that an Organisational Integrity Unit should be tasked to deal comprehensively and on a permanent basis with many of the issues which had arisen.

In El Salvador, the entire process of recruitment and training has been assisted and regularly monitored by the United Nations. The training and selection process were spelled out in the peace agreements. Recruitment programmes were carried out with international support, with the UN itself involved in organising training sessions with new police, judges, prosecutors, as well as in monitoring initial training for recruits (Call, 1996: 21). Both police and civilian interviewees agreed that UN involvement in oversight had played a vital role in ensuring that human rights remained central to training.

## Summary of Conclusions

CAJ's understanding of the RUC training programme, and more importantly its knowledge of RUC behaviour, suggests that the current police training programme needs to be thoroughly overhauled. Amongst other things, any police training programme needs to find effective and fair means to exclude recruits with an anti-rights disposition; to involve the community in determining the nature of policing (and therefore in decisions about police training); to put community relations and human rights issues at the heart of policing; and change the quasi-military culture currently imbued in recruits. The RUC fails to meet many of the principles of good practice outlined in this chapter. This is not to suggest that the RUC have ignored the problem of training - they have recognised the importance of greater cultural awareness and tried to address the issue in basic training. However, this analysis of the training debate in other jurisdictions has highlighted why anything less than a complete over-haul of the initial and in-service training practices will fail.

1.  Any changes to training must be made in the recognition that training alone will not ensure a totally impartial and accountable police service. Training is however an important component of the debate.

2.  The particular importance of training lies in its potential and actual impact on the organisational culture of policing. Training needs to contribute to the creation of an organisational culture of policing which is respectful of human rights, of cultural diversity, and of working closely with the communities served.

3.  The nature of police training must flow from decisions taken by society as to the kind of police service required.

Security-dominated policing and training are counter-productive; what is needed instead is training which will underpin and make possible the concept of policing by consent.

4.    Since training must derive from an over-arching analysis of the policing needs of the community, changes cannot be achieved in a piecemeal way, but will necessitate a holistic and strategic approach.

5.    Traditional methods of training are coming under increasing criticism.  The fairly widespread practice of training recruits in a closed institutional setting is considered problematic, as is the failure to involve the community effectively in the design and delivery of training, and the frequent marginalisation of human rights training.  Proposals for action are given below.

## Summary of recommendations

1.    International experience suggests that the delivery of training to police recruits should involve people other than just other police officers.  This can be done in a variety of ways:

-    involvement of civilian trainers in a police institute
-    a civilian training institute administered by non-police personnel
-    training outside of any formal institute e.g. placement in a community group
-    accredited courses run in universities and colleges

- mixture of formal police training intermingled with community service and/or work experience
- outside speakers
- practical courses offered by specialist groups etc.

Serious consideration should be given to all of these options.

2.    Training must be delivered by a variety of people so that the diversity of the community to be served is modelled in the very training process. There must for example be both male and female trainers, representatives from the ethnic minorities etc.

3.    Whether in the formulation of the training programme, in the setting of its objectives, in its delivery, in its evaluation, or in its location, civilianisation of the process is of crucial importance. Progress in this direction should be actively pursued.

4.    As part of this process of civilianisation of training, active partnerships should be built, perhaps along the lines of the local partnerships. Such groups could involve voluntary agencies, the statutory sector, local elected politicians, the youth sector and human rights activists. Consideration also needs to be given as to how best to involve the general public in monitoring and commenting on the training programme. (In other chapters we deal with issues of police oversight and local consultative mechanisms which are relevant to this question of society's involvement in questions of police training).

5.    It should be recognised that individual officers out on the street have extensive discretion. It is unwise to ignore this by training police in a quasi-military and strictly hierarchical fashion, and instead, training

methods should seek to inform and direct this discretion by:

- encouraging recruits to develop active problem solving approaches;
- teaching individual officers to be more self-reliant;
- emphasising team problem-solving, negotiation, consensus building and analytical skills;
- developing certain core-competencies and instilling good mental templates about – for example – the possibility and even desirability on occasion of disengaging from particular situations.

6. Training must not be restricted to new recruits, but must continue throughout the career of police officers. There has to be effective support from senior management for good training practices and the philosophy and practices of lifelong learning.

7. Human rights and cultural awareness training must be central to police training and should be integrated across the curriculum. Practical examples of good practice internationally include:

- the use of role plays especially to explore personal prejudices and stereotypes;
- the integration of human rights discussions into firearms training;
- the discussion of recruit reaction in stressful situations;
- the screening out of recruits with an anti-rights disposition;
- the application of international legal principles to practical everyday policing situations;
- presentations by outside groups;
- the use of professional actors, especially from minority ethnic communities, to facilitate debates around cultural awareness;

- the use of foreign lecturers to highlight the value of diversity and pluralism;
- the preparation and study of training documentation specifically addressing human rights issues;
- the evolution of a professional ethic which honours individual integrity and judgement rather than a simplistic and unquestioning loyalty to colleagues or to the organisation
- training support to be directed at police managers so that human rights perspectives are supported at a policy, managerial and supervision level and not merely amongst recruits.

8.      Evaluation of training must be routine and must, if it is to be truly effective, involve people outside of police institutions. The establishment of special research or policy arms, with civilian input, has proved useful in other societies.

# Chapter Three

# *Policing and accountability before the law*

In any democracy, it is vital to ensure that the police generally, as well as individual police officers, are accountable for their actions to the whole of society. The next chapter addresses systems of democratic accountability, but police powers also need to be clearly and tightly regulated by legislation. This chapter will look at the legal framework of policing under the following headings:

1. the rule of law and the issue of denial and impunity
2. international law and practice
3. benefits of a written constitution or bill of rights
4. emergency law
5. legal redress & complaints mechanisms

## 1. The Rule of Law

The single most important principle by which democratic societies can ensure security of person and property is that of the rule of law. The rule of law and in particular respect for human rights must operate as the defining dynamic in the relationship between the government and the governed. The concept of 'the rule of law' means that: no one should be above the law; everyone is equal before the law; the law itself should be clear, fair and comply with international human rights standards; law enforcement officials should apply the law impartially, and an independent judiciary should enforce the law without fear or favour. Very importantly, the rule of law means that policing gains its legitimacy by performing a legal rather than a political function, and by serving the law rather than partisan politics.

As the police draw their authority from the law, legislation providing powers to the police must be clearly and tightly drafted. It is accepted wisdom that sufficient legal and judicial checks and balances should be put in place both to prevent abuse of power and to provide appropriate sanctions when the law is disregarded.  If police are permitted to co-opt the law to their own ends (however valid those ends may appear to be), the law can come to treat certain groups of people as a suspect community (Hillyard, 1995) or underclass (Rose, 1996), simply because of who they are, where they live, their politics etc.  If laws are, or appear, unjust, certain police actions – whatever their technical legality - will be perceived and experienced by many of those policed as illegitimate.  Similarly, if the judicial process fails to detect or punish police wrongdoing, the rule of law can appear as little more than a cynical tool of political control.

Such dangers are all the more to be guarded against in places like Northern Ireland where political differences have spilled over into violent conflict.    Instead, the tendency for governments in such situations is to allow the law to develop in a narrow, security-led fashion which erodes rather than respects basic safeguards (Boyle & Hadden, 1996).  Whatever the perceived merits of such an approach in the short term, and we discuss the issue of "emergency" legislation and powers in more detail later, one of the consequences is that the law comes to be seen as a cover for official impunity.

Political conflict should not obscure society's legitimate demands of any police force to operate within strict parameters and be held accountable for any wrongdoing.  A desire to support the police in a 'fight against terrorism' should not lead to judging their actions less rigorously.  The stresses and difficulties of their job make it all the more important that independent and effective scrutiny take place. Otherwise, as Ralph Crawshaw (a former senior UK police officer and advisor to the Council of Europe), points out:

> *"one of the consequences...is that those who are subjected to [police abuse] become radicalised, and more prepared to join or support violent, subversive opposition groups. Another consequence is that such groups benefit hugely from the propaganda value of serious lapses of behaviour by state security forces. There are, therefore, practical, as well as ethical and legal reasons for respecting lawful human rights standards when confronting groups of that nature."*(Crawshaw, 1995).

Our research confirms that failure to draw and sustain appropriate boundaries to police action undermines faith, not just in the police, but in the law as an impartial arbiter of conflict. A variety of indicators (to be discussed below) suggest that the current checks and balances in Northern Ireland have not been effective in deterring, detecting, and punishing wrongdoing by the police. The following analysis shows that new and clearer forms of legal accountability are not something to be feared, but instead can benefit both police and public in enhancing respect for the rule of law.

## Denial and impunity

One of the problems faced in societies world-wide in securing the rule of law, is the temptation on the part of the police and government authorities to deny any wrongdoing, still less to take effective action to end it.

The process of denial of police wrongdoing is so commonplace that it can be seen within the ordinary criminal justice system and in jurisdictions of a more consensual nature. Very few courts in the world can claim to be blameless of the phenomenon of tending to believe a police officer's word in preference to all but the most respectable and middle class of defendants/witnesses (Chevigny, 1996; Brogden, 1988; Lea & Young, 1984).[79] The power of the police to exploit this privileged position in the judicial system is exemplified by what has been called the 'Contempt of Cop' phenomenon.   In his research, Paul Chevigny articulated a set of dynamics for police abuse that he identified in many culturally diverse countries. He consistently found that complaining about inappropriate police behaviour often results in charges being laid against the complainant since then any complaint made against the police can be portrayed as vexatious or indicative of 'anti-police' bias. Conviction becomes easier and in turn makes it less likely that any complaint will be substantiated, whatever its initial merit. Speaking at a Forum debate in January 1997, Councillor Gregory Campbell (of the Democratic Unionist Party) confirmed this to be a phenomenon in Northern Ireland also:

> *"All members here will know of cases, particularly in public-order situations but not exclusively so, in which charges are levelled.   First of all, a person makes a complaint concerning alleged action by a police officer. Initially the complainant does not have charges levelled against him, but subsequently he is charged by the police."*[80]

This in itself is a worrying trend and requires more research and analysis than this report permits. However, even more damaging to the credibility of the rule of law, is when a government chooses to respond to human rights concerns by

---

[79] This is due in part to the fact that criminal law tends to concentrate on crime perpetrated by the poor, but the traditional backgrounds, appointment process and training of the judiciary are also relevant.

[80] NI Forum for Political Dialogue, Record of Debates, Friday 24 January, no. 25, page 12.

denying them, rather than ordering a full impartial and public investigation of allegations of abuse. International experience shows that governments frequently prefer to deny wrongdoing in preference to acknowledging the possibility of police abuse. The reasons behind this phenomenon of denial may be varied, but the results are always detrimental for the rule of law.

Stanley Cohen has studied the practice of denial to the point of schematising the different methods practised by governments/police accused of human rights abuse (Cohen, 1995). To summarise briefly here, one form of denial is literal denial, where, in response to an allegation of wrongdoing by the security forces, the government/police initially deny that anything untoward happened. On other occasions, the raw facts might be accepted but denial is interpretive, in that the interpretation or news-spin placed on the situation by the authorities is very different from that of eyewitnesses or critics. Perhaps even more worryingly, implicatory denial is often used by the authorities to deflect attention from themselves by implicating the victim as a guilty party. A common feature of such denial is to displace blame completely on to the civilian victims (for a particularly blatant example of this, see the government response immediately in the wake of Bloody Sunday – Mullan, 1997). All of these forms of denial have been practised in Northern Ireland.

It is disturbing to see how common the phenomenon of denial is in many parts of the world, given that it can only compound the destabilising effect that the original crime/abuse has upon the rule of law. No matter how difficult the political or criminal situation faced, when police officers do not obey the law, they must acknowledge their wrongdoing and face the legal consequences of their actions.

Obviously the whole denial phenomenon can be much more subtle and nuanced. Cohen (1995), for example, illustrates how even Partial Acknowledgement can also be a form of denial.

Acceptance of some sort of blame is almost a last resort and still requires that the wrongdoing must be distanced from normal or current practice. Self-correction is deemed to be the solution, and outside intervention is argued to be unnecessary. This response of course risks perpetuating the same types of abuse, with the law being by-passed and the same lack of accountability continuing. In Northern Ireland, there have been a series of inquiries, reviews and commissions examining policing and police powers, established by successive governments. Some might point to such initiatives in response to charges of impunity. However, close scrutiny belies the claim that there has been significant political will deployed to ensure full police accountability before the law. These inquiries have often only followed mass public outcry or international pressure, and in most cases had a limited remit –

- not permitting the study to look beyond specific incidents;[81]
- others started from a contested premise, for example that the criminal law is insufficient to deal with the situation in Northern Ireland, and that emergency law is essential;[82]
- others were confined to making recommendations for the future rather than dealing with the past;[83] and
- yet others were expected to concentrate on technical and managerial issues without addressing deeper concerns.[84]

Often the only recommendations pursued appear to have been those acceptable to the authorities (Boyle & Hadden, 1994: 97-98). This does little to instil confidence in the rule of law.

---

[81] e.g. Scarman 1972.

[82] e.g. Review of NI (Emergency Provisions) Acts 1990, Cmnd 1115.

[83] e.g. Report of the Bennett Committee 1979, Cmnd, 7497.

[84] e.g. Reports by Her Majesty's Inspectorate of Constabulary.

# 2. International law and practice

There are many useful principles in international law that can be drawn upon in the formulation of domestic legislation governing police activities and powers. In company with key human rights legislation such as the European Convention (soon to be incorporated into UK law), and the International Covenants on Civil and Political, Economic, Social and Cultural Rights, the following examples reflect a number of concerns articulated by the international community in respect of policing. They have been selected on the basis of issues which have particular resonance in Northern Ireland.

Framers of legislation, and police officials, should look in detail at the good practice that is laid down in these international texts, with a view to overhauling the current legal framework governing policing.

## The UN Code of Conduct for Law Enforcement Officials[85]

- insists that policing must respect human rights and human dignity and that domestic law make specific reference to the relevant international and regional standards in this regard (Article 2).
- insists that force is only to be used *"when strictly necessary"* (Article 3) with emphasis on *"proportionality"*. The commentary on this article articulates that recourse to force should be *"exceptional"*, with the use of firearms *"an extreme measure"*.
- insists that all material gained in the course of a police officer's work must be kept confidential (Article 4).

---

[85] Adopted 17 December 1979.

- insists that neither torture, nor cruel, inhuman or degrading treatment are acceptable regardless of the level of security threat (Article 5).
- insists that effective mechanisms are available to police officers who believe that a violation of the Code has occurred, or is about to occur (Article 8).

Given concerns about the use of lethal force, collusion and interrogation methods, these principles are all relevant to policing practice in Northern Ireland.

## The UN Basic Principles on Use of Force[86]

- insist that *"governments and law enforcement agencies shall adopt and implement rules and regulations on the use of force and firearms against persons by law enforcement officials. In developing such rules and regulations, governments and law enforcement officials shall keep the ethical issues associated with the use of force and firearms constantly under review"*(Article 1).
- insist that governments equip their police with a range of equipment which would allow for a differentiated use of force; that they develop non-lethal incapacitating weapons *"with a view to increasingly restraining the application of means capable of causing death or injury"*; and that they provide safety equipment which would *"decrease the use of weapons of any kind"* (Article 2).
- insist that even the use of non-lethal incapacitating weapons be carefully evaluated and controlled (Article 3).
- insist that the police *"as far as possible apply non-violent means before resorting to the use of force and firearms. They may use force and firearms only if other means remain ineffective"*(Art. 4).
- insist that the police exercise restraint, act in proportion to the risk, minimise damage and injury, ensure medical

---

[86] Adopted 1990.

treatment is rendered to the injured as soon as possible, and that relatives are speedily informed of injuries (Article 5).

- insist that governments ensure that arbitrary and abusive use of force is punished as a criminal offence (Article 7).

Article 8 is worth citing in full: "*Exceptional circumstances, such as internal political instability or any other public emergency may not be invoked to justify any departure from these basic principles*". Further provisions relate to the use of firearms, policing unlawful assemblies, policing persons in custody, police training, and reporting and review procedures, all of which would be useful to draw upon in the establishment of domestic rules of procedure. A practical example of how the international standards in this area appear to be being ignored, and the failure to date of existing accountability mechanisms, can be found as regards the RUC's use of plastic bullets (see HMIC, 1996; CAJ, 1996 & 1997; HRW 1997).

## UN Principles on the Effective Prevention and Investigation of Extra-Legal, Arbitrary and Summary Executions[87]

The UN Principles lay down very clear parameters for the prevention and investigation of any illegitimate use of force.

Article 1: "*Governments shall prohibit by law all extra-legal, arbitrary and summary executions…Exceptional circumstances including a state of war or threat of war, internal political instability or any other public emergency may not be invoked as a justification of such executions….*"

Article 2: "*In order to prevent (such killings)… governments shall ensure strict control, including a clear chain of command over all*

---

[87] Adopted 24 May 1989.

*officials responsible for apprehension, arrest, detention, custody and imprisonment, as well as those officials authorised by law to use force and firearms."*

Later Articles talk of the prohibition on superior officers giving orders to carry out such killings, the right and duty of officers to disobey any such order, the necessity for police training to emphasise these principles and the need for effective legal remedies. In providing guidance regarding claims that an extra-judicial killing has occurred, the Principles talk of the need for *"thorough, prompt and impartial investigations... The purpose of the investigation shall be to determine the cause, manner, and time of death, the person responsible, and any pattern or practice which may have brought about that death..."* (Article 9). *"The investigative authority shall have the power to obtain all the information necessary to the inquiry...(including) the authority to oblige officials allegedly involved in any such executions to appear and testify"* (Article 10).

Examples abound of situations in Northern Ireland which would seem to violate these basic principles of accountability (CAJ, 1992a; Amnesty International, 1994).

## Other regional texts of relevance

In addition to these United Nations texts, the Moscow Declaration, produced by the Organisation of Security Cooperation in Europe (OSCE) in 1991, gives guidance as to how police officers should implement regional and international treaties such as the European Convention on Human Rights, the International Covenant on Civil and Political Rights, and the regulations which are laid down in the Standard Minimum Rules for The Treatment of Prisoners and in the Convention against Torture.

According to the Declaration on the Police issued by the Parliamentary Assembly of the Council of Europe in Resolution 690 in 1979 - it should always be possible to ascertain who is 'ultimately' responsible for acts and omissions of any and all police officers.

## Other jurisdictions

In addition to international and regional legal principles and institutions, it is worth looking at how other jurisdictions have attempted to put these principles into practice. One of the most interesting in this regard is El Salvador. In the major overhaul of policing in that country, there were both important negative and positive experiences worthy of study. On the negative side there was a failure to sufficiently reform the wider legal system. This lacuna led to an element in the police force slipping back into the repressive tactics of the old force without appropriate legal sanction or redress. This brought the whole force, and many other reforms, into disrepute. The obvious lesson to be learnt is that it is vital not to look at the police in isolation from the legal context in which they operate. Policing does not take place in a vacuum, and police abuse can only be sustained if supported by factors outside the organisation as well as within. Radical change therefore necessitates a much broader vision than making structural adjustments to one organisation.

On the positive side, however, El Salvador did create a new post of Human Rights Ombudsperson in the context of the National Peace Accords (see transition chapter). The present incumbent has shown how effective such a position can be if the person fulfilling the role is determined and committed to make sure that the authorities, are properly held to account for their behaviour. In the few years of her tenure she has to date: vetoed the appointment of a national police commissioner on human rights grounds; challenged the constitutionality of the newly-re-instituted emergency legislation; and developed a pro-active role in evolving less violent means of crisis resolution (the latter arose from the public outcry which followed a very heavy-handed police operation to rescue hostages) (WOLA, 1996). This highlights both the importance of extensive legislative powers to increase human rights protection, and the necessity of appointing a body/person with the courage to use those powers in a pro-active manner.

While the focus of much of the debate in many of the countries visited is on external legal checks and balances, it is worth emphasising that internal police checks and balances are also highly significant. International law emphasises the responsibility that each officer bears in carrying out his/her duties and yet, as discussed elsewhere (see chapter 2), it is often difficult for officers who wish to break rank and to challenge perceived abuses. To counter this, several jurisdictions have felt it necessary to enact domestic legislation which creates a duty on police officers to report misconduct or to co-operate with inquiries into police complaints. This in turn gives rise to the need for increased protection for 'whistleblowers'.

Queensland, Australia, for example, has introduced legislation[88]which requires even the suspicion of misconduct to be reported. A paper published by the Queensland Criminal Justice Commission in 1996[89] concluded that *"as a result of the Fitzgerald reforms, internal disciplinary processes in the QPS have been tightened up and police in management and supervisory positions have become more active in setting standards and initiating action against officers suspected of misconduct. There are also some positive signs that the code of silence has less of a hold over the rank and file of the QPS than in the pre-Inquiry era"*. The Queensland paper goes on to warn about the difficulties of achieving long

---

[88]e.g.Whistleblowers Protection Act 1994 and s.7 Police Service Administration Act 1991. Freedom of information legislation has also been deemed to be important in tackling abuse.
[89] Brereton & Ede: The Police Code of Silence in Queensland: The Impact of the Fitzgerald Inquiry Reforms.

term cultural and behavioural change. Whereas some change might be instigated following a particularly damning inquiry, strategies need to be put in place to maintain the momentum of organisational reform over the longer term. It is for this reason that internal and external oversight mechanisms need to be created and maintained.

## 3. The Benefits of a Written Constitution

One important mechanism introduced elsewhere which has been found to secure fuller legal accountability from the police is the introduction of a written constitution or Bill of Rights. Such an initiative formalises the responsibility of a state to protect the rights of all and to guarantee the rule of law. Legislation cannot of itself ensure good practice, but a Bill of Rights should codify in domestic law those obligations which a government has committed itself to under international law.

A framework for accountability based solidly on an entrenched Bill of Rights has certainly clarified and improved the situation of policing and human rights protection in a number of the countries visited. In the interim Constitution of South Africa, it was felt sufficiently important to write a number of detailed prerequisites for police accountability into the constitution itself, at least for a transitional period of a number of years.[90] Fundamental constitutional human rights protections were also commented on positively in discussions in Canada. The Canadian police had initially viewed the Charter of Rights and Freedoms with suspicion in the early 1980s, feeling it would make their job more difficult. Over the years, however, police forces have come to recognise the visionary value of such standards in helping them make difficult decisions and perform

---

[90] For example, constitutional provisions were made for Community Police Fora and an Independent Complaints Directorate.

their job more effectively at a distance from partisan political control.[91]

The decision of the UK government to incorporate the European Convention on Human Rights is an important step towards greater protection of human rights. However, the draft legislation is relatively weak, and as such will limit the potential for protecting human rights. Incorporation should mean that criminal justice (including police) training will, as a minimum, have to take into account the provisions of the Convention in a way it does not presently do. However, to ensure broad human rights protection, this measure ought to be seen, not as an end in itself, but as the first step en route to a Bill of Rights. The passage of such a charter of rights would allow us to adapt good international and regional standards to the particular needs of Northern Ireland.

# 4. Emergency law

A Bill of Rights would also be a standard against which to measure emergency powers, and ensure that any such legislation was informed by broader concerns than a narrow militaristic version of security. International law already lays down clear, if minimal, safeguards for the protection of rights. It recognises that exceptional circumstances may arise which threaten the life of a nation, and which require that some rights may need to be temporarily suspended. Accordingly, it distinguishes clearly between rights which can never be abrogated (for example, the right not to be tortured) and those rights which, for a temporary period, and with a view to protecting the rights of all, may need to be limited. The

---

[91] Interview with Barry Leighton, Solicitor General's Office, Ontario, Canada, October 1996.

essential point, however, is that there should be a return to normality in the shortest possible time. Permanent emergency legislation is not envisaged under international human rights law for although emergency legislation might appear to contain the problem of violent conflict in the short term, it does so at the expense of other long-term needs. Moreover, the experience of South Africa, El Salvador and many other countries around the world, is that the ending of emergency legislation is a prerequisite to the creation of a police service respectful of human rights, and of effective mechanisms of legal accountability.

This does not mean that police organisations easily cede such powers, particularly if they have never before had to police without them. In the case of El Salvador, for example, the police were at the forefront in arguing successfully for the re-introduction of emergency legislation in reaction to a wave of serious criminal activity. In response in part to the concern that these powers can all too easily become permanent, the Ombudsoffice for Human Rights is currently challenging the constitutionality of the decision to return to an emergency power regime.

Our research suggests that a major problem as regards securing effective legal accountability in Northern Ireland is the existence of emergency legislation. A whole array of powers is conferred on the police by the ordinary criminal law supposedly to assist them police society effectively. Emergency legislation means further powers and seriously risks a dilution of the safeguards usually taken for granted in a democratic society. The legislature's rationale in eroding basic civil liberties in this way is that the struggle against terrorism requires extraordinary measures. However, international experience (International Commission of Jurists, 1983) would suggest that it is these very powers which detract from the police's ability to do their job effectively and to "*respect and protect human dignity, and maintain and uphold the human rights of all persons".[92]* It is for this reason that international law[93] seeks to impose strict limits on the use, extent and duration of emergency legislation in any country.

Furthermore, particular problems arise in divided societies where the existence of wide legal powers for the police may come to be seen to have a disproportionate impact on one section of the community. Any such trend undermines the notion of policing by consent. In Northern Ireland, a divisive view of the role of the police has been bolstered by the historical and continuing perception in the eyes of many unionists, that the Royal Ulster Constabulary (RUC) provides the first line of defence for the Northern Ireland state against the reunification of Ireland (Farrell, 1976; Buckland, 1979; Brewer, 1991). For many nationalists, the RUC is, by the same token, deemed to be a political force. Rather than fostering respect for the rule of law, emergency powers and a lack of sufficient and effective legal safeguards have exacerbated conflict and make it more, not less, difficult to create the conditions necessary for impartial policing by consent.

Yet emergency legislation has existed throughout the seventy-five years of the life of the RUC and the need for it has been consistently argued by the authorities. The RUC has never worked solely within the framework of ordinary law. Instead, they (and other elements of the legal system) have operated a two tier criminal legal apparatus, with differing standards and safeguards[94] depending on the motivation of the crime allegedly committed. The work of the CAJ and other human rights groups, as well as that of major European and United Nations bodies, provides many examples (historic and current) of

---

[92]Article 2 of the UN Code of Conduct for Law Enforcement Officials.
[93] e.g. Article 15 European Convention on Human Rights.
[94] e.g. the standards of admissibility for confession evidence differ markedly as between Article 74 PACE (NI) Order 1989 and Section 12 of the Emergency Provisions (NI) Act 1996.

abuses occurring as a result of the existence of emergency legislation. For example, emergency legislation provides the RUC with extensive authority to stop and search people and dwellings and significant leeway in the matter of investigating suspected paramilitary crime. A person can be detained for up to 7 days without charge, can be denied access to legal advice for up to 48 hours at a time and, if tried for a crime, will not be entitled to jury trial but will have one judge sitting alone decide his or her fate. This emergency legislation fails to provide the minimal safeguards guaranteed by the European Convention on Human Rights and has necessitated the UK government exempting[95] itself from compliance with fundamental human rights obligations.

The impact of the violent conflict on individual officers, or the RUC as a whole, should neither be denied nor minimised. However, research[96] has shown that it is in precisely such circumstances that the existence of extraordinary powers renders any police force more likely to act in contravention of their own and international codes of ethics. Furthermore, in the absence of effective scrutiny, abuses which occur in an effort to contain or end conflict actually exacerbate it (Brewer, 1990: 78-91). It is, therefore, problematic and counter-productive to use the justification of violent attacks on the police force as a reason for short-circuiting the ordinary criminal justice system and subverting many otherwise guaranteed elements of the rule of law. To avoid the risk of succumbing to a security-led agenda, police conduct, particularly that of Special Branch and other units involved in what is termed counter-insurgency policing, needs to be more not less open to effective scrutiny than policing in less violent situations.[97]

---

[95] Through derogation under Article 15 ECHR, and currently in violation of the ECHR judgement in Murray v UK ECHR 1996, 22 EHRR 29.

[96] ICJ (1983) and see also Report to 35th Session of United Nations Sub-Commission on the Prevention of Discrimination and the Protection of Minorities, by N Questiaux, UN Special Rapporteur, 1982.

[97] For discussion of oversight of the intelligence services see chapter four.

> *"Police are law enforcement officials which means that they have a duty to enforce and respect law which protects human rights. They are certainly not entitled to violate this law when enforcing other law...in doing so they are not reducing criminality, they are adding to it"* (Crawshaw, 1995).

To counter criticisms of emergency powers, some would argue that all such legislation is safeguarded from any subjective political agenda, because it has been informed by parliamentary debate, and the police merely obey the will of the legislature in this respect. However, it is not so easy to disentangle the police from the legislation they enforce. Close scrutiny reveals that far from the RUC disinterestedly applying laws developed by a separate body, police influence has been key in designing the content of that legislation. It has been argued that *"It is hard to resist the conclusion that it is often the views of the security authorities on what should be permitted under emergency and related legislation that determines the law rather than the law that sets effective limits on what the security forces are permitted to do"* (Boyle & Hadden, 1994: 98).

Furthermore, once civil liberties have been eroded by statute, it has been almost impossible to reinstate them:

> *"The essentials of the structures put in place in 1973 and 1974[98] have not been changed. The most significant alterations have not been to limit or restrict police or army powers but to increase them whenever that has been demanded by the security authorities. In the review of the [Prevention of Terrorism] legislation prior to its re-enactment in 1989, for example, Lord Colville recommended the*

---

[98] This was when the Civil Authorities (Special Powers) Act of 1922 was replaced by the Northern Ireland (Emergency Provisions) Act and the Prevention of Terrorism (Temporary Provisions) Act.

> *introduction of a number of significant limitations*
> *and safeguards, including the removal of the power to*
> *reintroduce internment and the video recording of*
> *police interrogations, and a few extensions such as a*
> *new power to search documents. None of the*
> *limitations or safeguards were accepted, and all the*
> *extensions were approved"* (Boyle & Hadden, 1994:
> 97)

In short, emergency legislation has become normalised in Northern Ireland.[99] It has been deemed to be a good thing, largely because the security forces feel it is necessary. Police knowledge and opinions must be accorded their place. However, this is not the criterion upon which a democratic society should base legislative decisions. Normalisation of emergency powers has led to a large measure of acceptance without sufficient regard to the consequences for the rule of law or international obligations. Successive governments have failed to produce concrete evidence that the existence of emergency law, over and above the provisions of ordinary criminal law, assists the police to perform a difficult job in the most humane and effective way possible. Rather, the duration and extent of emergency legislation in Northern Ireland provide evidence of an abdication of civil society's responsibility to ensure a high level of protection for human rights.

---

[99] The law on the right to silence is a case in point. The government introduced the Criminal Evidence (NI) Order 1988 on the basis that that many suspects accused of paramilitary activity were remaining silent during interviews, although no evidence was produced to support this. However the legislation was framed in such a way that everyone arrested under the criminal law (emergency and non emergency) would be affected. This change then led in Britain to the Criminal Justice & Public Order Act 1994. A move aimed at 'defeating terrorism' in Northern Ireland was thereby 'normalised' and is currently used against suspects in all criminal cases in England, Wales and Northern Ireland.

# 5.  Legal redress & complaints systems

In Northern Ireland the phenomenon of denial of wrongdoing, broad emergency powers, and the lack of a Bill of Rights, is compounded by the paucity of effective legal remedies.

This is perhaps most starkly exemplified in the matter of killings by the security forces. Approximately 360 deaths have been attributed to the security forces, and in this most serious of actions, it is incumbent on the authorities to ascertain to their own and others' satisfaction that the force used was proportionate. However, the quality of investigation of such cases has been criticised,[100] and of all of the deaths, only a handful has resulted in criminal prosecutions.[101] No police officer has ever been convicted of murder committed while on duty, despite quite extensive evidence of foul play.[102]

---

[100] e.g. Former Deputy Chief Constable of Greater Manchester Police commenting on the obstruction of his investigation  said: "*It did not take us long to realise how unused RUC Special Branch officers were to any sort of outside scrutiny. Simple requests for explanations of basic systems and procedures were regarded with suspicion and resentment*".  He also said: "*the files were poorly prepared and presented. A...high level of inquiry...was shamefully absent...They bore no resemblance to my idea of a murder prosecution file*" (Stalker, 1988: 34,40).

[101] Prosecutions occurred in 22 cases of lethal force by the security forces, resulting in 4 convictions of military personnel for murder (18th SACHR Annual Report).

[102] For example, Sampson recommended in 1987 that a number of RUC officers be prosecuted for conspiracy to murder Michael Tighe in 1982. He apparently further recommended proceedings against MI5 officers for the deliberate destruction of a tape recording of the shooting of Michael Tighe considered by Stalker and Sampson to be crucial in deciding whether to bring charges for murder. No prosecutions followed. The Attorney General told the House of Commons (25 January 1988) that, despite evidence of attempts to pervert the course of justice, there would be no prosecutions "in the public interest". Amnesty International saw the government's inaction around the destruction of evidence in a murder investigation as an example of "*deliberate concealment of evidence of possible unlawful actions of state officials.*" (A.I.: Eur 45/10/91).

Often a family's only forum to discover the truth of what happened is a coroner's inquest, a legal procedure that has long been condemned as seriously flawed (CAJ, 1992a). In a number of cases such hearings have not been held (if at all) until years after the event, and do not attract legal aid to allow family representation. Furthermore, the person who allegedly pulled the trigger does not need to attend, the jury cannot reach a verdict,[103] and the imposition of Public Interest Immunity Certificates, has also frequently prevented the full story being aired.

Therefore, in addition to a legislative framework aimed at preventing abuse occurring, there must be effective legal mechanisms to discover and punish abuses once they have taken place. There are a variety of such mechanisms in Northern Ireland:

- judicial review;
- civil action;
- maladministration action;
- making a complaint against individual officer(s).

At the present time, however, all of these options provide very limited forms of redress. For example, the narrow grounds upon which executive decisions can be challenged, and the lack of onus on a Chief Constable to give reasons for decisions classed as 'operational' or affecting 'national security', make it difficult to mount an effective legal challenge through the courts. The judiciary has often been unwilling to intervene where decisions have been categorised as 'operational', or where they believe that policy issues are involved which are best left to the executive or legislature (Boyle and Hadden, 1994). It has been beyond the scope of this research to fully investigate the role played by the judiciary and wider judicial

---

[103] This is not the case in Britain.

system in either exacerbating mistrust or contributing to more impartial and honest policing. Our research does, however, highlight the need for much more substantive work in this area.

# Complaints - a case study

A formal police complaints system, which in Northern Ireland has recently been the subject of extensive review, can provide an important mechanism of redress as an alternative to judicial remedies. The move in many parts of the world to civilian oversight of police complaints systems has been strengthened by a growing recognition that dealing with police complaints as a purely internal matter is problematic. Civilian oversight is intended to sharpen police management practices - but also to provide a level of transparency and accountability not apparent when police are left to investigate police and enforce discipline without outside scrutiny or input.

> Chevigny has argued for *"a permanent tripartite system of accountability including a fact finding body for complaints, an auditor with power to obtain documents from the [police] department and an internal inspector general who can make sure that the findings of the other bodies are turned into working policy by the department...none of the devices taken alone has come close to being effective"* (Chevigny, 1996).

Various models of civilian oversight and review have evolved in the countries visited. Some were undoubtedly better than others - but even the best suffered to some extent from a negotiation process where police or police union opinion was accorded excessive weight in circumscribing the civilian body's powers at the outset.

Dr Lewis[104] in the course of doctoral research on the subject, came to the conclusion that this tendency means that many proposals for new and improved civilian oversight mechanisms fail because of a focus on a short-term political agenda, too placatory of police views and attitudes. This is not to say that police should not be involved in the consultation process. A sense of police involvement in the new system is extremely important, and the process must ensure that police desires and fears are met and accorded due weight. However, if this results in a watering down of the powers needed to secure effective oversight and enhanced accountability, the problem of accountability is exacerbated, not resolved.

## Police Complaints Systems: The Hayes Review

In response to fairly widespread concern about the efficacy of the police complaints system in Northern Ireland, the UK government in 1995 commissioned former Ombudsman, Dr Maurice Hayes, to review the present police complaints system and make recommendations. Following international comparative research, Hayes concluded (1997), in line with previous CAJ research (CAJ, 1990 and 1993) that the Independent Commission for Police Complaints (ICPC) had failed to perform a sufficiently credible and coherent role.

This failure can be blamed in large measure on the fact that the ICPC has very limited legislative powers.[105] Hayes concluded

---

[104] Dr Coleen Lewis, law professor at Monash University, Australia in address to IACOLE Conference, McLean, Virginia, USA, 26th September 1996.

[105] For example, the ICPC can only supervise investigations carried out by the police themselves; it has no independent investigative powers of its own; certain categories of investigation are dependent on a request for supervision coming from the Chief Constable; it can only substantiate a complaint where the case has been proved beyond reasonable doubt; and the Chief Constable chairs any subsequent disciplinary appeal.

that *"the (current) system focuses too much on innocence and guilt for the more minor cases, instead of customer satisfaction. Cases take too long; there is little systematic reporting back to the complainant [who loses sight of what he/she sees as his/her action], and there is insufficient action to draw lessons from the complaints and to use them as a tool of management"* (Hayes, 1997: 11). One further telling statistic of the lack of credibility of the ICPC is its failure to substantiate even one complaint of assault by the police on a civilian arrested under emergency legislation since the Commission's inception in 1988.[106] Despite this, legal settlements amounting to £500,000 per year for civil claims arising from assaults and various other incidents of abuse have been agreed and while there is no detailed breakdown *"it is reasonably clear that a number of cases relate to complaints or might otherwise have led to a complaint"* (Hayes, 1997: 20).[107]

The project's collation of extensive and up-to-date information about police complaints systems in over a dozen jurisdictions is timely, as it allows us to make a detailed commentary on the excellent work already undertaken by Dr Hayes. It is unnecessary in our opinion to reproduce here our country-by-country findings, or the arguments for civilian investigation of police complaints, since this would in large measure merely replicate information available in the Hayes' report and previous CAJ research. Instead, as Hayes' recommendations received widespread political and police acceptance at the time of publication of his report, our intention is rather to take these findings as the starting point of discussion, and indicate which of his conclusions were confirmed in the course of our own independent research. There are also a number of areas where, on the basis of our research, we believe that Dr Hayes' findings

---

[106] See reports of the ICPC.

[107] Viscount Runciman commented that it is *"unsatisfactory for the reputation of the police service when it is reported in the press that large sums in damages have been awarded or agreed to be paid in respect of serious misconduct by identified police officers and it then becomes known that no disciplinary action is to be taken against the officers concerned"* cited in Hayes, 1997:20.

could be further strengthened or would benefit from greater elaboration.

For example, our research concurs completely with Hayes that piecemeal reform of internal structures or external mechanisms is problematic, unless viewed as part of a wider and more holistic process of change. At the very outset of his report Hayes concludes that effective civilian oversight of complaints forms only a small part of improving police accountability and practice and acknowledges that:

> *"No complaints system, however sophisticated,*
> *will compensate for failure to reach a*
> *satisfactory resolution of the broader questions*
> *of structure, management and political*
> *accountability"* (Hayes, 1997, 2).

This said, the lack of an independent body, or its lack of credibility, can do untold damage to public confidence in the wider police service. Nor is it enough for such a system to be independent of police and impartial; its impartiality will be judged to a large extent on whether it is also perceived to be independent. Whatever system is in place to deal with complaints needs to be *"open, fair, easily understood and widely accessible"*(Hayes, 1997: v). Specifically, Hayes proposes a Police Ombudsperson who would have control of the whole process from the very beginning. All complaints would be made or referred to the Ombudsoffice which will decide on action.[108]

Hayes gave serious consideration to the problem most often cited as the main reason for the excessively low complaint substantiation rate in Northern Ireland – i.e. the need for a complainant to prove police wrongdoing 'beyond reasonable doubt'. Many interviewees in other jurisdictions were surprised

---

[108] Complainant surveys from elsewhere indicate confusion among 'users' as to what procedure was or should be followed (e.g. Landau, 1994).

to learn that this was the standard used currently. Most have the requisite standard as 'the balance of probabilities'. The proposal now that there be a sliding scale standard of proof depending on the seriousness of the allegation, is that which is de facto operating in many jurisdictions. Of all those consulted by Hayes, the Police Federation was alone in the view that the standard of proof should not be changed. Obviously, the Federation's concern to ensure that any police officer who is the subject of a complaint be guaranteed a fair hearing is entirely valid. This concern is, however, met adequately in Hayes' proposal. Furthermore, he specifically addresses the issue of vexatious complaints in an attempt to meet some of the genuine concerns of the police in this regard.

More than this is not required. The power and influence of police unions is something which has dogged many other civilian oversight agencies, and government must be careful not to jeopardise the chances of any new body by allowing any one constituency excessive influence. On a more positive note, it should be emphasised that, in many of the countries visited, it was the police themselves who propounded the advantages of an effective complaints system, as both ridding the force of individual corrupt officers, and securing public confidence in policing.

## Hayes: moving ahead

Hayes undertook his review in the context of a history of consistent government and police opposition to civilian investigations of complaints against the police. Therefore the broad acceptance of his eventual conclusion that the investigative function be an entirely independent one is highly significant. In order to ensure that this recommendation achieves its purpose of rendering the process more independent and effective, our research would lead us to propose the following steps.

## Appointment

Firstly, if the independent investigative function is to be respected as truly independent, much depends on the appointment made to the office of Ombudsperson and how that appointment is made. We comment elsewhere on the important work being undertaken by the Salvadorean Ombudswoman for Human Rights, and the need for the post-holder to have integrity. An ill-judged appointment to the Police Ombudsperson post, especially in its early days, could be fatal to the success of a new organisation, which must prove itself proactive and different from its predecessors in order to win over both police and public opinion. This problem will be dramatically heightened if, as seems possible, the current ICPC is simply transformed into the office of the new Ombudsperson. Hayes, somewhat surprisingly, given the priority he gives to establishing trust in a new complaints system, appears to accept this as a possibility (Hayes, 1997: vi). The recently appointed chair of the ICPC has spoken about the *"Members of the Commission and its staff, whom Dr Hayes envisaged as forming the nucleus of the Police Ombudsman's workforce…making every effort to contribute to the establishment of the new organisation"*[109]. The temptation to use currently available resources is natural, but it is difficult to reconcile this approach with the desire for a radical change in the public perceptions of the efficacy of the complaints system.

## The importance of resources for research

Another potential problem is that insufficient emphasis is given in the Hayes report to the importance of a well funded and professional research arm. The Queensland system would seem

---

[109] Letter from Chairperson inserted into Triennial Review 1994-1997, Jan.1997.

to suggest that it could be this element which could prove the most dynamic and effective part of the system in terms of complaint prevention and policy formulation. The El Salvador Ombudsoffice also reported the frustration of being unable to research important trends and practices because of limited resources. The importance of research, and the resourcing of research, cannot be overstated, and new legislation should make explicit mention of the research component of the Police Ombudsman's office.

## The benefits of Independent Audit
Working in tandem with a research arm, a system of independent audit has proved an extremely valuable feature of many other complaints/quality service monitoring systems.[110] Again, detailed legislation would need to provide powers and guidelines to ensure the Ombudsperson would have access to all materials deemed necessary, and the right to see police files without prior warning. Audit systems have the advantage of dealing with bad practice in a more systemic way and focussing attention on management. Audits can provide a body of knowledge which, as long as it goes beyond just technical or administrative issues, can be very beneficial.

## Independent Investigation
One means of creating this trust is recognised by Hayes in his recommendation of the need for non-police investigators to have charge of complaint investigations. However, he moves quite quickly to the idea of 'sale and lease back'[111] as a dynamic

---

[110] e.g. San Jose, USA.
[111] i.e. the Ombudsperson would have power to investigate all complaints, but would delegate minor issues to the police. Gradually,more serious complaints could be delegated. The risks lie in the RUC investigating the majority of complaints, and many complainants continuing to distrust the system, or in the fact that many so-called minor complaints hiding more sinister patterns which would not necessarily be picked up if dealt with as police matters.

to encourage police co-operation with the new system. The reality of the initial sifting of complaints by the Ombudsoffice will undoubtedly lead to the police continuing to conduct many investigations themselves - unless substantial resources are put into recruiting and training non-police investigators (such as lawyers, DHSS and customs officials, etc). Hayes does mention the dangers associated with a hierarchisation of complaints which could leave police dealing with many 'low level' issues which are actually indicative of a much more widespread problem. For example, minor complaints of incivility could amount to a very serious pattern of harassment affecting whole groups and causing serious difficulties. However, little is said to alleviate fears that this could quickly become the norm under the new system.

An alternative way to achieve co-operation from the police is the model provided in, Queensland, Australia. There, there is a requirement that police officers report their colleagues if they even suspect misconduct has occurred. If officers do not fill in the appropriate form for their supervisor, they may end up facing proceedings themselves for failure to do so. Failure on the part of middle management to follow up would also place them in a difficult position.

**Selection and Training**
Another issue arising from Hayes' recommendations, but worthy of particular emphasis here, is the benefit to be gained by the development of appropriate in-house and independent training for civilian investigators. The success of such investigators is vital to real change. Many bodies have turned to former police as their civilian investigative team, but this has led many commentators to wonder if this is not at least part of the reason why the number of prosecutions or successful

actions does not improve.[112]  In Ontario, the policy to date has been for the Police Complaints Commission only to hire trained investigators. This has resulted in about half their recruits coming from a police background. Now with the development of in-house training, reliance on former police officers would seem not to be so necessary.  Several investigators spoken to did not see the need for investigators with previous policing experience. The types of issues dealt with called not for specific and technical expertise, but instead good analytical skills, a step by step approach and the ability to think logically.   One interviewee stated: *"I brought with me a civilian approach to policing. They have a difficult job but they are trained to do that job and that does not excuse them. I expect professionalism. Ex police are more likely to be sensitive to the difficulties of the job and let things pass. As a black woman, I bring to the job the fact that I may see other issues. We bring to the job what we've experienced."*[113]

### The benefits and dangers of Informal Resolution
Part of a built-in defect in any complaints system can be a failure to deal with people as individuals and with individual expectations of the system. Complainants are not necessarily looking for vengeance or severe punishment; some merely want an acknowledgement that the incident happened, and that the officer was informed of their concerns; others might be satisfied with an informal apology or some commitment to ensuring the same thing will not happen to others in the future. Many complaints might have the potential for informal resolution as Dr Hayes emphasises, and as confirmed by international experience.  However, informal resolution, if the system is not

---

[112] See Andrew Goldsmith, What's Wrong with Complaint Investigations? Dealing with Difference Differently in Complaints against the Police; *Criminal Justice Ethics*, Vol 15 No.1 Winter/Spring 1996, 38.
[113] Interview with civilian investigator, Toronto, October 1996.

to be abused, should be closely monitored.[114]   Alternative Dispute Resolution (ADR) undoubtedly has its place but it is crucial that any patterns (in a particular officer, unit, or type of duty) be tracked.   Given the frequent charges of harassment made against the police by certain groups in society, it is crucial that patterns of this kind not be overlooked as minor complaints to be channelled via the ADR conduit. Furthermore, there is the question of who is to mediate and what training they receive.   Hayes proposes that designated police officers be informal resolution officers, but there are also clear advantages in having independent conciliators.   These reservations aside, ADR can be an important part of a system of rehabilitative rather than simply retributive justice – where early warning systems, counselling, and retraining form part of an abuse prevention policy that will help police officers struggling with the many often conflicting demands made on them.

## Dealing with the past & moving ahead
In considering how to bring Hayes' recommendations further forward, consideration needs to be given to the outstanding problems of the past – serious allegations of police abuse which were not satisfactorily addressed at the time, and which will cast a pall over any future complaints system, however effective.   Whether this takes the form of a Truth Commission or some other mechanism to deal with specific major incidents, it is difficult to see how any new body which fails to deal in some measure with the legacy of the past can be expected to deal credibly with the future.

Nor can the transition process be ignored.   Moving from the current problematic complaints system to a more credible and

---

[114] Hayes cites approvingly a study which argues that ADR is positive but would reduce the risk of abuse if there were *"more formal and more rigorous monitoring of informally resolved complaints by independent outsiders"* (1997: 26).

authoritative system will require careful planning. To ensure police acceptance of a new body, governments in many instances have actually succeeded in stripping the embryonic complaints structure of the very attributes intended to be at the core of the change process. The result is to thwart the objective of enhanced public confidence in the police, and to fuel mistrust and suspicion. The Police Ethics Deputy Commissioner in Quebec cited early difficulties faced by her organisation in establishing itself.[115] On the day it opened for business, it already had an 18-month backlog of cases left over from its predecessor. At the very time when it needed to be most dynamic and show a real break from the past, it did not have the capacity to do so. Following a period of very low substantiation rates, a decision was taken to employ very senior and experienced lawyers. This financial and political commitment secured the necessary professionalism and prestige for the new body. Without this commitment, international parallels suggest that the process of transition will fail, however well intentioned the goals.

## Summary of Conclusions: police and the law

From a study of international theory and practice in this area, the following conclusions can be drawn about policing and legal accountability:

1. Policing gains its legitimacy by performing a legal rather than a political function, and by serving the law rather than partisan politics. Accordingly, a situation of serious political and violent conflict makes vigilance more, not less, necessary. A major concern in divided societies is that domestic law may develop in a narrow security-led fashion, and in doing so undermine any hope of policing by consent.

---

[115] Marlene Jennings, Interview, Montreal, October 1996.

2.  The measure of whether police accountability mechanisms are working effectively, is the extent to which the current checks and balances are deterring or punishing any wrongdoing by the police.

3.  The fairly widespread phenomenon of denying wrongdoing can only compound the destabilising effect that the original crime/abuse has upon the principle of the rule of law.

4.  The introduction of written constitutional protections of rights formalises the responsibility of the state to protect the rights of all, whether they be part of a majority or a minority, whether they be police or civilian. Furthermore, it protects these rights regardless of the prevailing political or security climate and provides a yardstick against which legislation and state action can be judged.

5.  International law recognises that exceptional circumstances may arise which threaten the life of the nation and that certain rights may be curtailed for a temporary period, with a view to protecting the rights of all. International law however demands that any resort to emergency powers should be of as short a duration as possible.

6.  While there are different forms of legal redress available to the public, the existence of a strong, effective, and accessible civilian complaints/research/audit system is particularly important.

# Summary of Recommendations: police and the law

1.  Police legislation which is currently being drafted (and any future proposals which are forthcoming) need to be informed by the important principles laid down in

international law. Specifically, it is recommended that all domestic legislation relating to the police incorporate explicit reference to the international and domestic human rights standards relevant to policing.

2.  These international principles lead us to recommend that any domestic legislation governing policing should:

- outline the nature, philosophy and practices expected of the police;
- clearly define the remits of all those involved in providing policing to ensure that effective accountability can be ensured;
- define controversial concepts and words such as 'operational' which lead to much ambiguity as to current responsibilities;
- delineate powers as well as functions;
- review, redraft and give a statutory basis to the police disciplinary code;
- and impose a statutory requirement on the police and relevant agencies to consult effectively with and be influenced by the community (the importance of which is explored in more detail in chapter four), and provide appropriate guidelines to facilitate such communication and involvement.

3.  Police legislation should also require officers to report any misconduct by their colleagues.

4.  It is recommended that, in addition to incorporating the European Convention on Human Rights into domestic law, the government move urgently to encourage a broad society-wide debate with a view to introducing a Bill of Rights for Northern Ireland.

5. The government should end its reliance on emergency legislation which, we believe, is in contravention of international human rights law.

6. An effective and credible police complaints/audit system must be introduced without delay. In the legislation now being canvassed with regard to policing, and police complaints, commentators should measure the proposals against the good practice evolved from a study of other jurisdictions. Detailed recommendations are given below. Particular care should be taken to ensure an effective transition so that police and public can have confidence in the new complaints system.

(a) The police complaints system should not be designed to address exceptions to the rule, but to recognise that bad practice (even where it is not widespread) is often systemic. Legislation needs to achieve a balance between individual accountability and management responsibility.

(b) Any body set up must be completely independent of government, political influence, and of the police. All members must have the degree of credibility and integrity necessary to win/restore public confidence in the system. To underpin this principle of independence, there must be a guaranteed and sufficient budget independently controlled.

(c) The Ombudsoffice needs to be able to investigate the whole process of a case from start to finish. This would include pointing out any weakness of the judiciary or broader legislative framework where necessary. The Ombudsoffice needs to be able to comment on the whole picture to tackle causes as well as symptoms.

(d) The Ombudsoffice needs to access the same information available to police and steps need to be taken to avoid and deal with any police obstruction that might occur.

(e) There is a need for widespread dissemination of information about this form of redress – all too often the public are kept in the dark about investigations about police behaviour. One of the best aspects of the Ombudswoman in El Salvador's role is that she has published and distributed free copies of pamphlets on the most controversial cases.

(f) The complaints body must have the power to decide what is and is not a complaint, it must have power to investigate incidents of its own volition even in the absence of a complaint, and investigators employed must all be independent of the police. (There remains some argument as to whether the investigative team benefits from the presence of former or seconded police as well as civilians).

(g) The complaints system must be accessible and effective, both in dealing with members of the public, and police officers who may be the subject of vexatious complaints. A complainant needs to feel involvement in the process.

(h) The standard of proof necessary to substantiate a complaint should always be the 'balance of probabilities', though for the purpose of any criminal proceedings arising out of the same incident the standard would become 'beyond a reasonable doubt'. A criminal prosecution should not be an automatic bar to internal discipline.

(i) Any appeals procedure should be independent, transparent and respect the rights of officer and complainant alike.

(j) The system should not be overly legalistic and the appropriate use of Alternative Dispute Resolution (ADR) procedures should be encouraged and facilitated through appropriate training. However, care should be taken that ADR is not abused allowing particular officers, or practices, to escape scrutiny.

(k) The body should have power to recommend appropriate action in respect of individual officers and police systems, and be provided with some sanction if recommendations go unheeded. This function also suggests that the body should have a power to issue special reports, make recommendations, and take other steps to raise public and government awareness of relevant matters.

(l) The complaints body should have a research arm with a view to being pro-active, and tracking trends beyond individual incidents.

(m) Audit and advocacy functions need to be integrated into its operation and, perhaps most importantly, the investigative body must be fully integrated into broader accountability mechanisms so that complaints are not boxed off as a discrete area with no implications for other oversight structures.

# Chapter Four:

# *Policing and democratic accountability*

*"Where there is no dialogue there can be no understanding; where there is no accountability, there is no compulsion to serve."*
John Alderson, former Chief Constable, Devon and Cornwall[116]

## Introduction

Effective accountability structures are crucial to policing for two reasons. First, they provide oversight mechanisms which ensure that police powers are not abused; second, they enable society to influence and monitor police policy and practice. In a democracy, it is crucial that unfettered power does not reside with any one individual or group. This principle has a particular importance for policing, since police officers already have much greater powers than the average citizen (including the right to carry weapons). Around the world, systems of democratic accountability have therefore evolved, alongside a framework of legal regulation, to provide mechanisms for public input into policing and to act as a restraint on the powers of the police. In the previous chapter, we looked at the issue of legal accountability; this chapter focuses on issues of democratic accountability and local community involvement.

Democratic accountability in essence is about society being able to choose the type of police service it wants. As John Alderson argues (in the quote above), effective systems of communication and dialogue are necessary if society is make informed choices, and if the police are to know what society expects of them. However, consultation alone is not enough. Effective oversight

---

[116] Cited in Roach & Thomaneck, 1995: 26.

structures are also vital to ensure that the police provide the quality and type of service agreed upon, and to ensure redress if the police do not carry out their duties as agreed. Effective structures of accountability should mean that communities and individuals become more than simply 'the policed', and the objects of a policing process. Instead, the public should have an active role in designing and monitoring how policing is carried out.

It is a basic premise of all democratic societies, that society has a role to play in designing and monitoring the police service. All of the countries visited had some form of accountability structures external to policing, although the structures varied extensively depending on constitutional, political, social, cultural, economic, and historic circumstances relevant to the jurisdiction studied. There are no direct parallels to be found, but the study confirmed our belief that democratic accountability is necessary and important, that the current structures of democratic accountability in Northern Ireland fall well short of the ideal, and that there are valuable principles and examples of good practice from elsewhere that could prove useful.

In an attempt to clarify what kind of democratic involvement in the decision-making process around policing would be appropriate, a graph indicating different levels of involvement is reproduced overleaf. A responsive police service can be created only if the public enter into partnership with their police service, and are situated at the top levels of the graph's ladder – consulted, involved, and helping to design the service.

## Table: Levels of decision making[117]

**High power**: Controls
    Helps design service
        Partner
            Participant
                Involved
                    Consulted
                        Informed
                            Placated
                                Manipulated
                                  **Low Power:** Powerless

As our analysis of existing arrangements in Northern Ireland will show, citizen participation in police decision-making is currently found along the lower/middle rungs of the ladder. The Police Authority of Northern Ireland (PANI) and local Community Police Liaison Committees (CPLCs) are sometimes consulted and informed, but the system falls well short of a true partnership. To understand and critique police accountability structures in Northern Ireland, it is necessary to provide a brief overview of the English model, as this is the model on which our current system is based.[118] In particular, Northern Ireland's commitment to the tradition of civic oversight, to a tripartite structure of democratic accountability, and to the concept of a police chief's 'operational independence', all have their roots in an English policing model.

This chapter will look at the relevance of English structures and debates to the issue of democratic accountability, the current situation in Northern Ireland, proposed changes to the current structures, and then finally useful international parallels. It will

---

[117] "Ladder of individual participation, Thoburn and Shemmings, 1995, cited in Horgan, G. & Sinclair, R, 1997, Planning for Children in Care in Northern Ireland, National Children's Bureau. The ladder refers to decision making in social work situations but is just as relevant in relation to policing.

[118] This is not to ignore the many differences, discussed later in the chapter.

also address the specific question of democratic accountability and the intelligence services.

# The English model of civic oversight and police accountability

The tradition of civic oversight of policing goes back to some of the earliest days of professional police institutions. In the first half of this century local council 'watch committees' were responsible for over-seeing policing in their areas, and played an important role in directing police policy and determining priorities.[119] The role of local authorities was, however, substantially reduced by the 1964 Police Act which laid the basis for the current structures. Since then the system of democratic accountability in England and Wales has been based around a tripartite structure made up of the Home Secretary; the local Chief Constable; and the local (partially elected) Police Authority. [120]

The Police Authorities have responsibility for maintaining an adequate police force, and have the power to appoint, discipline and fire senior officers (subject to the Home Secretary's approval). Under the Police and Criminal Evidence Act (PACE, 1984) they also have a responsibility to consult with the local community on policing. This emphasis on community consultation, and civic oversight, was strengthened as a result of Lord Scarman's report into the 'Brixton Disorders' of 1981. Lord Scarman proposed the setting up of consultative or liaison committees and argued that it was possible to achieve community involvement in the policy and operations of

---

[119] For further discussion of the role of watch committees see CAJ, 1988. These committees evolved in England but such a system never existed in Ireland, pre- or post- partition.
[120] An important exception to this model is the Metropolitan Police, accountable only to the Home Secretary.

policing, without undermining the independence of the police. However, under Scarman's proposals, communities would be consulted and could advise the police, but the police would not be obliged to follow this advice. As Mike Brogden et al comments:

> *"Since he (Lord Scarman) fails to specify what statutory powers the new committees might have to force Chief Constables to discuss operational policies, since he insists Chief Constables should retain their independent decision-making over policing, and since he even qualified what might be a fit matter for committee discussion… it was hard to be optimistic about what such bodies might achieve."* (Brogden et al, 1988).

Alongside the concept of civic oversight, and the tripartite system of democratic accountability sits, somewhat uncomfortably, the English doctrine of the operational independence of the Chief Constable. The 1964 Act made Chief Constables responsible for the direction and control of their forces. Chief Constables are expected to have regard to the local policing plan produced by their Police Authority, but there is no legal obligation on them to accept the Authority's advice. During the 1980s there were a series of disputes between Police Authorities in England, the respective Chief Constables and the Home Secretary. Some local authorities were unhappy with the increasingly quasi-military methods used in inner city areas which they felt were an important contributory factor in the inner city disturbances. It appeared to some elected Councillors that they had no effective means of holding the police to account when it really mattered, as the policy of "operational independence" could always be called upon by the chief constable.[121]

The policing of the miners' strike of 1984/85 in Britain highlighted the inner tensions of the tripartite system. Some Police Authorities objected to the deployment of their forces outside their areas, but found that they were powerless to do anything. The revelation that there had been regular meetings between members of the Association of Chief Police Officers (ACPO), Home Office representatives and the Home Secretary led to accusations that the policing of the strike was politically driven.[122] Lady Margaret Simey, chair of Merseyside Police Authority from 1981, described the frustration felt when the Authority had exercised their powers to the full, and still found that they had no impact on the direction taken by the police:

> *"We were well on the way to mastering the art of driving our 'old banger' and were in the process of making sure that it was roadworthy. But what use was that if we were flatly refused the right to sit in the driver's seat or even to issue instructions as to where we wished to go? Obviously the mechanical act of driving must be left to one person, but surely we must retain the responsibility for deciding in which direction we wished to be taken?"* (Simey, 1988).

Since the mid-1980s there has been a further erosion in the extent of democratic accountability over policing in England and Wales. The abolition of both the Greater London Council (whose police committee had played an important role in monitoring local police activity) and the Metropolitan County Councils in 1986, deprived local communities of an important

---

[121]For an account of the problems facing police authorities during this period see Scraton, 1985; for an intriguing personal account, as chair of Merseyside Police Authority from 1981-1986, see Simey, 1988.

[122]See Scraton (1985: chapter 7). There have been many insightful discussions of the policing of the miners' strike eg Fine and Millar, 1985; Green, 1990.

source of accountability. In 1994 the Police and Magistrates' Courts Act shifted the balance further away from elected representation. Until then, elected councillors comprised two-thirds of the Police Authority membership,[123] now elected representatives are in a majority of just one.[124]

Ironically, at the very time there is a burgeoning debate about more local democratic control of policing in Northern Ireland, there has been an erosion of electoral representation in Police Authorities in England and Wales, and an increase in the power of central government and the Home Secretary over policing. It remains to be seen if this trend in Britain will be maintained under the new government, or whether the commitment to devolution, and more local autonomy, will also have an impact on the structures and nature of policing oversight.

# The current structures of police accountability in Northern Ireland

## The tripartite system

As stated, Northern Ireland also has a tripartite system of accountability: the Police Authority for Northern Ireland (PANI), the Chief Constable of the RUC, and the Secretary of State for Northern Ireland.[125] PANI's twin roles are to act as an

---

[123] Appointed magistrates made up the remaining one third.

[124] Police Authorities have seventeen members, nine councillors from local government, five appointees chosen by the other members of the Authority from a short list drawn up by the Secretary of State, and three magistrates. Conservative plans to make elected representatives a minority failed.

[125] Police Act (NI) 1970. This followed the 1969 Hunt Report. Hunt also recommended elections to the Police Authority, regular inspections and a Inspector of Constabulary specific to NI, the end of emergency laws, unarmed police, and ending links to the Orange Order on the grounds that membership in the loyal orders was seen as incompatible with serving in the RUC. None of these recommendations were implemented (see Oliver, 1997:121).

oversight body supervising the actions of the Chief Constable on issues relating to efficiency and use of resources, and to act in a consultative role by liaising with local communities about policing issues (Walker, 1990). The system is built along the same principles as the English model with one important exception: unlike Police Authorities in England and Wales, PANI has no democratic input - its members are directly appointed by the Secretary of State.[126]

For some time, CAJ has argued that there are several shortcomings with the current Police Authority (CAJ, 1988, 1995a, 1997). Secrecy is one problem. Minutes of meetings were not available until recently and PANI continues to meet in closed sessions, though an open annual meeting has been recently introduced. Another problem is that PANI is unrepresentative. Both the Social Democratic and Labour Party (SDLP), and the umbrella trade union organisation (Northern Ireland Committee, Irish Congress of Trade Unions), have refused to put forward candidates to PANI because of their reservations about its work. These reservations are due in part to a further shortcoming, which is that PANI is ineffective in holding the Chief Constable to account. There is some disagreement as to whether this ineffectiveness is due to the limited powers of the Authority, or to its decision to exercise its powers in such a limited way.

One limitation which particularly hampers PANI is the fact that it does not appear to intervene in matters concerning security policy objectives. Given that anti-terrorist policing is the RUC's top priority, this places severe restrictions on the work of the Authority. A further problem is the relative weakness of PANI within the tripartite structure vis-à-vis both the Chief Constable and the Secretary of State. The policy of the 'operational autonomy' of the Chief Constable, and its practical

---

[126] For duties of PANI see Oliver (1997: 147). The Police Authority composition is intended to be representative of the community (ibid. p.145).

interpretation, allows the Chief Constable the opportunity, should he or she choose to use it, to place important restrictions on the Police Authority's capacity to become involved or exercise effective oversight. The full implications of the operational autonomy of the Chief Constable, in terms of his relationship with the third element of the tripartite structure, the Secretary of State, and therefore by implication with PANI also, became particularly clear as a result of a series of events in the summer of 1996.

The controversy centred around the respective roles of the Chief Constable and the Secretary of State in relation to a series of proposed parades by the Loyal Orders, some of which planned to go through predominantly nationalist areas. In several areas, nationalist residents' groups organised in protest against the parades. Much of the public speculation surrounding the 1996 marching season focused around the extent to which the Secretary of State had, or had not, intervened in the process of deciding whether or not to ban or re-route some of the parades. Particular controversy surrounded a parade on the outskirts of Portadown scheduled for 7 July 1996 by members of the Orange Order. The route of the parade was to be from Drumcree parish church down the Garvaghy Road, and was opposed by nationalist residents. The then Chief Constable of the RUC, Hugh Annesley, first banned the parade and then, following widespread loyalist protests, allowed it to take place. There followed major disorder in nationalist areas, which met with a harsh response including the firing of thousands of plastic bullets.[127] Strenuous efforts were made by the then Secretary of State, Sir Patrick Mayhew, and the then Chief Constable, to insist that the decision to deny permission for the march down the Garvaghy Road, and then the decision to reverse that earlier decision, were purely operational matters. As such, the argument ran that they were decisions to be made by the Chief Constable alone.

---

[127] For detailed account see CAJ, 1996.

In a CAJ commentary on these events (CAJ, 1996), it was queried why decisions about the policing of contentious parades are treated as purely operational concerns, since the political ramifications of such decisions are so clear. In the summer of 1997, the new Secretary of State, Dr Mo Mowlam, played a much more active and public role in trying to negotiate a local settlement. However, again, she made it clear that if no mutually acceptable agreement was reached between the concerned parties, the final decision was a purely operational one, and one which would therefore rest with the Chief Constable. Once again, the Chief Constable (now Ronnie Flanagan) allowed the march to take place.[128]

In future years, it has been proposed that the Parades Commission be given the necessary legislative powers to provide some external input into decision making on contentious parades. However, the draft legislation currently before parliament, proposes that the Chief Constable be allowed either, in advance, to appeal a Parades Commission decision to the Secretary of State, or alternatively be allowed to determine, on the day itself, that a Commission decision needs countermanding. [129] This approach risks making the doctrine of operational autonomy even more all-encompassing and ill-defined. At the very least, any move in this direction must be counterbalanced with clear procedures governing how the Chief Constable is to be held to account afterwards for the decisions taken.

---

[128] A further controversial decision (as to whether an Orange parade would be allowed down the Ormeau Road) was avoided when the Order decided to abandon their plans and avoid further disorder. Both decisions (to allow the march down the Garvaghy Road, and to abandon the march on the Ormeau Road) appear to have been made on the sole criterion of public safety. While an important issue, prioritising public safety as the sole criterion encourages a resort to violence, or the threat of same, to achieve one's ends. This gives no consideration to the need to balance the rights involved on both sides, to act in a proportionate manner, and to uphold the rule of law.

[129] See the Public Processions etc. (NI) Bill, 1997.

The parades issue exemplifies the fact that the Secretary of State, as well as the Police Authority, has chosen to interpret the Chief Constable's operational autonomy widely. It is evident that clarity is needed about the precise powers of the Chief Constable and the Secretary of State in the tripartite structure. At the same time, while arguing for more clarity in their respective powers, it should be pointed out that we have no evidence of conflict between the Chief Constable and Secretary of State.  Rather, there is evidence of close co-operation on security issues with regular meetings involving them both, as well as the army's General Officer Commanding and members of the security services (Walker 1990:115).  In 1976, PANI apparently sought permission to participate but this was refused by the Secretary of State (Ellison, 1997).  Our point here is that PANI is clearly the 'poor relation' in the accountability triangle.

The issue is not only, however, a lack of powers.  There is also disturbing evidence that PANI does not flex the weak muscles that it does have.  The Police Authority does not make a habit of commenting publicly on issues such as allegations of collusion, or threats to lawyers, or the use of super-grasses. It is worth looking in some detail at a recent example of a matter of grave public concern (the use and abuse of plastic bullets) where PANI clearly has authority to intervene and exercise leadership but, in our view, has singularly failed to do so.  Any effective civic oversight body must not only have the necessary powers to intervene, it must have the will to exercise those powers to the full.[130]

PANI is responsible for authorising the purchase of equipment for the RUC and therefore has the potential, if the Authority chose to exercise it, to refuse an RUC request to supply plastic

---

[130]In commenting on similar problems exhibited by English police committees, Martin Kettle talked of *"the voluntary misuse of responsibility"*(cited in Scraton, 1985: 59).

bullets.[131] To date, PANI has chosen not to exercise this option, on the grounds that this would interfere with the Chief Constable's operational autonomy. This stance is maintained despite 17 deaths from plastic and rubber bullets and several thousand injuries and maimings; despite the fact that police in England and Wales have never used such weapons even when faced with serious riot situations; and despite the fact that Her Majesty's Inspector of Constabulary commented negatively on the fact that the RUC practice in this area was subject to less strict guidelines than those agreed by the Association of Chief Police Officers (ACPO), whose remit covers England & Wales.[132]

Even leaving aside the principled question of whether to keep supplying plastic bullets to the RUC for use, the Police Authority has an undeniable responsibility to ensure that the plastic bullets, if they are to be used, are subject to stringent control and accountability. Yet in this highly controversial area, where there is much public concern, the Authority has shown itself unable to reassure people that it is pursuing an effective oversight role, still less having an impact on policing (see Appendix 3 for an account of CAJ/PANI exchanges relevant to the issue of scrutinising plastic bullet usage).

PANI demonstrates a lack of will in overseeing police policy and practice, but has also failed to accommodate within the Authority those with a more pro-active approach. PANI chair

---

[131] Though what would be the consequences of them refusing to supply plastic bullets is not clear. In an English court case (Ex parte Northumbria Police Authority (1988) 1All ER 556) it was established that the government has a prerogative power to equip the police regardless of the Police Authority's wishes. During the Toxteth disturbances in 1981, it became clear that if police authorities refused to agree spending for police equipment, central funds would be available to the police. Chief Constable Kenneth Oxford was admonished by his police committee for having over-spent on riot control equipment, particularly given the committee's concerns about the use of CS-gas. He ignored the committee and received financial help from the Home Office and 'mutual aid' from other forces (see Scraton, 1985:70-86).

[132] HMIC, 1996: recommendation. 16.

David Cook, and Authority member, Chris Ryder, were sacked from the Authority by the Secretary of State following a vote of no confidence. It was argued that they had seriously undermined PANI by discussing 'politically sensitive' issues (e.g. display of the union flag, oath) in public, without raising them first with the Authority (*Irish Times*, 21 February 1996).

## Legislative proposals for changes to the tripartite relationships

At the time of writing, the government is understood to be drafting legislation to address the ambiguities and weaknesses in the current system of democratic accountability. It will be clear from much that has gone before in earlier chapters that the scale of the change that is required in policing is very great. Certainly any legislative proposals must address the problems we highlight in the foregoing critique of the current tripartite arrangements, but we are concerned that the proposals (especially if they replicate those made in earlier consultative documents) will not go far enough.

For example, the consultative paper "Foundations for Policing", a White Paper on Policing in Northern Ireland, noted the confusion about the respective roles of PANI, the Secretary of State, and the Chief Constable, and proposed that PANI have a role in setting Northern Ireland policing objectives, and in approving and publishing an annual policing plan drawn up by the Chief Constable. This would mean that PANI would be able to seek reports from the Chief Constable on the achievement of the objectives, and would monitor and report to the community and the Secretary of State on the implementation of the policing plan.

Clearly these measures are intended to give PANI a greater involvement in, and responsibility for, setting and monitoring the strategic objectives of the police. In the same White Paper, it was proposed that the Secretary of State be responsible for resolving any differences which might arise between the Chief Constable and PANI in relation to policing objectives. If the Secretary of State decides to reject PANI's proposals, then reasons must be given for this. The intent presumably here is to strengthen the role of PANI in its relations with the Chief Constable about the overall direction and priorities of policing. However, there was no suggestion that the Chief Constable's 'operational independence' be clearly defined, or in any way restricted, and it is this which is at the heart of his/her relationship with the other elements of the tripartite structure.

Nor is it clear whether the civic oversight body will be given, or will exert, more authority in the area of security or related matters than PANI has to date. Security policing is central to what the RUC does, and the way in which security policing is carried out impinges on every other aspect of policing. Therefore, while recognising the potential conflict between security considerations and open and transparent mechanisms for public accountability, it is unclear why a civilian oversight body should not seek to hold the Chief Constable to account for security policing. As a general rule, secrecy should be kept to a minimum and, even when people's safety requires confidentiality, there is no justification for the police themselves alone deciding what should or should not be secret. A civic oversight body must have the wherewithal to contribute to decision making with regard to the use of plastic bullets, the policing of contentious parades, and the use of emergency legislation, to list but a few examples of issues of broad public interest.

If it were proposed, despite all these arguments, to retain a limited civic oversight role in the operational area, the principle of retrospective accountability becomes all the more important. Whatever arguments are made for allowing the police an important margin for discretion in operational decisions, there can be no argument against officers having to experience rigorous scrutiny in retrospect for their decisions to act or refrain from acting.

In the preceding chapter on legal accountability, it was noted that any new legislation governing policing should be measured against a series of international principles. Below we recapitulate the principles specific to the issue of democratic accountability which need to be codified in law. All new legislation should be measured against the following criteria as a minimum:

- explicit reference must be made to the philosophy of policing and its responsibility in international and domestic law to protect human rights;
- protections for officers choosing to disobey illegitimate commands should be enunciated;
- mechanisms to ensure police accountability, particularly in the use of force, should be provided for;
- the respective remits of the different bodies involved in overseeing policing should be clear and unambiguous;
- in particular, potentially amorphous concepts such as operational autonomy should be defined, as should oversight mechanisms;
- powers as well as functions should be established;
- a statutory basis for a revised police disciplinary code should be provided;
- and it should be made a statutory requirement on the police and relevant agencies to consult effectively with the community, and provide appropriate guidelines for such consultation.

## Community Police Liaison Committees (CPLCs)

Alongside the tripartite system that provides leadership and a central overview of policing, there is a local network in Northern Ireland of Community Police Liaison Committees based loosely around District Councils.[133] These committees are co-ordinated by PANI as part of its brief of community consultation (PACE (NI) Order, 1989). They are designed to give locally elected representatives input into policy matters. However, there are many deficiencies in the system. There is no formal representation from the nationalist community: the SDLP do not take part, nor do Sinn Fein. The committees have no powers and, as their title suggests, are intended to be consultative. The consultation process is voluntary on the part of the police and, while some committees report that useful discussions are held, the committees have no power to demand answers from the police. Security policing is not part of their remit, and the focus tends to be on relatively mundane local issues (Weitzer, 1992; Hamilton et al, 1995).

The RUC (in its Fundamental Review)[134] has proposed changes in its own structures which will have an impact on the CPLC's. These changes include turning sub-divisions into area commands based geographically on District Council boundaries. The divisional tier of command would be removed, and the superintendent in charge of each subdivision would have ultimate responsibility for the provision of policing in that area. It is proposed that this change occur in conjunction with a strengthening of CPLC's, allowing them to advise local police about the policing of the area. While such organisational changes appear to make administrative sense, and may lead to

---

[133] There are three types of committee: District Council committees made up of Councillors and police; District Council committees made up of Councillors, police and invited community representatives, and in nationalist-majority areas there are RUC sub-divisional committees with community representatives and police (CPLC, 1997).

[134] A Fundamental Review of Policing: Summary and Key Findings, RUC.

increased efficiency, they are unlikely (based on experience to date) to bring about real local accountability. Unless important changes are made to policing along the lines discussed elsewhere in this report, relatively small changes in the powers of the CPLC's are unlikely to win over those communities currently unrepresented on the committees. And yet, without their participation, the unrepresentative nature of the CPLC will continue to be a major obstacle to effective scrutiny.

## Policing, democratic accountability and the army

This report concentrates on policing and devotes little space to the work done by the security forces working alongside the police. However, although the RUC is the predominant police organisation in Northern Ireland, no discussion of the democratic accountability mechanisms can afford to ignore the fact that other security services work with the police and have important and wide-ranging powers and responsibilities. Charges that there is insufficient accountability exerted over the police are all the more problematic when that policing function is performed by the army (including the locally recruited Royal Irish Regiment). In common with most military forces elsewhere, the army – unlike a police service - has no tradition of democratic involvement, and limited civic oversight. Yet the army is performing policing functions. Since 1976, there has existed a system of 'police primacy' whereby the RUC has operational control of security policing, even when carried out by other security services.

The problems which arise may best be illustrated by reference to an exchange of correspondence between the CAJ and the General Officer Commanding and the Civil Secretary.[135] In response to questions, the army confirmed that within Northern Ireland there were two sets of guidelines (army and RUC)

---

[135] CAJ/army correspondence dated 18 July, 5 & 15 August, 3 November 1997.

governing the use of plastic bullets. This was apparently not considered problematic since, according to the army's Civil Secretary *"Both the RUC and Army guidelines on the use of plastic baton rounds are framed in accordance with the (Criminal Law) Act and, though the language may differ, the rationale is the same"*. The CAJ, however feels that there is likely to be confusion on the ground, given the important discrepancies between the army and RUC guidelines, and is pursuing this correspondence. To quote from one CAJ letter in the exchange of correspondence:

> *"...Surely it cannot be the case that the army can only fire plastic bullets in response to a threat to life, while the RUC can shoot when property is at risk? And, in any event, how would this work on the ground? Given that the army is working in support of the RUC, surely it is the RUC guidelines which would take precedence, and does this not mean that army officers are failing to comply with their own guidelines regarding nature of threat, authority levels, prior warnings etc. when operating subject to RUC control".*

The police are ultimately accountable for the activities of the army. However, the plastic bullets discussion exemplifies just how complex the interface between military and policing functions renders any debate about accountability

# International experience: policing and democratic accountability

Part of our research remit was to explore how other countries deal with the issue of policing and democratic accountability. In general, it was discovered that systems of accountability are very different in most other European countries (and those like El Salvador and South Africa that are based on European models). The key difference lies in the fact that in many of these countries, the police are put directly and deliberately under ministerial control.[136] In these jurisdictions, the police are clearly subject to close democratic scrutiny: police chiefs are responsible for the everyday decisions about the running of the police, but in terms of general priorities, policies and strategies, he/she must act according to ministerial instructions.

On the negative side, however, it can be claimed that increased ministerial control politicises policing in a way that is avoided by the English model, because the latter is based on the independence of the constabulary. We have not devoted space here to exploring the debate over the advantages and disadvantages of these very different approaches. Nor are we proposing a specific model of accountability. Rather, we have tried to elicit key principles of participation and accountability that must be present in any system if it is to be effective. Three key principles which we explore below are: the need to define clearly the powers of the police; to strengthen the role of oversight bodies; and to ensure effective community participation at local level.

## 1.    Defining clearly the powers of the police

A key lesson from other jurisdictions is that the definition of the term 'operational independence' is at the heart of the debate of democratic accountability and policing. If operational independence is defined in its broadest sense, or there are weak or non-existent systems of accountability after the event, then there is little room for anyone other than the police to judge whether certain actions/policies are or were appropriate. The police can use the concept as a 'trump card', negating all other arguments. There are two ways of preventing the potential

---

[136] As indeed was the RUC under the Stormont government before Direct Rule.

abuse of the concept: there can be effective retrospective mechanisms for holding the Chief Constable to account, and this option is explored later in the context of police oversight bodies. A second option, however, it to recognise that while in the UK, and specifically in Northern Ireland, operational independence has been consistently defined very broadly, this is not true elsewhere. In continental models, 'operational' is understood much more narrowly to refer to day-to-day policing decisions, and there are clearly advantages in this approach.

An obvious conclusion from this is that whether one chooses to define operational independence and autonomy broadly or narrowly, it is such an important concept that it should be defined by statute. The term should be defined by society (via legislation), not by the police. Furthermore, any society wanting to exert effective democratic control of its police, would be well advised to interpret the concept narrowly to cover technical concerns of day to day policing and not issues of general policy and direction. Experience from elsewhere shows that effective democratic scrutiny of the police does not necessarily result in the politicisation of the police - the challenge lies in finding the right balance so that democratic control does not become partisan political control.

In this regard, the example of the Netherlands is very helpful. As in Northern Ireland, the system of accountability in the Netherlands is based on a triangle of accountability. However, in the Netherlands the relationship between the chief of police and civic representatives is seen very differently. In each of the country's 25 regions, the mayor (known as the burgomaster) of the largest city in the region is the force manager. He/she shares formal command of the force with the chief public prosecutor of the district. The third point of the triangle is the chief of the force who is responsible for day to day running of the police. These triangles are replicated in each city with local representatives dealing with local problems.

Authority over the police works on two levels: for public order policing they are responsible to the burgomaster, for criminal proceedings to the public prosecutor. As the Dutch National Police Institute explains *"The police are ... required to serve two masters."* Decisions on public order are not considered 'operational' matters, and are therefore not left to the sole responsibility of the police chief. Instead, major policy decisions are taken by the regional executive - made up of all the burgomasters of a region and the chief public prosecutor.

Detailed formulation of policy is the task of the regional triangle - burgomaster, public prosecutor and chief of police. They meet regularly (in some regions weekly, others monthly, depending on need) to discuss policy. In planning for a potentially difficult situation for example, the arrival of rival groups of football supporters, or a large demonstration, all three interested parties would meet to discuss the matter. Here a policy would be developed for the policing of the events, and decisions would be taken in principle regarding how the event will be policed - how the police should react in particular scenarios, how many police officers are required, etc. The Police Chief would then be answerable to the burgomaster for the public order side of the situation, and to the public prosecutor for criminal concerns. In the event of disagreement about the handling of public order situations within the triangle of authority, the burgomaster has final decision making power.

The system in the Netherlands is not without its shortcomings. This dual system of control can lead to some confusion and overlap. There is also a democratic deficit in the system as, despite their community role, the burgomasters are not elected but are appointed. The influence of elected local councils is formally non-existent, and in practice diffuse.[137]

---

[137] The council could penalise the burgomaster through budgetary constraints but in practice this does not happen. However, as Dr Kees van der Kijver noted, public Council meetings are not easily ignored (Interview, Nov. 1996).

The important lessons from the Netherlands for Northern Ireland is that public order policing does not have to be left entirely in the hands of the police. The Netherlands example also demonstrates the potential of developing tripartite mechanisms at different levels: national, regional; city/local council area. Policing policy can be developed at the higher levels, and local policing strategies decided in local fora. is not coincidental that the issue of police accountability has come under particular criticism in Northern Ireland in the context of disputes around the marching season and concerns around public order policing. Finding mechanisms for effective democratic control of the policing of such divisive events will be difficult but essential to the maintenance of the rule of law.

The Goldstone Commission (1992) panel on the policing of mass demonstrations in South Africa sought to address explicitly this issue of public involvement in decisions about public order policing. The panel argued that the right to demonstrate also implied responsibility. They stated that those organising mass events should be required to submit to the municipal authority, and if necessary a judge, plans to indicate that they have the effective capacity and knowledge to police the event (for example through the deployment of lay marshals). The process of setting up such an event would involve 'triangles of security' - organisers, the police, and municipal officials. The police would advise the organisers, but municipal officials would have the final decision making role as to policing arrangements. Such decisions were to take place within an agreed framework of national standards, and the process should be transparent and not take place in secrecy (see Shearing, 1991).

## 2.    Strengthening the role of oversight bodies

An important component in ensuring effective democratic accountability lies in strengthening the role of oversight bodies.

This means increasing their representative nature, their own accountability, and their authority.

Ideally, the most democratic way to establish police boards/authorities is to elect them. McCabe et al express this effectively when they argue that :

> *"the primary purpose of accountability is to ensure that representative views influence or determine policy. Therefore institutions which are representative of the local community should be the primary basis of accountability. This means – despite well-known police misgivings about 'sectional interests' – elected bodies"* (McCabe et al, 1988).

The US model provides an interesting comparison when addressing the issue of electoral accountability and policing. In the United States, in a majority of forces, police chiefs are selected and appointed by the elected local mayor. In theory, citizens can hold candidates accountable by taking their policies and record on policing into account when electing mayors. However, Brewer et al note the drawbacks of this system:

> *"The close relationship between police chiefs and elected mayors in American cities makes it difficult for the former not to curry favour with what is perceived as the 'majority view' within his [sic] jurisdiction ... The police chief fears that his appointment could be terminated if he carries out policies that impinge directly on the interests of the mayor's political supporters: electoral considerations and impartial policing thus make awkward bedfellows."* (Brewer, 1988: 116).

Despite these difficulties David Waddington argues that in some cases there have been positive results from this electoral control:

*"... some of the tension which existed between the police and black communities in the 1960s appears to have been relieved by an increase in the number of elected black politicians and their moderating influence on police policy."* (Waddington, 1992).[138]

The US system is based on a different philosophy from the UK model and is clearly not transferable (nor would we wish to recommend bringing the police under the control of a single individual, whether elected or not). What we can learn from the American experience is that it is crucial to involve those on the receiving end of policing in the decisions about how policing should be carried out.

The difficulties which would be involved in creating an elected police authority for Northern Ireland are obvious (danger of majority domination, difficulty in agreeing an electoral system, abstentionist politics of different kinds etc).[139] However, the establishment of strong electoral representation on the body responsible for police accountability should be a goal. Perhaps the District Partnerships (created within the framework of the European Peace and Reconciliation Programme) can serve as some kind of a model, since they bring together elected political representatives as well as a broad range of sectoral and constituency interests. Even this model, however, requires a commitment to working together for the common good, and the application of clear and objective principles and criteria to the work, so that sectional interests are not allowed to predominate.

---

[138] In Waddington's view, the Rodney King incident (in which Mr King, a black motorist, was assaulted by members of the Los Angeles Police Department in March 1991- an incident which was caught on video) was the exception which proves the rule. In this case the city's black mayor called on the police chief to resign but was unable to insist that he do so because of the accountability structures in the area.

[139] Lord Hunt recognised these difficulties, but believed that his proposals for an elected Authority dealt with the problems (see Oliver, 1987: 118).

As long as members are to be chosen by appointment, then the process must be as transparent as possible, and some advances in this regard already in relation to PANI are to be welcomed. Security concerns, which have been cited to justify why PANI membership has historically been shrouded in secrecy, are hopefully a matter of the past. If electoral representation is not the basis for the police oversight body, it is all the more vital that those appointed to any intermediate civic oversight body be people who will be prepared, when necessary, to raise criticisms of policing. Whatever powers are given to this body, much will depend on the calibre of people appointed or elected to it, and whether or not they are willing to exercise their powers for the good of all. Furthermore, evidence of their good faith and their desire to hold the police accountable lies to some extent in a willingness to render themselves accountable to the public for their action, or lack of it. Recent initiatives to seek information about public attitudes to policing are to be welcomed; regular public consultations of this kind should be instituted, as should report-backs on the Authority's findings and, most importantly, the action taken as a result.

Powers and representation are integrally linked. The surest way of increasing interest in, and support for, a civic oversight body is to ensure that it can exert proper accountability from the police. Anything less than this ensures that the most qualified candidates are unlikely to be attracted to work on the body. Indeed, the continued existence of a body not fulfilling this basic function exacerbates distrust and a lack of confidence in policing in general. As with so many other discussions, an effective civilian oversight body is in the best interests of the police as well as society in general.

## 3.  Ensuring effective community participation at local level

Although somewhat distinct, effective civic oversight is greatly facilitated by good local community participation in policing matters. The issue of consultation – and the limitations of the present system - has been discussed in relation to the Community Police Liaison Committees (CPLCs) in Northern Ireland.  The White Paper proposed a strengthening of these bodies so it will be interesting to see if this proposal is pursued in the legislation currently being drafted.  A very similar debate is going on in South Africa where community police fora have been set up to increase local participation in policing.

Under the South African (Interim) Constitution all police stations were obliged to establish community-police fora (CPF's) and to embrace the philosophy of community policing. These fora must by law be "broadly representative of the community" and the police must by law participate in these fora.  A draft policy document on Community Policing encourages a contract of service between the police and community.  Community fora in South Africa have the right to ask about public order policing in their areas and not just about routine local policing issues.  Local fora elect representatives to inform thinking at a regional level, but this does not permeate any further through to the national level.  The fora involve many of those people in South Africa who would have previously been excluded from participation.  The black majority population were previously the 'policed' – the object of the policing process – now the fora provide a way of involving local people.

However, there remain some difficulties. In some poor black areas, fora are finding it difficult to get funds to carry out their work and police resources still tend to be concentrated in affluent white areas.  Most importantly because the law delineates the functions but not the powers of the CPFs, they have been deemed to be purely consultative bodies. According to the Institute for a Democratic Alternative for South Africa (IDASA): [140]

> *"Government still sees police transformation as an internal process. It could be redesigned to ensure that communities are able to drive some of the changes. The boundaries on CPFs are still strict. We need more inter-connectedness between the CPFs and the police. We need to co-create policing, not just look at policing activities".*

Monitoring and evaluation are needed as well as participation – otherwise the CPFs remain a loose coalition of disparate individuals very much dominated by the police. IDASA has campaigned to re-visit the concept of community participation: *"We have a consensus on words but we have never unpacked the meaning of them – this discussion needs to happen".* Until it does, the fora may provide an important source of information for the police about what local people want, but they do not provide a means of making the police truly accountable.

In New South Wales (NSW), Community Consultative Committees were formally adopted as a community-based policing strategy in 1987 (in some areas, committees had been informally operating for some time previously). The aim of the committees was to encourage a closer relationship between the police and Aboriginal communities. Committee members were to include representatives of minority ethnic groups, young people, people who live and work in the area, representatives of non-governmental organisations and community organisations. By 1990 almost every patrol had established Community Consultative Committees but there were reported 'teething problems', for example lack of interest in the committees on the part of local communities, and in some cases

---

[140] Interview with IDASA staff, Pretoria, December 1996.

lack of interest by local police officers. Janet Chan describes some of the views of critics of the committees:

> "Critics of the police felt that members were not truly representative of the interests of the community; they mainly represented business interests, or interests of conservative middle-class sections of the community. Others saw the whole activity as a mere public relations exercise which was not meant to do anything" (Chan, 1997: 150).

In his report on race relations and policing, the Ombudsman evaluated the community consultation efforts made by NSW police. The Ombudsman found dissatisfaction among Aboriginal, ethnic and other minority groups about the make-up and running of the consultative committees. Some groups were not represented on the committees and there were suggestions that those who were chosen were selected for their compliance. One difficulty in establishing the effectiveness of the consultative committees was that there had been no monitoring of their practice. The Ombudsman suggested that the operations of the committee be monitored to ensure that they were providing effective two-way communication.[141]

Janet Chan found that in some cases the existence of community consultation committees was actually creating more distance between the police and marginalised groups. By attending the meetings, some police officers were able to say that they were consulting the community and ignore the views of those groups not represented. However, one positive outcome of consultation cited by Chan came when the police held a meeting with representatives of Koori (Aboriginal) people to discuss policing issues. A police officer told her that:

---

[141] See Landa report (1995) Race Relations and Our Police - a special report to Parliament under section 31 of the Ombudsman Act.

> *"There was ... an agreement to provide a support group – by that I mean a group of Kooris would be on a roster system. Were a Koori offender taken into custody, the police would automatically ring them, they would attend and assist"*(Chan, 1997: 202).

One key lesson from the Australian experience is that the establishment and running of Community Consultation Committees is not an end in itself. If consultation is to mean anything, then police must be prepared to make significant changes in the policing service to suit the needs and wishes of local communities. Thus, the setting up of structures of community consultation should be seen as the beginning and not the end of the process. As a senior police officer told Chan:

> *"People are out to tell you that (community based policing has) failed. I'm out to believe that it's yet to begin. We certainly mouthed the words. We have certainly talked about community involvement, and we have established community consultative committees, and we have got Neighbourhood Watch, we have these banners we wave around, but the core notion of policing with the community, solving problems with the community, having the community involved in solving its own problems with police assistance – is almost as far away as it ever was"* (Chan, 1997: 203).

The lessons for Northern Ireland appear to be:

- local fora are in principle a good idea, bringing police and communities together at the local level;
- there must be an enforceable contract between police and community;
- fora must be able to discuss issues relevant to local people, such as security and public order policing, if they are not be rendered ineffectual;

- fora must be representative of people in the area including minority interests;
- fora must be accountable for their activities to those who appointed them;
- the police must be legally obliged to give proper consideration to and to respond to the community's views;
- proper funding is necessary if fora are to work;
- the local fora must be in a position to forward their concerns to a regional/national authority with greater oversight powers, and they must be entitled to expect some report back on concerns raised.

Granby Labour Group developed principles which suggested a useful division of roles between the civic oversight body and local community fora. The Police Authority, they proposed, should have powers to determine police policy in relation to issues such as deployment, police training, equipment, discipline and recruitment, but no authority to intervene in individual prosecutions. Community Police Councils (CPCs) should be set up to make recommendations to the Police Authority, and the police would be legally obliged to consult the CPCs on all matters which have a bearing on policing operations in their area (see Scraton, 1985: 87).

Whatever eventual oversight and consultative structures are eventually agreed, it is particularly important that young people have a voice in designing and monitoring policing in their areas. All too often young people are 'the policed' and suffer harassment and suspicion from the police. Channels must be created for young people to be able to influence policing. Consideration should be given to the best way of doing this (some young people will feel intimidated in a meeting dominated by adults). It is crucial that young people, the unemployed, and other marginalised groups are included within the accountability structures. This is notoriously difficult to achieve.  As research on police-public partnerships in Lancashire found:

> *"The exclusion of disorganised interests impacts differentially on the politically marginalised and socially disadvantaged: the unemployed, the homeless, black and lower-class youths and many trapped in abusive family relationships"* (Jemphrey et al, 1997: 45).

Inclusivity must be a key principle in any community police forum.

# Independent Monitoring

Somewhat distinct from, though obviously related to formal civic oversight mechanisms, is the principle of independent police monitoring.

There have been a number of important police monitoring projects in the UK.  In 1981-2 following a summer of disturbances, six London boroughs developed local police committees or sub-committees which urged the government to set up a metropolitan police authority for the region.  Some of these police committees co-opted representatives from local independent monitoring groups, others directly funded their own research officers to carry out a monitoring function.  The committees acted as a resource for people who wished to complain about police activity and some recruited volunteers to act as witnesses to police operations.

During the 1984-85 miners' strike, an important monitoring operation involving some 40 volunteers was set up in Sheffield in response to local concerns about the policing of the strike including the use of road-blocks, mass arrests and violence against demonstrators. (see Field in Fine & Millar, 1985; Brogden et al, 1988: 190-193). One important aspect of this independent monitoring work has been the dissemination of information about police activities to the wider society who are normally excluded from possession of this knowledge. For example, the Greater London Council Police Committee produced a monthly *Policing London*, free to all Londoners. The Manchester unit delivered their *Policewatch* to all Manchester households.[142]

In Tottenham, England, an encouraging development has been the commissioning by the local police consultative group of independent monitoring of stop and search powers. Haringey Community and Police Consultative Group contracted the National Association for the Care and Resettlement of Offenders (NACRO) to conduct an independent evaluation of the effectiveness of a stop and search leaflet. Each time police carried out a stop and search, the person concerned was given a leaflet describing police powers and individual rights. The leaflet was jointly signed by the local MP, Bernie Grant, and a police chief. NACRO's evaluation covered police stop and search statistics, a survey of police attitudes, an attitudes survey of people who were stopped and searched and comparison with a similar London police division.

The project came up with a series of recommendations. Commander Gilbertson of the local police was enthusiastic about the results of the project: *"I hope that the lessons learned will. .. serve as an example of what can be done when local communities and their police service work together"* (NACRO, 1997). It is only when the police and police authorities open up to independent monitoring and evaluation, and take on board the

---

[142] Secrecy Acts in Britain limited this work, as did resources (Brogden et al, 1988:191).

results of this process, that the barriers between police and local communities will begin to break down.

Another interesting monitoring initiative is provided by the Joint Forum on Policing in the Western Cape, South Africa. Here, a number of non-governmental organisations came together out of mutual concerns regarding policing in the new dispensation. The 22 organisations involved published a major report detailing evidence of serious abuses by members of the new South African Police Service in their different areas. This initiative is all the more important in that it came at a time when many were unwilling to criticise the new regime and many former activists had been "co-opted" into government departments and agendas. Given the stake South Africans have in needing Mandela's government to succeed, and the faith people have in "Madiba" rescuing them from the oppression of apartheid, this type of critical action may not have proved popular. However, it demonstrates that no matter how "benign" or popular the government, problems with policing continue and must be challenged. In fact, for a society to really leave the past behind - it is vital that analysis, critique and evaluation occur even during the most difficult of transition periods. Otherwise the "new dispensation" might in many ways grow to be not too different from the old.

The value of monitoring work in Northern Ireland was demonstrated by CAJ's activities in the summer of 1996, and again 1997, when teams of independent observers represented the organisation at a large number of contentious parades and demonstrations. Observers were asked to monitor whether the policing of these events was being carried out in an even-handed way, respecting the rights of both marchers and protesters. In addition, statements were taken from over 160 people who witnessed events. The result was an important bank of information on the policing of the marches and protests which led to the publication of *The Misrule of Law,* and helped the CAJ to develop concrete proposals for future events, see especially *Policing the Police* (CAJ, 1996, 1997, 1997a). In the absence of local police committees with real powers, it may be useful for local councils and community organisations to develop their own monitoring exercises.

## Democratic oversight of intelligence services

The gathering and use of intelligence is perhaps the most sensitive aspect of security work, and little information is available on the subject. The RUC's Special Branch (SB) employs a range of special investigative measures such as the running of informants and police officers working undercover. Intelligence-gathering of this kind often results in fewer direct complaints or grievances from the public, with the exception of the numerous complaints from people who are detained under the Prevention of Terrorism Act and allege that attempts were made to recruit them as informers. This intelligence-gathering is of paramount importance to all security-related activities, and it is most relevant from a civil liberties point of view, as it can intrude deeply in the private lives of large segments of the population in Northern Ireland.[143] Whether it be the RUC's Special Branch, the army's intelligence network, Government Communications Headquarters, or MI5, they all exercise extensive powers of information-gathering regarding individuals in Northern Ireland, and any discussion of police accountability is meaningless without addressing the activities of these groups also.[144]

Although the Security Service Act of 1989 established an elaborate complaints system, the Tribunal responsible for

---

[143] There is less accountability for telephone surveillance activities in NI than in Britain; no statistics are available as to the extent of such surveillance.

[144] In a notorious case, the police, investigating leaks of security documents, discovered that army agent Brian Nelson was also working for the paramilitary UDA providing loyalist hit squads with confidential information on targets. He was sentenced to 10 years jail in 1992 (HRW, 1997).

investigating complaints did not uphold a single one of the 175 complaints studied in 1994.[145]  There is also a committee dealing with the Intelligence and Security Services (ISC) established by the Intelligence Services Act of 1994 intended to give some parliamentary oversight to intelligence activities.  However the committee does not enjoy the prerogative of calling witnesses, is not empowered to examine actual operations, does not decide what information will be made available to it, and submits its reports to the Prime Minister not parliament.  In practice, this means that the committee has very limited powers.

In seeking good practice models regarding the democratic accountability mechanisms which could oversee the work of the intelligence services, the Canadian experience seemed to be particularly interesting.  There is also some academic work of interest looking into the principles which should govern such work, and that is reported upon after a brief review of the Canadian model.

## Canada: a case study

The Canadian Security Intelligence Service (CSIS), the country's federal domestic security service, was established in 1984[146] following a series of severe problems with security work done by the Royal Canadian Mounted Police. The same 1984 Act also created CSIS's oversight body, the Security Intelligence Review Committee (SIRC). The Committee is completely independent of the government, and is responsible to parliament. Its members are appointed by the Governor General, after consultation by the Prime Minister with the leaders of the larger political parties. SIRC reports to parliament through an annual public report, which contains a fairly detailed evaluation of

---

[145] Background paper by Peter Klerks for CAJ (1996).
[146] Canadian Intelligence Service Act.

CSIS operation. SIRC also has the power to investigate complaints relating to any act or thing done by CSIS, including vetting activities. For these purposes, SIRC has its own research staff.[147]

SIRC has a statutory power of access to any information held by CSIS or, where relevant, by government departments. It also has the power to conduct reviews and inquiries, and produce reports for the Minister. In practice, SIRC deals with a wide variety of matters such as broad policy issues, questions of competence and management effectiveness, security breaches, and compliance with legal directives and principles of human rights. SIRC's annual reports contain extensive discussions of its investigations into alleged wrong-doings, often involving the behaviour of CSIS informers. SIRC also investigates certain operational and policy matters at its own initiative, the results of which are normally presented in the form of secret reports which are summarised in the public annual report. While differences of view remain, CSIS management has repeatedly expressed satisfaction with its watchdog. In recent years, the security service has developed a new mode of working in a more professional and transparent way while maintaining its effectiveness. This has resulted in dozens of publicly available publications and reports on security assessments, economic espionage, domestic and foreign terrorism, immigration, etc., which in turn have sparked public debates in which journalists, various professionals, academics and the general public have further contributed to an enhanced awareness and understanding of security-related issues.

SIRC was deliberately not created in 1984 as a parliamentary committee, since it was feared that this would mean partisan politics would play a role in the review of CSIS' activities. Certainly SIRC's relationship with the parliamentary

[147] SIRC consists of five part-time members who are supported by a full-time staff numbering about a dozen, of whom half are researchers (Lustgarten et al, 1994).

subcommittee on National Security is far from perfect and has deteriorated in recent years. The fact that SIRC as a controlling body has been given the power of full access to CSIS's information, but that its subsequent findings must often be 'taken on faith', has failed to satisfy some of its critics. Most of SIRC's investigations are not made public other than in brief summaries. This seems a basic dilemma in any intelligence oversight system. The existence of (some) secrets is inevitable, and the majority of people will always have to put their confidence in a limited number of others. The question is only whether this be left entirely within the purview of the service's own employees, or whether it is better that this role be performed by an appointed or elected external body.

Apart from oversight through SIRC, CSIS is also scrutinised by an Inspector General (IG) who has no public role but in fact functions as the Ministry's eyes and ears inside the agency, thus ensuring that ministerial responsibility has real substance. The IG is appointed by the government and responsible to the Deputy Solicitor General. His/her task is to monitor and review CSIS' operational activities with particular reference to their compliance with ministerial policies, legality and reasonableness. The IG, supported by his staff of about twelve, engages in elaborate research projects into CSIS' s practices and also comments on the CSIS director's annual report, sending a 'Certificate' to the Solicitor general in which satisfaction and/or criticism over the report are recorded. The Inspector-General's Office and the Security Intelligence Review Committee may on occasion assist each other and there is significant informal co-operation between the two offices.

A further interesting element in the Canadian intelligence control structure is the Target Approval and Review Committee (TARC), a body chaired by the Director of CSIS and consisting of senior officials of the Service together with representatives of other relevant ministries and an Independent Counsel (Lustgarten et al, 1994: 81). TARC oversees the application of intrusive investigative measures and the role of the Independent Counsel is to challenge the factual basis of the individual warrant requests. SIRC has actually advised the government to enhance this system by establishing a veritable 'Devil's Advocate,' who would have to challenge the need for a warrant in the first place. SIRC already has a somewhat similar procedure regarding security clearance refusals. Here, an independent outsider is called upon to act on behalf of appellants, arguing their case. A list of about two dozen counsellors fulfilling this role, mostly full-time practitioners but some academics as well, is printed regularly in SIRC's annual reports.

### General principles

Clearly it is difficult to devise a system of oversight that ensures the confidentiality of security work, while satisfying the need for public trust. All intelligence operatives are by nature extremely wary of sharing the nature and identity of their sources even with superiors and colleagues. This is quite understandable, since lives are often at stake. Yet, it can be done. In other countries where these same vital interests are also recognised, legislators have introduced various mechanisms to try and ensure that no uncontrollable centres of power exist, and that professional zeal does not prevail over the rule of law. In countries such as the United States, Canada, Australia and some European nations, oversight bodies have access to security-related and police information. This allows them to correct mistakes, and improve the professional functioning of the intelligence and law enforcement services under scrutiny, without releasing more information than is absolutely necessary.

From a study of the literature and a series of interviews, we can summarise a series of basic principles concerning democratic accountability and the intelligence services. We have brought here together a series of issues derived from the work of the McDonald Commission in Canada, Dr Alfred Einwag, the Federal Data Protection Commissioner in Germany, and the Belgian Ministry of the Interior.

The experience in Canada,[148] argues that:

- in the gathering of information, there should be no violations of the criminal law;
- the investigative means to be employed should be proportionate to the threat posed and the probability of its occurrence.
- the need to use various information-gathering techniques, even if lawful, must be balanced against the possible damage they cause to civil liberties;
- the more intrusive the technique, the higher the authority that should be required to approve its use; less intrusive techniques should always be employed in preference to more intrusive techniques.

Dr Alfred Einwag, the Federal Data Protection Commissioner in Germany, adds that:[149]

- basic to the philosophy of accountability in modern policing is that the functions of control ('steering') and oversight ('reviewing') should be seen as separate;[150]
- the state shall define exactly the tasks and powers of an intelligence agency by law; in particular, intelligence

---

[148] Conclusions of the McDonald Commission.

[149] See "The Proper Role of an Intelligence Agency in a Democracy", conference paper in Sofia, Bulgaria 8-10 April, 1992, p.23.

[150] This doctrine contains a warning against a too intense involvement of overseeing bodies in the actual policy-making and operational processes. An intelligence committee called upon to give prior approval to sensitive decisions such as bugging or infiltration operations cannot be expected afterwards to have the impartial position necessary to review such matters.

agencies shall not have any executive powers, for example the power to arrest individuals or to seize goods;

■ the use of methods for obtaining information which seriously infringe the privacy of an individual (for example wiretapping) must be authorised by a different body and on a case-by-case basis;

■ an intelligence agency shall collect and store only that information which is actually necessary to fulfil the specified task, and will erase or purge information which is no longer needed;

■ the collecting, administering, and storing of personal data must be scrutinised by authorised institutions. The secrecy of information is no reason to limit independent supervision.

The Belgian Ministry of Interior concluded that supervision of the police and intelligence services must.[151]

■ be exercised by bodies outside the police and intelligence services themselves;

■ pervade the regular work of the intelligence services so it needs to be carried out continuously rather than intermittently;

■ be exercised by bodies with sufficient authority, means and powers to carry out a thorough investigation;

■ be done openly, and while there has to be a balance between openness and confidentiality, the results of an investigation must be publicly reported as much as possible.

It is clear from the debate in other countries, that there are no easy solutions as to the balance between open democratic accountability and the efficient functioning of a country's intelligence services. It is equally clear, however, that there are

---

[151] Belgische Kamer van Volksvertegenwoordigers, 1305/1-90/91;Wetsontwerp tot regeling van het toezicht op politie- en inlichtingendiensten. Memorie van Toelichting pp. 6-7.]

minimal safeguards being evolved which can and should be applied in Northern Ireland.

# Summary of conclusions – democratic accountability

1.  Mechanisms for democratic accountability complement the legal framework in ensuring that the police provide the quality and type of service agreed upon, and the possibility of redress if they do not do so.   Such community involvement ensures that individuals and groups in society become more than simply the 'policed' but have an active role in designing and supporting the policing function.

2.  Weaknesses in the current mechanisms for democratic accountability derive from the ambiguous division of authority between the Secretary of State, the Chief Constable and the Police Authority, and in particular the generous interpretation of the Chief Constable's 'operational autonomy', and the 'poor relation' status of the Police Authority.

3.  Any effective civic oversight body must have the necessary powers to secure accountability from the police, but must also be prepared to exercise those powers energetically and responsibly.

4.  The establishment of more localised fora  can be useful as long as the police are under some obligation to listen to community views, and the fora  are able to forward their ideas and concerns to regional or national bodies with legal powers of oversight.

5.  Police accountability requires that the powers of the police are clearly defined; that the powers, representative nature and accountability of the civic oversight body are defined; and that there is effective local community participation in the process of democratic oversight.

6.  The democratic oversight of the intelligence services poses particular problems, but is also particularly important. Other countries have found mechanisms for balancing genuine security concerns against the need for transparency and democratic accountability; we need to be equally creative.

7.  Independent monitoring of police is a valuable contribution to the process of community involvement and oversight.

# Summary of recommendations – democratic accountability

1.  While there is no single model of how a democratic society might hold its police to account, there are a number of important principles, the most important one being the need to define clearly in law and in practice the powers of the police. In Northern Ireland, this requires specifically a clear definition of operational independence as it applies to the Chief Constable.

2.  The role of civic oversight bodies should be strengthened in any forthcoming legislation. In addition to clarifying the meaning of 'operational independence' (which by restricting police powers, strengthens other elements in the oversight structure), there needs to be a genuinely representative civic oversight body, with

clear and effective powers of control.  If the members of such bodies are to be appointed rather than elected, then special care should be taken to ensure that the process is as transparent as possible.

3.      As a way of giving practical expression to the above two recommendations, new policing legislation, if it is to be effective in ensuring democratic accountability, should be measured against a number of criteria:

-       explicit reference must be made to the philosophy of policing and its responsibility in international and domestic law to protect human rights;
-       mechanisms to ensure police accountability, particularly in the use of force, should be provided for;
-       the respective remits of the different bodies involved in overseeing policing should be clear and unambiguous;
-       powers as well as functions should be established;
-       a statutory basis for a revised police disciplinary code should be provided;
-       and it should be made a statutory requirement on the police and relevant agencies to consult effectively with the community, and provide appropriate guidelines for such consultation.

4.      Local systems of communication, consultation, and decision making should be encouraged with a view to creating stronger relationships between the police and the local community served.  There must be an enforceable contract between the police and the community, the issues discussed must be relevant to the community, the composition of the group should be inclusive and representative, sufficient resources must be provided, there must be a legal obligation on the police to listen to and respond to community concerns, and a mechanism whereby local concerns can be

pursued at senior levels within policing and police oversight.

5.  The intelligence services cannot be excluded from this move to greater democratic accountability. Principles drawn from international experience show that there are ways in which effective democratic control can be exerted without undermining the functioning of such services. These should all be pursued energetically.

6.  We have argued for the need for more effective structures of accountability over policing. Until such structures are in place, and possibly even thereafter, we recommend that efforts to secure an independent monitoring of police activities be maintained.

# Chapter Five:

## Devising new structures and forms of policing

### Introduction

One of the key themes of this report is the complex nature of the policing problem in Northern Ireland. On the one hand, issues of justice and fairness are central to the conflict and therefore the creation of peace over the longer term requires that fundamental questions of policing and legal reform be effectively addressed and resolved. However, on the other hand, an accountable and representative police service cannot come about in isolation, and is to some extent dependant on changes in the judiciary and in the criminal justice system, and on the expectations society places on the police. As such, major change may be dependent upon the larger peace process and political negotiations (Pollak, 1993). Devising new forms of policing will both affect the political process, and be affected by the process.

However, the fact that changes to policing and the long-term search for peace are integrally linked, is not a recipe for doing nothing until the conflict is resolved, and a political settlement arrived at. Rather, moves towards more democratic, representative policing could make a major contribution to peace, and indeed a failure to move constructively on these issues could undermine potential advances on other fronts.

Given that CAJ takes no position on the constitutional status of Northern Ireland, it falls beyond the organisation's remit, and the brief given to the authors, to propose specific structures for policing which may impact on constitutional questions. It is therefore not our purpose to recommend any particular option for policing structures. However, CAJ's work over many years on the principles of policing, and most importantly the comparative research carried out for this report, do give vital insights into the principles which should underpin any new policing arrangements. This chapter will look briefly at the framework already agreed by the British and Irish governments for policing, and will then discuss some of the specific structural proposals being canvassed and the international parallels.

## The search for agreed structures

In "A New Framework for Agreement" the British and Irish governments, with a view to assisting discussion and negotiation among the Northern Ireland parties, set down in writing their shared understanding of a series of issues.[152] Insofar as policing is concerned, paragraphs 18 and 19 of the Joint Document are particularly important:

> "18. .....(*The governments*) *acknowledge the need for new arrangements and structures to reflect the reality of diverse aspirations, to reconcile as fully as possible the rights of both traditions, and to promote co-operation between them, so as to foster the process of developing agreement and consensus between all the people of Ireland.*

> "19. *They agree that future arrangements relating to Northern Ireland and Northern Ireland's wider relationships, should respect the full and equal legitimacy and worth of the identity, sense of allegiance, aspiration and ethos of both the unionist and nationalist communities there. Consequently both Governments commit themselves to the principle that institutions and*

---

[152] Joint Framework Document of British and Irish Governments, 1995.

*arrangements in Northern Ireland and North/South institutions should afford both communities secure and satisfactory political, administrative and symbolic expression and protection....".*

It is with this in mind that we study below some of the options already put forward in public debate. It is interesting to note that, to date, few very concrete structural models have in fact been proposed. Furthermore, those models which have been proposed have largely come from nationalist voices – the Social Democratic & Labour Party, Sinn Fein, and other individuals within the nationalist community. The option of rank-flattening and police restructuring in line with District Council areas has been suggested by the Royal Ulster Constabulary (RUC),[153] and there has been some (albeit limited) academic debate around specific models. It may therefore be most useful to draw out general principles against which these, and any models proposed in future, can be measured. Prior to doing that, we can summarise briefly the proposals which have been most publicly and frequently raised to date as follows:

-       The creation of two-tier policing. This model would create a local 'community police' for local areas, and a federal force for the whole of Northern Ireland. A geographical division in policing often involves a division of functions, so the consequences of two-tier policing needs to be considered simultaneously in terms of both geographical and functional separation.

-       The development of community policing based on the 'informal policing systems' already in existence. Some might argue that such systems be integrated into formal policing structures, others that they complement such structures.

---

[153] See RUC's Fundamental Review.

Both of these models have parallels in other jurisdictions, and the following discussion draws extensively on this international experience to assess what the implications of either option are for human rights protection and democratic participation.

# Creation of regional police organisations

## Rationale for reform

The desire to create policing institutions which are closer to the people policed, on the assumption that this will make them more responsive to local needs, is a very natural one. In Northern Ireland, the proposal is often additionally motivated by the belief that this is a necessary move if one is to move away from the current situation wherein the Royal Ulster Constabulary (RUC) is seen as monolithic and, as such, is deemed to be largely representative of the majority population, which is Protestant and unionist.[154] The force has few Catholic police officers, and few officers live in nationalist areas. While the reasons for this are complex, the institution is therefore seen to be far removed from Catholics and nationalists, and their concerns. Given the extent of residential segregation in Northern Ireland, the creation of regional police organisations would allow a more pluralist force to develop. However, the argument is not just of relevance in addressing the communal divides within society. Many working class communities, Protestant as well as Catholic, exhibit signs of alienation which might be somewhat assuaged with more localised access to the police. According to this argument, if policing was restructured along regional lines, it would be possible to establish policing entities composed of local people, who lived locally, and were in tune with local needs.

---

[154] For further discussion of the culture, ethos and make up of the RUC see chapter one.

The proposals are also based on the recognition of the difficulties of combining quasi-military and community functions within the one organisation. It is clear from our previous discussion and from the work of many experts that the predominance of security functions over community policing has been a problem for the RUC. Lord Hunt, for example, commented on this issue when putting forward proposals to professionalise and civilianise the force in 1969:

> *"The RUC has had to perform what is in fact a dual role. In addition to carrying out all those duties normally associated in the public mind with police forces... it is responsible for security duties of a military nature"*

The same report described the military role of the RUC as having been:

> *"of first importance ...(it) has played a significant part in the training, equipment and traditions of the force..."*

Yet he also went on to conclude that:

> *"Policing in a free society depends on a wide measure of public approval and consent. This has never been obtained in the long term by military or paramilitary means. We believe that any police force, military in appearance and equipment, is less acceptable to minority and moderate opinion than if it is clearly civilian in character."* (Hunt,1969).

Hunt, of course, did not recommend dividing the functions of the RUC - rather he argued for the professionalisation and civilianisation of the entire organisation. Yet, despite Hunt's recommendations, the RUC has remained a highly armed and militarised force during the great majority of the past 28 years of political violence. Security policy predominates over community policing in the force's priorities. Nor is this a recent development reflecting the serious conflict in recent years; it has been true throughout the history of the force. Policing expert, John Brewer, has written extensively on the problems which the conflict has caused for the policing of 'ordinary' crime in Northern Ireland (Brewer, 1993). He identifies three key problems:

1.  The high profile given to politically-motivated crime means that the RUC's public image tends to be based on its handling of terrorism and public order rather than on its handling of ordinary crime.

2.  The dominance of anti-terrorist policing detracts from the effort and resources put into 'ordinary' crime.

3.  The militarisation of ordinary crime fighting even in less dangerous areas e.g. routine carrying of arms, joint police-army patrols.

The Opsahl Commission also found that *"the problems created by the RUC's conflicting security/policing roles is felt by police and public alike . . . The absence of community policing because of the security situation was a cause of regret"* (Pollak, 1993: 62-63).

A separation of functions has been argued to be an advantage by some people. This functional division of roles would, for example, allow the police to distinguish in structural terms between their community role and their security/military role. Local police services in this scenario could be unarmed, but a federal body (with less direct community responsibilities) could be armed.

## Proposals for structural change

Specific proposals for the greater regionalisation of policing have come most notably from the Social Democratic and

Labour Party (SDLP). The party has proposed a multi-tiered police service organised on a regional basis. In this model, military functions would be strictly separated from civilian policing. A further key element would be the disbandment of specialist units which operate outside local police control. In proposing this regional devolution of policing, the SDLP look to the examples of other European countries, such as Spain, France and Belgium. They point out that unitary structures (like the RUC) are the exception rather than the norm in European policy.[155] The party also argues that there must be a north-south dimension to any policing arrangements if nationalists are to identify with the new policing service.

The SDLP is not the only voice calling for regionalisation of policing. The Opsahl inquiry heard several proposals on the theme. For example, Rev. Raymond Murray, a Catholic priest and author from Armagh, urged consideration of regionalisation and a separation of policing according to function. In this model the 'military division' would be separate from an unarmed civilian, cross-community police service. Similarly, Rev. Brian Lennon of Portadown argued that while political divisions persist, the possibility of creating separate unarmed, community police organisations for politically divided areas should be explored (Pollak, 1993: 277-278). Mike Brogden, drawing on South African parallels also talked of "*a local police force acceptable to both local democratic community structures and subject to the final discipline of a reconstituted 'Northern Ireland Police Service*" (Brogden in CRD, 1994). Sinn Fein, while arguing for an all-Ireland police service, calls in the interim for the disbandment of the RUC, and the establishment of a Police Commission which would oversee the creation of special police sections to deal with serious crimes, drugs, and

---

[155] See "Policing in Northern Ireland" presented at the SDLP's annual conference, 18 November 1995.

sex offences, and of localised police services based on the District Council electoral boundaries.[156]

Aware of these concrete proposals for structural change, we interviewed many policing experts about their experiences of police regionalisation, both in countries which face political violence and divided loyalties, as well as those with distinct and sometimes geographically segregated communities. What follows is not a full account of the structural arrangements in each country. Rather we have highlighted particular issues of interest for the protection of human rights in any new structures which transpire.

## Basque Country/Catalonia

The Spanish experience of creating devolved police structures is especially pertinent. As noted elsewhere, following Franco's death, and as a result of nationalist pressure, the Spanish government devolved power to newly created local parliaments in Catalonia and the Basque Country, although the Spanish state retains overall sovereignty. This limited autonomy included the right to raise police institutions.[157] A local Basque police organisation, the Ertzaintza, was officially formed in 1981. In Catalonia, the Cuerpo Mossos d'Escuadra, took responsibility for policing functions from 1994.

In both the Basque Country and Catalonia, the Spanish state forces have continued to play a role - particularly in relation to the policing of anti-terrorist activities, borders, and drug

---

[156] See "Policing in Transition", discussion document for Sinn Fein Ard Fheis, 1996.

[157] The situation is somewhat unclear as Articles 148 and 149 of the Spanish Constitution declare the Spanish state's exclusive responsibility for public security but also allow for the creation of autonomous police forces in the regions. The Statutes of Autonomy, both in the Basque Country and Catalonia, include the right to raise a police force.

control. While this arrangement works smoothly in Catalonia, where the Spanish state forces and the autonomous police co-operate well, in the Basque Country there has been conflict and confusion. This is partly because in Catalonia the local autonomous police do not have the remit of policing terrorism or drugs - anyone arrested for either offence is handed over to the Spanish state forces. In the Basque Country, however, both the local Ertzaintza and the state Guardia Civil have responsibility for anti-terrorist policing. Police experts interviewed spoke of considerable competition between the two agencies. Theoretically in the Basque Country, co-ordination of security policing should be managed through the Public Security Council, made up of representatives from the Basque government and the Spanish government. However, in practice this has proved ineffective.[158]

A further problem with having regional police organisations alongside a national force could be that of over-policing. In Spain and Catalonia, new forces have been created while the old still exist. This results in an extremely high ratio of police to civilians. In Catalonia, the Guardia Civil are very under-employed in some areas - this inactivity and over-lap constitutes a gross waste of public funds, and a threat to civil liberties.[159]

There is also some ambiguity in terms of the powers of the respective forces. The Spanish state forces can intervene when asked to by the Basque government. However, Spanish state forces do not come under the jurisdiction of the Basque

---

[158] The head of the Ertzaintza, Juan Maria Atutxa, believed that those in command of the Guardia Civil had been reluctant to accept that the Ertzaintza had taken over responsibility for most policing functions, and that lack of co-operation was a direct result of this. Interview, February 1997.

[159] Questionnaire response from Francesc Guillen, Research Director, Police Training Academy of Catalonia noted that while there is a commitment to reducing police numbers, there have been difficulties involved in reducing the numbers of state forces officers in the region.

government, so though the Basque government is responsible for their intervention, it cannot hold the police to account once they do intervene. Furthermore, they can also intervene at the request of the Spanish state itself in cases of emergency (this occasion has not yet arisen and it is unclear exactly what these circumstances would entail). These powers create an important gap in local accountability structures.

In Catalonia, the devolution of power to the local parliament, and the creation of a local police service, have been relatively successful in meeting national aspirations. But then the conflict in Catalonia has not been a violent one.[160] In the Basque Country, the creation of the local parliament and local police have met the aspirations of many people. The constitutional nationalist PNV party is heavily involved in the running of the state, although it continues to argue for more autonomy. However, other Basque nationalists (particularly those involved in the Basque nationalist political party Herri Batasuna, and the paramilitary organisation ETA) remain opposed to participation in the new police force, and indeed ETA has killed police officers as part of its armed campaign. Overall, there has been an increase in democratic rights and in civil liberties with devolution and the creation of the new police structures. However, the conflict continues and in some ways is more internalised, bitter and entrenched than ever. Whereas the Spanish state forces were the object of hostility for many years, now the situation can be described as Basque against Basque.[161]

---

[160] As Raymond Carr notes in reviewing a new book on the difference in the two struggles the Catalans, unlike the Basques *"obtained their Generalitat without violence, thereby accepting the legitimacy of the Spanish state"*.

[161] In the Basque Country it was also considered important that members of the Ertzaintza live in local communities. This was in contrast to the Spanish state forces who had been stationed in barracks, separate from the people. In the Basque Country this civilianisation has largely been successful. Ertzaintza do live normal lives in local towns and villages. However, the threat of ETA violence and hostility between certain groups and the police has meant that some Ertzaintza have left their areas and gone to live in safer districts.

Limited autonomy has assisted the management of conflict - it has not ended it.

Indeed, even the Ertzaintza, conceived of as a local community police organisation, providing a service more than a force, has increasingly used methods of repression in quelling dissent. This is of course both a product and a cause of the continuing conflict, and is a worrying trend for human rights (see chapter 6 for more details).

There is at least one vital difference between the policing problems of Northern Ireland and the examples cited here. Even in comparison to the Basque Country, we face a much more internally divided society. As such, there is a risk that the creation of local forces for local areas could institutionalise and strengthen existing social divisions and residential segregation. Certainly, there are many lessons we can draw on directly from the Spanish experiences:

- There is a danger of confusion and competition between regional and national forces – in any new structures of this kind there would need to be clear agreement on responsibilities and powers.
- There is a danger of lack of accountability of the state forces. Attention focused on the local organisation may detract from sufficient attention being directed at the need for accountability of the non-local force(s).
- There is a danger of over-policing if new forces are created in addition to old ones.
- If some sections of population are hostile to the new policing organisations, conflict may well persist.
- Despite the best of intentions, continuing conflict may still lead to the new police structures resorting to the same repressive tactics as their predecessors.

More positively, one can also note:

- Policing and democracy are integrally linked – the creation of new policing structures was able to take place because new democratic political structures had also been created.
- It is possible and practical for policing functions to be devolved downwards.
- It is important to civilianise policing and the philosophy, training and practice of the new police was more civilian than the miltarised federal state forces.
- It is important that human rights are at the heart of policing.
- Local people will join the force once consent for the policing institutions is won.
- Training practices must be open to civilian input and evaluation.

## Palestine/Israel

In Palestine, the Israeli security forces have had a serious problem of legitimacy, and there have been consistent complaints of abuse and harassment at the hands of the Israeli police. The Oslo Accords, in an attempt to try to resolve this long-standing conflict, laid the basis for the creation of the Palestinian autonomous police force. It should be noted that the creation of the Palestinian National Authority and the Palestinian Police Force is not the end product of the peace process in the region; instead their establishment is seen as an interim measure pending further negotiations.

Of the police, the Accords state: *"the Council will establish a strong police force, while Israel will continue to carry the responsibility for defence against external threats, as well as responsibility for overall security of Israelis for the purpose of safeguarding their internal security and public order."*[162] This has led

---

[162] Declaration of Principles, Oslo Accords, Article VIII, September 1993.

to a very unusual policing model by which the Palestinian and Israeli police operate in parallel on the same territory - a form of Dual Authority. Furthermore, the Palestinian arrangement is unusual in that it is based around citizenship rather than territory. The Palestinian police are responsible for policing Palestinians, and in principle do not have powers over Israelis, including those residing in Israeli-established settlements in the Occupied Territories. The Palestinian police operate in Palestinian areas of the West Bank and Gaza Strip, and have limited powers both in relation to territory and function.[163]

An additional problem is that the legislation which the Palestinian police are enforcing is not Palestinian in origin. Thus the police are enforcing legislation, the legitimacy of which is challenged by sizeable sections of the Palestinian community. Furthermore, the Palestinian police are policing alongside the Israeli police, and sometimes in co-operation with them. Given the continuing allegations of human rights abuse directed at the Israeli police, such close co-operation by the new Palestinian force undermines their credibility. As Mustafa Mar'i of the Palestinian human rights group, Al Haq, notes:

> *"the joint policing role itself is quite problematic since it means that the Palestinian police has to jointly patrol certain areas and has to carry out many of its activities with close co-ordination with the Israeli occupation troops at the time the Israeli troops are still carrying out their violations of the rights of the Palestinians living under Israel's occupation."* (Mar'i, 1997).

In a paper comparing the importance of policing in the peace processes of Northern Ireland and Palestine, Milton-Edwards (1996) points out that it was not long before the Palestinian police were using strong-arm tactics against its own

---

[163] Background paper prepared for CAJ by Mustafa Mar'i (1997).

opposition.[164]    The setting up of the Palestinian National Authority and police force were opposed by radical sections of the Palestinian community, and the police has since been used to quash opposition.   As Milton-Edwards (1996) comments: *"The PNA, in order to establish and maintain its authority has had to take action against its own opposition including extremely coercive measures, simply to comply with Israel's demands".*

From the Middle East experience, lessons of special relevance for Northern Ireland would appear to be:

- The law must be changed as well at the same time as the police who implement it: a repressive legal system will undermine any chance of creating a police service respectful of human rights.
- Human rights safeguards must be put in place for all forces involved in policing.
- If a new police service is created alongside an old unreformed police service, it may well emulate the bad practices of its predecessor.
- New police bodies can soon start using illegitimate force if not effectively controlled.
- A multiplicity of forces can lead to a splintering of authority, which can be as dangerous, anti-democratic, and narrowly politically partisan, as police structures which are monolithic and over-centralised.

## Belgium

Like Northern Ireland, Belgium is a divided society.[165]   With a view to better representing the needs of its French and Flemish

---

[164] This is also the case in the Basque Country where the Ertzaintza play an important role in policing of political violence and have broken up political demonstrations with rubber bullets.

[165] The population is divided between Flemings (58%) who speak Flemish and Walloons (42%) who speak French (Benyon et al : 3).

speaking communities, Belgium has federalised both its political system and its police.[166] There are three types of police organisation in Belgium: the gendarmerie (formerly a military police force, now a federal civilian force responsible for public order, disasters etc); the judicial police (concerned with criminal investigations); and the communal police (local, civil forces). Every local community with at least 10,000 inhabitants can have its own police force, and there are 589 formally independent forces (Klerks in Bunyan, 1993). The authority of the communal police is limited to their own local area, although they can be given special authorisation for cross-commune policing if circumstances require. Local forces tend to be comprised of local people, and so people will be policed by policemen and women using the language of their community. In bilingual communities, like Brussels, the police are expected to speak both languages.

As in other European countries, policing in Belgium is ultimately under the responsibility of political ministries. As a way of ensuring adequate representation of both communities, police and judicial appointments have been divided between political and linguistic candidates. This appeared to create consensus. However the failure of the police effectively to investigate the paedophile ring of recent controversy raised doubts about the success of the system. Stephen Bates writing in the English *Guardian* newspaper said that the process of appointing according to political allegiances led to "mediocrities" being appointed to top positions, and rivalries between local forces. Police in Liege, where some children disappeared, never passed on their information fifty miles down the road to Charleroi, where their alleged kidnapper was living.[167]

---

[166] The 1993 Constitution stipulates that Belgium is now a federal state made up of communities and regions.
[167] *Guardian*, 27 September 1997.

The Belgian government has spent energy, attention and money in the process of federalisation. However, although powers have been devolved on many issues there are limits to the process. The gendarmerie continues to play an important role in Belgian policing. Formerly a military police force, the gendarmerie has been demilitarised since 1991 (although Peter Klerks notes that it continues to be characterised by a *"strong esprit de corps and little accountability to the outside world"*) (Klerks, 1993: 42). Despite demilitarisation, the gendarmerie continues to play a 'heavy' policing role, with its duties including support to local forces at soccer matches, demonstrations etc, preventive patrols and identity checks, territorial defence in case of war. Despite the existence of local policing for local areas, the state has retained for itself an important force for containing social disorder.

Professor Cyrille Fijnaut, Leuven University, argued that federalisation was used to contain the crisis in Belgium, but warned that the centralised state recognises the need to keep key powers and resources to itself: in particular, it would be impossible for the state to exist without a centralised police force: *"to federalise the gendarmerie would be the end of Belgium. You cannot endlessly split up the system."*[168]

Finally, the Belgian system of local police for local areas has been manageable in a country where many towns are exclusively French or Flemish speaking. While Northern Ireland is very residentially segregated, it is rare that the lines of social and political division are as geographically distinct as they appear to be in most parts of Belgium. Apart from wondering if this kind of segregation would be further exacerbated by a move to regionalised police services, the key lessons for Northern Ireland from Belgium would appear to be:

---

[168] Interview, Brussels, November 1996.

- The creation of local police institutions for local people may prove possible where there is peaceful co-existence generally.
- There needs to be some close institutional co-operation built up between local forces so that serious crime does not go undetected.
- Corruption may evolve more easily, and be less detectable, in small close police forces and precautions would need to be taken to avoid such a trend.
- The process of devolving autonomy to local areas is generally limited by the state's need to retain key powers for itself.
- Accountability structures governing the powers of the federal force should not be neglected.

## International lessons regarding police regionalisation:

The experiences of the Basque Country, the Middle East, and Belgium, show that while a degree of autonomy and self-government has been granted to regions, central government has retained key powers to ensure the cohesion of the state. There is a clear danger from a civil liberties perspective in this approach. On the one hand, it is positive that people have more control over the policing of their local areas, even if this is generally in relation to 'ordinary' neighbourhood crime. On the other hand, localised forces may not be aware or respectful of human rights norms, and the most important powers of the state are likely to become even more obscured from public scrutiny and removed from local democratic control. Thus, the Guardia Civil in the Basque Country, the Israeli police in Palestine, and the gendarmerie in Belgium remain largely outside of the control of those they are responsible for policing.

Furthermore, unless the political conflict in Northern Ireland is resolved it is likely that, despite the best intentions, security policy is likely to predominate over community policing priorities, whether they be the responsibility of the same force or separate forces. Of course, there is little doubt that in some cases the fact that a police organisation only has powers over the 'service' function can add to its popularity. For example, the Basque police were extremely popular when they dealt only with service issues e.g. traffic duties. Although they retain the support of most people, it is since they took over public order functions and security policing functions that there has been more controversy about their role.[169]

Certainly, if we choose to pursue the idea of a more regionalised police service in Northern Ireland, this must not be done at the expense of proper democratic accountability for state policing. In addition to finding ways to give people in communities an opportunity to influence decisions about the policing of 'ordinary crime' in their areas, ways must be found to allow people to have an input into security policing, public order policing, intelligence policing etc. Anything less will be counter-productive, for it is in precisely these most controversial areas that the police and the policed most often come into conflict. It is in these areas that civil liberties and human rights are most likely to be infringed.

To sum up some of the foregoing, the chart on the next page cites some of the potential strengths and weaknesses that derive from the creation of different forces.

---

[169] An opinion poll carried out for the Basque government in 1993 found that 56% of respondents agreed that the *"Ertzaintza respects human rights"* compared with 70% in 1991. Having said that, most people questioned were happy with Ertzaintza's anti-terrorist policing (only 2% in 1993 thinking it excessive, whereas 28% found it insufficient). Interviews with prisoners' families spoke of their unhappiness with Ertzaintza treatment of relatives and their breaking up of peaceful demonstrations (Interview with Senideak, February 1997).

## Creation of separate forces by region and function: strengths and weaknesses

| Potential Strengths | Potential Weaknesses |
|---|---|
| Local police for local people | Institutionalises existing divisions |
| Representative of local community | Confusion over different powers and responsibilities |
| Demonstrates willingness to change | Problems of over-policing |
| Easier for community police to operate | Problems of co-ordination |
| Local community police can develop positive relationship with public without contamination by public order/security concerns | National force may be left unchanged |
| Allows for diversity | Increased possibilities of "political" appointments in local areas |
| | Potential for political rivalries between forces |
| | New force may quickly become repressive |
| | Danger of officers in security division becoming hardened |
| | Difficulty to centrally set human rights norms for following at local level |
| | Officers from community forces may become targets |
| | Difficulty of ensuring accountability of federal/security agency |

## Building policing upon 'informal justice' systems?

This report has focused on the changes necessary in the formal criminal justice system, and lessons to be learned from elsewhere in this regard. It is, after all, states which are held to account under international law for the protection of human rights in their jurisdiction. It is states, therefore, which are under a specific legal obligation to create and maintain the rule of law for the benefit of all.

However, in recent years, a variety of alternative and informal approaches have arisen with regard to policing. Some of these approaches draw their roots from deep indigenous traditions of social justice and community responsibility – for example, the experiences of the Canadian, Australian and New Zealand Aboriginal peoples. Other approaches are seen as entirely complementary to the formal policing structures, providing resources from within the community which would not be available otherwise (for example, Neighbourhood Watch/'youth at risk' services/restorative justice schemes, etc). Yet others are established because they reject the policing offered by the state (and the reasons for this can be numerous) or because, having started to work alongside regular police structures, they have become disenchanted with the latter. In these categories, one might include the so-called 'community policing' engaged in by paramilitaries in Northern Ireland, and the anti-drug vigilante groups operating in numerous inner-city areas in Britain, Ireland and elsewhere.

In their very different ways, all these forms of alternative justice systems arise because of real or perceived inadequacies in the policing provided by the state, or as alternatives to it. The inadequacies may be explained in terms of culture, of politics and sovereignty, of class, or simply in terms of lack of resources or expertise to do everything expected of the police function. Nor should one ignore the fact that alternative justice systems can also arise as a means of paramilitary groups securing alternative power bases within local communities.

There are at least two very different responses possible. On the one hand, one might conclude that policing should be a formalised and centralised responsibility, that any inadequacies discovered should be addressed as a matter of urgency, and that thereafter certain alternative or complementary justice systems would prove unnecessary. On the other hand, one might argue that there is a value in the community as a whole taking on a greater responsibility in the matter of their policing, by putting their energies positively into self-help projects and working effectively alongside formal policing. If one accepts this option, the challenge is how to ensure that 'community policing' is respectful of human rights and does not descend into the horrendous cruelty and violence that has been witnessed here and elsewhere.

While the focus of our research was on making the formal policing structures responsive to community needs, we would certainly not want to suggest that a focus on complementary community policing is misguided. Indeed, we would argue that the creation of a healthy formal policing service (i.e. one which is accountable, responsive, representative, and respectful of rights) is a necessary pre-requisite if one is to develop a healthy and complementary (rather than alternative) community policing model. We have not the space here to devote to a very lengthy discussion of complementary community policing networks. However, the following account of informal policing approaches in different jurisdictions does help in the development of some core principles.

## Canada /Australia/New Zealand - Aboriginal groups

Before the colonisation of their land, Aboriginal people in Canada, Australia and New Zealand, had their own organised societies, their own rules, and their own systems for dealing with breaches of these rules. These communities have struggled to maintain their culture and societies against a background of extreme repression and discrimination. Historical tension between state police institutions and First Nation communities, and the struggle of those communities to retain their culture, have led in recent years to an acceptance by some police institutions and government bodies that they must develop ways of meeting the communities' needs. Strategies for achieving better relations must happen at different levels. Police training has been developed to create a better awareness among officers of Aboriginal cultures and, in some communities, self-policing has been adopted, for example within the reservations.

In Canada, the RMCP, in response to a recent incident involving armed and barricaded Aboriginal people, intervened with assistance from an Aboriginal spiritual leader. Canadian justice systems are looking at the 'healing circles' of Aboriginal justice where the community sits in judgement of the offender. Alternative forms of sentencing are increasing. The Aboriginal Justice Inquiry of Manitoba and the Donald Marshall Inquiry in Canada both affirmed that the adversarial justice system in Canada is in conflict with the spirit of Aboriginal systems, which focus on healing and reintegration of the offender into the community.

In Australia, Family Group Conferencing has emerged as an important trend. Family Group Conferences were first developed in New Zealand and are based on the traditional restorative system within Maori culture. The restorative justice approach was formalised in legislation in 1989 in New Zealand when Family Group Conferences were made a means for dealing with both civil and criminal matters. These conferences involve the young person alleged to have carried out the crime, their family, the victim, and a professional co-ordinator. A mutually acceptable plan of restoration is developed (Maxwell & Morris, 1996). In Australia the police have embraced the restorative justice model as having potential for improving relations with Aboriginal communities.

In a critical overview of restorative justice movements internationally, Kevin Haines observes that there are two ways in which restorative justice has tended to come about. Firstly, there are officially sanctioned, state sponsored national developments, as exemplified by the case of New Zealand, and to a lesser extent parts of Australia. Secondly, there are more 'bottom up' developments where projects have *"blossomed on an otherwise barren plain, as in most Western European countries and the USA"* (Haines, 1997). Haines highlights the problems which can arise when a 'mix and match' scenario emerges, i.e. when some parts of the system are restorative and others are not. It is self-evidently problematic for young people to be involved in a restorative project but with the threat of the official system (and perhaps a custodial disposal) hanging over their head. The concept of voluntarism, so important in restorative justice, can become rather meaningless.[170]

This insight has valuable lessons for us in Northern Ireland. We have argued throughout this report that piecemeal change is insufficient and at times dangerous. There are discussions underway in Northern Ireland about restorative justice approaches. If we are to learn from the Australian (and even more the New Zealand) experiments in restorative justice we need to recognise that whatever principles we adopt need to permeate the whole system. Otherwise contradiction and confusion emerge. One positive lesson from Australia is the way in which the police have attempted to work with

---

[170] This would be even more so in Northern Ireland were a paramilitary punishment the alternative waiting for anyone refusing to co-operate.

communities in developing restorative approaches. This is not to say that there are no longer tensions between the police and Aboriginal communities. However, there is evidence of a willingness to change on the part of the police. This may mean a re-thinking of the police role, and a recognition on the part of the police that it is the community themselves and not the police who are the key people in fighting crime in local areas.

## Informal justice systems in Ireland - north and south

There is a long history of informal justice systems in Ireland. The emergence of these alternative justice systems tends to coincide with periods of political unrest. Alternative systems have emerged when the legitimacy of not only the criminal justice system, but also of the state itself, is contested. For example, during the campaign for the Repeal of the Union in the 1840s, Daniel O'Connell initiated the establishment of arbitration courts which were further developed during the land war of the 1880s. Johnny Connolly notes that the Land League *"soon came to be seen as the legal authority in rural areas."* (1997: 19).

During the War of Independence, Sinn Fein through its policy of non-cooperation with state institutions, established its own courts and police. Arbitration courts had spontaneously emerged throughout many parts of Ireland from around 1917, as people boycotted the official criminal justice system. These tribunals were developed into an alternative justice system through the authority of the unofficial government of Dail Eireann. The judgements of the courts were generally enforced by the IRA. The popular courts were judged by the *Manchester Guardian* to be fair, popular and effective.[171]

During the civil rights struggle of the late 1960s and early 1970s, 'no-go areas' for the police were created in the Bogside and in parts of Belfast. The RUC and B-Specials (a reserve police force) had dealt harshly with civil rights campaigners (and had been seen doing so on national and international media), and they found themselves barricaded out of certain neighbourhoods. 'People's Courts' were established in some Catholic no-go areas with punishment by the IRA as the ultimate sanction (Conway, 1997: 111). The phenomenon of 'self-policing' has continued throughout the past two decades. In areas of Northern Ireland, a feeling that the police have failed to protect people from crime has led to alienation, and to particular groups and communities turning towards policing by the paramilitaries in the area.

This has occurred in both loyalist and republican areas. The brutal effects of this have been well documented. Pat Conway describes the 'tariffs' meted out by the paramilitaries:

> "*In terms of the republican tariff system, this ranges from cautioning and includes reparation, painting, tarring and feathering, placarding, curfewing, exiling (both locally and out of Northern Ireland), beatings, gradated shootings (knees, ankles, elbows, or a combination of these) culminating in some individuals being shot dead. The loyalist tariff system is much looser and more truncated involving reparation, exiling, beatings, shootings, and death*" (Conway, 1997: 109).

More recently there has emerged a number of 'community/neighbourhood watch groups' in areas of North

---

[171] Cited in Mitchell, A. 1995, Revolutionary Government in Ireland: Dail Eireann, 1919-1922, Gill and Macmillan, p.141 – see Mitchell for a full account of the development of the Dail court system.

and West Belfast.[172]    However, vigilantism and a violent
response to crime in local areas remain a serious reality.[173] For a
fuller reading list on this phenomenon see below.[174]


## South Africa

In South Africa, street committees and people's courts
developed during the mid 1980s at the height of the struggle
against apartheid in predominantly black townships.[175]    The
administration of justice in these areas had totally broken down
and ordinary policing was impossible, and gradually the
vacuum came to be exploited by criminal elements within the
community.  To counter this, street committees and people's
courts were formed so that members of a community could lay
a complaint which would be investigated by the street
committee, and the culprit would be brought before a people's
court for the matter to be adjudicated.  The punishments meted
out by these Peoples' Courts by no means always met human
rights standards:

> *"Most of the cases concerning the youth were dealt with
> on the spot where the offender was found, or the nearest
> place from there.  If, for example, you were found and it
> was discovered that you had stolen half a load of bread,
> then you would get fifteen lashes on the spot over the
> buttock, or if it was said that the price of bread was 25
> cents, then you would receive 25 lashes.  There was, for
> example, a guy who had stabbed a dog and he could not*

---

[172] see Adams, G *"We need democratic alternative to RUC"* in *Irish News*, 8
October 1997.   Alternatives to paramilitary punishment have also been
explored in loyalist areas, see for example Winston (1988) and below.
[173] see *Andersonstown News*, 11 October 1997.
[174] Bell, 1996; Munck, 1988; Kennedy, 1995; Conway, 1997; Winston, 1997;
Human Rights Watch, 1992; Thompson & Mulholland in Kennedy, ed. (1995).
[175] By 1987 around 400 People's Courts had been created. Brogden & Shearing
(1993:149) provide a comprehensive report of the self-policing initiatives.

> *explain why he did it. So he was found guilty and was*
> *given five lashes there on the spot"* (Moses in Brogden
> & Shearing, 1993: 149).

However, in some areas, appeals committees drew up codes of conduct stressing the need for due process and, in some, the emphasis was on education and re-integration rather than punishment (Brogden & Shearing, 1993: 151-157). In South Africa (as is currently happening in Northern Ireland) during the period of transition, informal structures existed alongside and sometimes in opposition to the formal system.

This led to the creation of a dual system of justice, wherein these mechanisms for local policing became part of the struggle against the state and were seen to challenge the hegemony of the apartheid state. *"In the medium and short term it represented an attempt to settle disputes between members of its community in an organised and peaceful way, thereby creating harmonious relationships and peace within its community."*[176] These measures were initially supported by local communities, but as many of the senior positions within these structures came to be taken over by the youth, the result in some places was an abuse of power, with an accompanying dwindling of support from the communities (Brogden & Shearing, 1993: 162). Many of the structures were crushed by the state during the states of emergency. As Brogden notes, there was not a peaceful co-existence in South Africa between the formal and informal structures. This is therefore unlike the New Zealand model (see above). In such situations tensions and contradictions will occur. There are some crimes which the formal system may be best placed to deal with, and good relationships between the two are necessary (e.g. in the area of child protection). Creating alternate structures is not therefore an alternative to accountable, state policing.

---

[176] Questionnaire response, Joey Moses, South African lawyer

Trying to adopt "western style" policing on top of or alongside informal justice systems has proved problematic for South Africa. The Community Police Fora, that were legislated for in the Interim Constitution, have not fully integrated indigenous structures such as these. In particular, the Self-Defence and Self-Protection Units (SDUs and SPUs) of the townships have been largely sidelined. These were made up of militant youths who had given up their education and much else in order to defend and protect their community. These young people have now been marginalised and alienated by the very system they fought to put in place. Many interviewees spoke of the dangers of failing to give these young people a stake in the new dispensation. Now unemployed, and with low socio-economic status, many of these young people have turned to crime. From having a place in the community, the youth now feel betrayed by the government which kept the new policing structures closed to them. In losing the SDUs and the SPUs, the government has failed to recognise that these provided a *"container for the war-psychosis of youth"*.[177] Although integrating a mass of uneducated, largely unskilled and undisciplined youth into the new police service would be problematic on many levels, leaving these same youths without their previous place in society could cause even longer-term problems for policing in South Africa.

The South Africa experience shows that communities can and do police themselves where state structures of policing break down. This leads us to ask whether some of the formal aspects of policing are necessary or best carried out by the police or whether there are functions which communities can best perform themselves e.g. mediating between young people who offend and the community. As Brogden argues, it is not just the police but the whole process of policing which must be re-examined.

---

[177] Interview with IDASA, Pretoria, 3 December 1996.

## Palestine

In Palestine, in the late 1980s during the period of uprising (known as the Intifada), police or guardian committees were formed. These aimed to provide an alternative to the Israeli forces, and carried out policing of the local area. A Palestinian activist said *"we meted out justice in front of our people. We proved we were the true Palestinian police"* (Milton-Edwards, 1996). In commenting on the positive and negative aspects of this informal policing, Beverley Milton-Edwards cited as positive the fact that such activities:

■ harnessed the energy of otherwise disaffected local youth
■ were built on historic practices and law and encouraged open discussion within the community
■ were effective in filling what would otherwise have been a law-and-order vacuum.

Overall, she notes: *"The community also felt empowered by this experience and relieved that state control was marginalised to such an extent"*.

However, there were also some serious disadvantages, most importantly:

■ the criminalisation of the committees led to a rise in armed gangs associated with political factions
■ human rights organisations reported abuses associated with this trend
■ in time the committees became increasingly autonomous of community authority.

## El Salvador

In some societies the issue about whether or not to build upon the alternative justice system is integrally tied into the debate about political transition. In the following chapter, we report on the decision in El Salvador to completely disband and build an entirely new police service. Part of the rebuilding process involved deciding formally, and in terms of specific quotas, to incorporate former guerrillas into the new police service. Obviously the former activities of guerrillas fighting a 12-year long civil war cannot be directly equated to the activities of disaffected youth in some of the societies alluded to above. Nevertheless, there are some parallels, in that in all of these societies, the conflict has brutalised many people, especially those with a limited economic stake in the future. Attention now needs to be devoted to ways in which these young people can be channelled into constructive initiatives.

# Beyond Present Structures

Many of our interviewees voiced concerns about how far democratic expectations of policing can be met while the police remain a hierarchical body and report solely to national government. Stef Snel of UMAC in South Africa saw a problem in that *"police come out of a militaristic structure where creative thinking is not encouraged".*[178] The onus therefore lies beyond the police. Instead:

> *"Communities need to take primary ownership and accept that the police are an extension of their (the communities') power, rather than an extension of the state. While we are still sitting with classic policing*

---

[178] Interview, Cape Town, 28 November 1996.

> *models, community policing cannot be real. In the next decade, policing will change because countries cannot afford classic models. We need to be much more inventive".[179]*

Professor Clifford Shearing, Director of the Centre of Criminology at the University of Toronto, also spoke to us[180] of how thinking about policing forms needs to push beyond existing boundaries and structures. Community policing as presently propounded runs the risk of being little more than *"free volunteer labour to support a police agenda"*, whereas it should be a means of enabling the police to respond effectively to community needs. If we are serious about breaking down the 'us and them' dynamic between police and community, then we need to experiment with new forms of partnership that integrate a state police force more fully into the community.

Shearing feels that the policing budget should be given to communities to decide how they want to use it. The relevant community organisations could then enter into a contract with the state police for the services they need. *"The police could give a figure for how much an emergency response service would cost. The contract would stipulate expected response times etc."* The remainder of the budget could be used by the community to run their own rehabilitation centres, joy-rider schemes etc. This ought to be a much more efficient use of resources in that local people could target money where they knew it was most needed.

This brief resume does not claim to do justice to all the thinking in this area, and there are obvious problems apparent in this approach. Who defines the community? Who in the community would have authority in financial matters? How could any tendency to vigilantism be prevented? Would

---

[179] Ibid.
[180] Interview, Toronto, 11 October 1996

money be wasted on extra administration? How would the different needs be negotiated and prioritised? Nevertheless, it is an exciting and very different vision of how policing might be organised in the future.

# Summary of Conclusions

As noted at the very outset of this report, this research project did not seek an ideal model for policing. Indeed we believe that no single ideal model exists, since policing must be responsive to local needs and realities. At the outset of this chapter, we furthermore emphasised that that we would not be proposing specific structural models for policing.

Proposals about the future form and structure of policing in Northern Ireland will presumably form part of the political negotiations. It is very important, however, that such discussions not be restricted solely to politicians but that there be a wide-ranging discussion of how best we want to ensure effective policing in future.

The international research provides a series of very important principles which provide the framework against which any structural model proposed, now or in the future, should be measured. Whether one is examining the Sinn Fein proposal for localised police services in an all-Ireland framework, the RUC's proposal for a reduction in number of ranks, or community policing models, any proposal for re-structuring policing must be tested for its ability to:

■ put a respect for human rights at the heart of the policing process. This applies to the institution(s) as such, but also to individual officers.[181]

■ provide accountability. This is a complex concept, but it must include accountability 'upwards' to an oversight body representative of the broad community, and 'outwards' to local communities. It must also mean that local communities can secure accountability on the issues which are important to them, and not solely trivial issues of purely local concern.

■ provide a police service which is civilian rather than military in philosophy, training and practice.

■ ensure that any different forces which are created (e.g. along regional or functional lines) co-operate effectively. This will require careful legal codification of the different responsibilities of the different units/forces.

■ secure a diverse and representative composition. People from both major traditions (and indeed all traditions) in Northern Ireland must be able to participate both in policing institutions and, just as importantly, in the structures of accountability. The creation of insular and non-representative police forces at the local level (with Protestant police working in Protestant areas etc) would run counter to all the principles enunciated elsewhere in this report.

---

[181] It is interesting to note that in interviews with the police in New South Wales (NSW), Australia, they referred to themselves, somewhat tongue-in-cheek, as "the uniformed branch of the Civil Liberties Union". Few, if any, police services would see themselves, or be seen by those policed, in these terms; yet the gap thus highlighted between the conceptual ideal and the reality on the ground is a challenge to us all.

■ provide an effective, responsive and efficient police service, adapted to the needs of the community served.

■ undermine rather than reinforce the institutionalisation of existing social divisions and residential segregation patterns.

■ implement a legal system which is itself framed according to international human rights standards and democratic principles.

■ avoid either excessive centralisation and hierarchisation of authority, or a splintering and fragmenting that can lend itself to narrow "cronyism" or corruption.

■ effectively harness the commitment of local people to providing safe, crime-free environments for their communities.

■ keep decision making as close as possible to those being policed.

To conclude, there are great advantages to be gained from developing a concept of policing which goes beyond the formal and highly structured policing provided by the state, and sees this as only one part of a common responsibility for society's welfare. Community policing which is accountable and respectful of rights would be an enormously beneficial complement to the more traditional view of policing. As we approach the 21$^{st}$ century, we must recognise that policing, like many other social institutions, may need to dramatically change and diversify if it is to meet all the expectations placed upon it.

# Chapter Six:

# Transition and Management of Change

## Introduction

The thrust of the research findings to date, is that change is required in a number of areas if we are to ensure a police service which is truly representative, responsive, accountable and respectful of human rights. Yet change is a difficult challenge for most institutions, and particularly police bodies imbued with a sense of tradition and organisational loyalty. At the very outset of our research, an Assistant Chief Constable in the Royal Ulster Constabulary (RUC) epitomised the difficulties by saying of the project: *"Come to us when you have got your proposals together, and we will tell you why they won't work!"*. Recognising the inherent difficulty of institutional change, the authors were specifically concerned to study how other jurisdictions have gone about introducing and managing fundamental change. Some of the jurisdictions were explicitly chosen because they had undergone important transformations. Even where the change had been less fundamental, there were lessons to learn, since any healthy organisation is constantly evolving, and even evolutionary change needs careful management.

Our research confirmed that not only is change possible, and indeed necessary, but that the police themselves, once convinced of the need, can become active proponents of change. What is required is a combination of the right planning, a willingness to be open and accountable, good leadership, and the right structures in place to manage change. Unfortunately, for the most part, the police are sometimes initially hesitant. International experience shows that real innovation generally requires input from outside agencies, but the changes that are initially resisted so strongly by the police, can eventually come to be welcomed by these very same critics once it is seen that they contribute to the legitimacy of policing and therefore improved police-community relations.[182]

So far in this report we have highlighted basic principles for effective, responsive, accountable and impartial policing, no matter what system of governance is in place. We have also considered discrete areas (such as representation, training, and accountability) where the present system of policing in Northern Ireland either does not conform to, or actively hampers, the attainment of such principles. This final chapter assumes that once decisions have been made about the kind of changes to the policing service which are required, it will be useful to have studied how other people have gone about introducing fundamental changes to policing. What, in their different societies, has helped (and hindered) the process of transition and the management of change?

The general conclusion from elsewhere is that if we are unable to meet realistic and desirable goals in the present dispensation and with current structures, we need to look honestly at the benefits and potential pitfalls of radical change. In some countries, people have seen the merit in meaningful and far-reaching reform which nevertheless leaves much of the institution and/or personnel intact.[183] In yet other countries, people have concluded that they needed to start entirely afresh, since a process of thoroughgoing change would be easier and ultimately less painful than attempting to reform an agency

---

[182] For example the introduction of the Police and Criminal Evidence (PACE) legislation in Britain in 1984; civilian oversight agencies in Canada and Australia (see on); and the South African adoption and development of a concept of community policing that allowed for a political settlement without disbanding the police  (interview with Peter Gastrow, Special Advisor to Minister for Safety and Security, South Africa), December 1996.

[183] See South Africa & Queensland (Australia) entries in particular.

steeped in a particular tradition, culture or subculture.[184]  In turn, we will examine the management of change in:

- Australia
- Canada
- The Netherlands
- Palestine
- Spain
- El Salvador
- South Africa

In looking at policing change throughout the world, it is important to stress again that we are not advocating mechanistic or simplistic comparisons. Rather we are seeking to distil what lessons we, in Northern Ireland, could usefully glean as to how others have broached controversial issues, and have managed the dynamics of change.

## Australia (New South Wales and Queensland)

Australia holds some interesting lessons for Northern Ireland. While the change there came about because of charges of police corruption, an allegation not often levelled at the RUC, the impetus for and process of change are very instructive.

An example of a police force which initially did not concede that a commission of inquiry, still less radical change, was necessary was the force in New South Wales (NSW). Allegations of police corruption in the media were the first public signals of how the various oversight bodies had failed to prevent massive, systemic and entrenched corruption. After

---

[184] See El Salvador and Spain entries in particular.

some delay, parliament[185] set up a Royal Commission headed by Justice Woods. He was assured by police leaders, at the outset of his far-reaching and revealing investigation, that the Commission would find nothing wrong, since there was nothing wrong to be found.[186]

Only when covert surveillance produced video evidence, and when hi-tech investigation led to confessions by corrupt officers, did many police colleagues stop maintaining the organisational culture of solidarity, which in reality had led to cover-ups.[187]   Once the Commission's investigation confirmed that massive corruption existed within the NSW force, attitudes did change.  A high level "change implementation team" was created, and with it came the opportunity to be involved in extensive re-formation and re-structuring of a system that many police officers had previously been very proud of.   From defending the organisation strenuously against critics, police officers moved to a more open and self-critical public stance. The process has been painful but is now widely accepted as having been necessary.

The Queensland Police Service is another provincial Australian force regaining confidence in itself following a similar Commission of Inquiry led by Justice Fitzgerald in the late 1980s.  This Commission also came about as a result of media allegations of police vice and inactivity.   As Fitzgerald commented in his final report[188]: *"Similar controversies had surfaced and subsided from time to time for many years. The*

---

[185] This was as a result of extensive campaigning by one MP in particular (Hatton) who at the time was one of a few independents who held the balance of power in the NSW parliament.  Doubtless, without this particular political dynamic, the Royal Commission would not have happened as it did.

[186] See Royal Commission into NSW Police Service, Interim Report, p. 3.

[187] See interim reports of Wood Royal Commission

[188] Report of a Commission of Inquiry pursuant to Orders in Council dated 26th May 1987; 24th June 1987; 25th August 1988; 29th June 1989.

*spokesmen for the Police Department routinely ground out stereotyped denials and hit back at critics".*

Given this all too common history, this 'scandal' might also have faded completely into the background, had newspaper reports not been quickly followed by a television documentary[189] which raised the possibility that the *"Police Force was lying or incompetent or both"*. It was particularly telling that much of the evidence outlined in the film was information that should easily have been available to police had they been doing their job properly. After years of denial, there was a response and the day after the TV showing, an inquiry was ordered.

Initially this inquiry did not have Royal Commission status and looked as if it would be just another ineffectual and cosmetic response. However, Fitzgerald was appointed a short time later to satisfy public outrage. Thanks in large part to the calibre and independence of the Commissioner and his staff, and the fact that these events took place in the run up to a Queensland election, forcing all parties to guarantee implementation of all of Fitzgerald's recommendations ('sight unseen') should they be elected, the investigation and the subsequent report were extremely influential. Justice Fitzgerald discovered early on that the *"Justice Department and the Police Department did not intend to lose control. They seemed to think that the standard responses of secrecy and obstruction would still apply" (Fitzgerald, 1989 : 3)*. The police have now, however, accepted the need for change and are, for the most part, appreciative of Fitzgerald's main legacy - an effective Criminal Justice Commission (CJC).

This body has statutory[190] civilian capacity to monitor and report on the implementation of the original inquiry proposals, and the result has been extensive transformation of the

---

[189] "Moonlight State", broadcast by Australian Broadcasting Corporation, 11th May 1987.
[190] Criminal Justice Act 1989.

Queensland police.[191]  The police have found the CJC very useful.  One initial police argument against CJC was that its existence would inhibit the police from doing their job effectively because officers would feel that they were having to constantly look over their shoulder.  However, this concern was disproved by subsequent research.  If the concern had been valid, one would have expected to find that in areas where police have discretionary arrest powers (e.g. drunkenness etc), which are often also the areas where most complaints are likely to arise, there would have been a fall off in the number of arrests made.  Instead, CJC Research division statistical survey showed that arrests for these potentially contentious offences had actually increased at a higher rate than other arrest categories.  A general consensus appears to have emerged that the Criminal Justice Commission working independently of, but in tandem with, the police has had a transformative and beneficial influence on the policing of Queensland.[192]

## Canada

In Canada also, the views of some police officers, and managers in particular, when challenged to change ranged initially from open scepticism to complete hostility. The idea, for example, that policing could be enhanced by respect for the Charter of Rights and Freedoms was largely dismissed. Fifteen years later, while most agree there is still some distance to travel in realising all their aspirations, it would now be an anathema to

---

[191] See Criminal Justice Commission evaluation report: Implementation of Reform within the Queensland Police Service, August 1994 " *In summary, there has been substantial reform in the QPS over the last five years.  The bulk of the Fitzgerald inquiry recommendations have been implemented, at least partially, and there has been considerable movement towards the organisational model which underpinned these recommendations"* p. 207.

[192] Ibid.  Details delineate changes in extensive regionalisation and devolved accountability; improvements in community policing; processes for determining police deployment; civilianisation; transfers and promotions; management of information services etc

suggest to the police that the protection of human rights was other than at the core of policing service in Canada.[193]

In Canada, it was the growth in multiculturalism and a sense that society's needs were changing, which prompted an in-depth study of Canadian policing, amongst other things. The main engine of change lay in the increasing public debate about the introduction of a Bill of Rights and Charter. This in turn encouraged the national, provincial and municipal forces within the country to accept that policing is integral to the protection of basic human rights. Alongside this society-wide debate, different incidents prompted the different forces to embark on a process of change, albeit with varying degrees of commitment. With some, the impetus was the public outcry which followed the shooting of young black people;[194] with others, particular miscarriages of justice[195] have paved the way for new thinking. Major Commissions of Inquiry[196] have made far-reaching recommendations which have meant that the nature and structures of Canadian policing have undergone, and are continuing to undergo, massive change. This said, there are still occasions when such commissions' recommendations have been left to gather dust on shelves when sufficient political will has been lacking to implement them.

A particular emphasis within the Royal Canadian Mounted Police (RCMP) as elsewhere has been on moving away from a quasi-military and hierarchical structure, and civilianising the organisation, to respond to the changing needs of society, where police are not just "bandit catchers" (Brogden & Shearing, 1993). This is evidenced by an increased embrace of Canada's Charter of Rights and Freedoms, and dynamic changes in recruitment and training. With this has come a newly

---

[193] Interviews with Barry Leighton and Frum Himmelfarb, Canada, October 1996.
[194] e.g. Toronto Metropolitan Police.
[195] e.g. Halifax, Nova Scotia.
[196] e.g. Oppal in Vancouver, B.C.

developed recruitment and training model based on the identification and acquisition of core competencies as vital to effective and impartial policing. Policing is now looked at as an area where certain key competencies (some of which the candidate must exhibit before selection; others of which can be taught) are more essential to good policing than a command/control, hierarchical structure.[197] It is not, however, just in the area of recruitment and training where change has been undertaken. Accountability mechanisms embracing extensive forms of civilian oversight of police complaints are now an accepted and welcome fact of life to most police officers in Canada, both within and beyond the RCMP.

## The Netherlands

Policing in the Netherlands underwent a radical process of change as a result of the passage of the Police Act in April 1994. Prior to reorganisation, there had been 148 municipal forces, a state police force, and a small Royal Military Police. The system suffered from lack of co-ordination and inefficiency. A crisis of policing had arisen in Amsterdam in the 1960s leading to a series of government recommendations, but few were implemented. However, by the mid to late 1980s, it was clear that change was inevitable, and the system was overhauled. A national police force was created with 25 regional forces and one National Police Service Agency (see Jones; Wintle, 1993).

The scale of the reform was dramatic. Over 80% of police chiefs no longer had a force to run and had to be demoted to lower ranks, and more than 12,000 officers being moved to different jobs within policing, sometimes in different cities. There were many difficulties arising from the reorganisation, but while no-

---

[197] See Chapter on Training for further detail.

one would claim that the new system is perfect, the general consensus is that it is better co-ordinated, functions more smoothly, and has resulted in improved police-public relations.[198]

In discussing with interviewees how such radical reform was able to take place, and with apparently few problems, several explanations were proffered. The first component for successful transition appears to have been a recognition of the need for change. Whereas for over twenty years there had been a lot of dissatisfaction about the former system and its ineffectiveness, the crucial pre-requisite to recent changes was the fact that the police themselves now recognised the need for change. So the debate centred around how to make the changes, and no longer on whether or not change was needed.[199] A further component for change appears to have been the existence of sufficient political will in support of change. Thus, commitment to change from the highest echelons ensured that any opposition to the reforms (however limited, or serious, it might be) was undermined. The police leadership emphasised not only the need for change but also that change should occur with minimum delay. Policing unions were encouraged to try to get the best deal for their members rather than to create obstacles to change (for example police officers who were old enough were encouraged to take early retirement). It was the speed of reform, combined with the lack of organised resistance, which was said to have ensured the success of the process.[200]

Concrete evidence of the positive effects of change for both police and the general population can be found in the development of an independent complaints system in

---

[198] Interviews with Jan Naeye, Peter Klerks & Amsterdam police officers, Netherlands, November 1996.
[199] ibid.
[200] ibid.

Amsterdam. The current complaints system has evolved from a grassroots informal system originally organised by radical law students. Despite their initial hostility, the police were persuaded to take it seriously, and are now keen to mediate as many complaints as possible via this now formalised complaints mechanism. The view of most interviewees in Amsterdam was that rather than an adversarial approach to complaints - 'us and them' - the key task is to get the police to take complaints seriously. The police have discovered that they can learn important lessons from complaints and be more effective as a result.[201]

A final conclusion from looking at the Dutch experience is that the impetus of change often comes from several different directions simultaneously. Any examination of the efforts to improve the representation of women and minority groups within the Dutch police, for example, shows how it was the combination of different elements which secured change. On the one hand, the European Network of Policewomen (which is based in Holland and has been given great support from the government) has been a vital source of pressure on the local police and the political establishment. There has, however, also been top-down pressure from the Ministry of the Interior on the police leadership to reach target figures for female and minority representation. Whereas sometimes it is the police hierarchy which recognises the need for change, and the benefits of developing a more representative service, at other times the pressure comes from police at the local level.[202]

The demand for change in the Netherlands came initially from outside the police - from dissatisfied communities and protest

---

[201] see Amsterdam Police Complaints Handbook
[202] *"Often the initiators were not primarily senior police ranks, but smart young cops working at the grass roots who began experimenting with new models of policing and gradually succeeded in winning senior management over to their ideas."* (Questionnaire response from Peter Klerks).

movements. However, once the need for change was recognised, the police became supportive. The transition was managed smoothly because the necessary political will existed to see it through, and there was an understanding within the police of the benefits that flow from an improved service, and of closer relationships with the general population.

## Palestine

In 1991, following the Madrid Peace Conference, peace talks began to resolve the long-standing Israeli/Palestinian conflict. Secret negotiations then led to the signing of a Declaration of Principles and a number of other agreements in the early 1990s. These set down a framework of interim measures in pursuance of a final settlement, with the establishment of the Palestinian National Authority (PNA) in 1994 to exercise limited control over much of the West Bank and the Gaza Strip. Many of the arrangements have breached existing international obligations, and could be "categorised by non-respect for international law and human rights". (Mar'i 1997: 6; Campbell, 1996) This has had grave consequences for the peace process which is currently in a state of disarray. As regards policing, the interim arrangements stated that there should be a "strong police force".

In 1994, the Cairo Agreement came into force and gave Palestinians responsibility for their own internal security arrangements in those areas under the jurisdiction of the PNA. The Palestinian police was set up in a relatively short period of time, consisting largely of members of the Palestinian Liberation Army, political activists, and former detainees. Most recruits supported the Israeli/PLO agreements, and for the most part, members of those Palestinian opposition groups hostile to the peace accords did not apply to join the new police service.

In effect, several police forces have sprung up but they have a limited jurisdiction in terms of the territory covered. Of particular note is the fact that the Palestinian police have no jurisdiction over Israeli citizens.

Initially the Palestinian police were warmly welcomed, since people felt that this was at last their own force. However, over time, a number of factors have led to brutal and repressive policing.

(a) There is the fact that the Palestinian police are enforcing Israeli laws which are seen by many as unjust laws of occupation.

(b) There is the requirement that the police have to work in conjunction with and in support of Israeli police.

(c) The paramilitary background of many recruits has not prepared them for peacetime policing.

In theory, the Israeli and Palestinian police are supposed to co-operate and co-exist. In practice, the relationship has been fraught to say the least. Accountability structures are obviously deficient so that, although the various departments of the security forces are in theory under a unified command, they act like separate police forces. This has led to situations where police have turned up to arrest someone already arrested by another unit. The various units also appear to serve a highly politicised role,[203] which helps neither their credibility nor good practice.

---

[203] e.g. Al-Quds (the Jerusalem-based Arabic daily newspaper) has called on Palestinian youth to perform their "national duty" by joining the police as a means of building the Palestinian State. (3 October 1993). A question that applicants are asked is whether they view the authorities as more important than human rights. Even more problematic are the divided loyalties of various functions within the police.

The Palestinian police have been provided with an inappropriate level of resources and training (particularly in respect of human rights). Although some improvement has been made in this latter area, the human rights dimension still seems to be an after-thought. This creates the impression that *"policing is one thing and respect for the rule of law and human rights is something else"* (Mar'i, 1996).

There are a number of lessons to learn from the failures to date of the Palestinian experience. Thus:

■ narrow political and group interests should have no part to play in the setting up of a police force;

■ good police/community relations are vital for the success of any police force and particularly within a complicated and sensitive political context;

■ the police must be prepared to refuse to apply laws which violate human rights. This did not happen in the Occupied Territories, but would have been in keeping with international law;

■ there must be a recognition that militaristic behaviour must be unlearned and that soldiers do not make good police officers unless totally retrained. This does not just apply to those who have previously been in armies outside the police structure, but also to police who have operated in a quasi-military structure and environment;

■ systems of accountability must be a priority;

■ it is impossible to ignore past human rights abuses and assume that they will not resurface. Some mechanism for dealing with the past must be carefully thought out and instituted for any peace process to be successful.

## Spain, the Basque Country and Catalonia

The Basque Country and Catalonia have undergone two major periods of transition. Firstly, there was the transition to democracy following the death of General Franco in 1975 and, secondly, in response to nationalist pressure, there has been a devolution of political power during the 1980s, from the central state to the regions. Of particular interest has been the creation of autonomous police organisations in the regions - the Ertzaintza in the Basque Country and the Mossos d'Esquadra in Catalonia.[204]

In April 1980, after the victory in the elections of the Basque National Party (PNV), the first autonomous government was installed. The government set out to create its own police force. The process began secretly and in small numbers but by February 1982 the new Basque police academy at Arkaute officially opened. Since then, there has been a gradual process of handing over power from the state security forces to the autonomous police and the emphasis for the new police body was to be part of the people. Although they would carry arms, they were to be based on the notion of the 'British bobby', and would patrol local areas alone, on foot. As part of this process of civilianisation, the Director of the Ertzaintza and the Director of the Academy were both civilians - appointed by the Basque government.

However, the process of devolving power has not always gone smoothly. From the outset there has been friction and lack of co-ordination between the embryonic Ertzaintza and the state forces.[205] There is no doubt that the Ertzaintza are much more popular than the state forces ever were and are closer to the

---

[204] The process of devolving responsibility is now complete in the Basque Country but still has some way to go in Catalonia. There, deployment is just starting and it is expected to take six to ten years to cover all the territory.

[205] Interviews, San Sebastian, April 1997.

population.[206] They are also better trained in human rights and are subject to closer scrutiny in this regard. This alone has not, however, guaranteed their acceptability and in recent years ETA has targeted and killed members of the force. A growing militarism has meant that all police members are trained in the use of rubber bullet guns, and these are routinely fired at both rioters and demonstrators and have resulted in death and injury.[207] On 15 February 1997, the police fired lead bullets at a nationalist demonstration in Bilbao. While the threat posed by violence is cited as a reason for this increasing militarisation, photographic evidence of Ertzaintza members in balaclavas pointing guns at unarmed striking truck drivers[208] suggests that these tactics have also been adopted in much more routine policing situations.

The principles on which the new force are based are a vast improvement on the militarism and brutal tactics of the previous state forces. However, the increasingly militarised tactics of the Ertzaintza, and the lack of co-ordination between the state and autonomous forces, are instructive regarding the dangers inherent in this process.

The autonomous police in Catalonia have only recently resumed a formal policing role and powers. However, the Mossos d'Esquadra ("boys from the squad") can trace their history back to the 18th century making them the oldest police force in Spain.[209] Over the 20th century the Mossos d'Esquadra appeared and disappeared in parallel with the development of

---

[206] See survey carried out by the Basque government – Resultados del Estudio de Opinion llevado a cabo en Vitoria-Gastriz acerca del nuevo desplieuge de la Ertzanta en la capital, Julio 1995 – which shows more support for Ertzanta than for the state forces.
[207] For the Basque government's response see Comparencia parlamentaria sobre los sucesos accedidos en Bilbao el 15 de febrero de 1977, Juan Maria Atutxa.
[208] *El Mundo*, February 1997.
[209] Interview with Director of Police Training Academy.

democracy. During periods of democratic development they re-
emerged only to be crushed again during Franco's dictatorship
- during this time they existed mainly as a folkloric police with
about 20-25 police officers wearing disguise.[210] After Franco's
death, the Mossos d'Esquadra were again revitalised. This
connection between the autonomous police and the struggle for
democratic rights within Catalonia has been crucial to the
development and philosophy of the police.[211] The creation of
the autonomous police has been inextricably linked to
devolution of power to the Catalonian parliament.

In 1983 the autonomous police was formally legislated for. Over
the next decade they slowly grew from 100 officers at the
beginning to more than 1,000 in 1993. The aim is to create an
optimal force of 10,000.[212] At the same time as the autonomous
police grew it was intended that the Spanish state forces would
reduce in number, however, this has failed to happen.[213] Unlike
the Basque autonomous police the Catalonian police are not
responsible for 'anti-terrorist' policing. There has been an
agreement of division of functions between the Catalonian and
Spanish state police.

In Catalonia the new police are not controversial in the way that
the Basque autonomous police have been. The Director of the
Police Training Academy in Catalonia explained this as being in
part due to the fact that there has been less hostility within
Catalonia for mainstream Spanish parties. In Catalonia all of
the parties except the conservatives are in support of
Catalonian Home Rule. In the Basque country, however, the
socialists (in power for much of the 1980s) have been opposed
to Basque nationalism. In Catalonia people have not boycotted

---

[210] ibid.

[211] ibid.

[212] ibid.

[213] Discussed in more detail in chapter five.

Spanish state forces *"they prefer local forces - but the local population are not fighting with the state police."*[214]

The very different experiences of Catalonia and the Basque country demonstrate the links between policing and the building of democracy. Without consent for democratic structures there is likely to be a lack of legitimacy for the police who are seen as defending the state.

## El Salvador

El Salvador provides an example of a jurisdiction where existing policing institutions were entirely disbanded as part of a political agreement, and a new policing service created.

To set the context, it is important to understand that policing was a central element in the negotiations which lasted from 1989 to 1992 in El Salvador, between the government of President Cristiani and the armed opposition group, the Frente Farabundo Marti de Liberacion Nacional (FMLN). The 12 year civil war which preceded the political negotiations had been horrific. By the end of the war, an estimated 75,000 people, mostly non-combatants, had been killed. The war had reached a stalemate, since the army could not defeat its armed opponents, but neither could the opposition take power. This stalemate, however, meant that both sides were willing to negotiate and prepared to make compromises. The degree and nature of the subsequent reforms was determined largely by the need on the part of both sides to get an agreement which would be mutually acceptable. Negotiations around the issue of policing played a key role in the overall peace process.

---

[214] Interview with Director of Police Training Academy.

Among the central demands of the FMLN, ever since the early 1980s, had been the need to cleanse and eventually dismantle the armed forces. Peace could not have been agreed without fundamental changes in policing. The final Accord[215] recognised this reality but was, of course, a result of compromise and negotiation. Accordingly, while the FMLN had given way on the question of the demobilisation of the army, they insisted that the police be disbanded and that a new force be created, drawing its membership from both former guerrillas and former security forces. The form which the new police was to take was clearly determined by the give-and-take of political negotiations. FMLN presidential candidate, Ruben Zamora, explained[216] that there were two objectives involved in the negotiations around policing. First, there was obviously a need to replace the old, corrupt police force. Second, the form of the new police had to be designed with a view to incorporating a series of confidence-building measures.

Crucial in this regard was to be the make-up of the police, which was to be composed as follows - 20% former FMLN fighters, 20% former security force members, and 60% civilians[217] (ie people who had no previous military involvement). There was disagreement among those interviewed for this report as to whether the incorporation of former combatants had been a positive experience. Some felt that it created competing loyalties within the police, but others argued that, once people joined the new police, their old loyalties were subsumed, and they brought with them vital experience. There was however a unanimous sense that, whatever the practical arguments for and against incorporating former combatants into the new police service, the political reality in Salvador had required that this occur.

---

[215] Chapultepec Accord 1992.
[216] Interview February 1997.
[217] Background paper prepared for CAJ by Chuck Call, 1996.

Yet, one factor which militated against the development of confidence-building measures around policing, was the fact that the political negotiations were being carried out with great confidentiality. The secrecy of the negotiations was problematic for several reasons. This meant that, for example, civil society, including non-governmental organisations, was unable to play an active role in proposals or discussions of the police reforms. It also came as a great shock to many FMLN activists that the demand for the abolition of the army was dropped. Secrecy may have helped to ensure the success of the negotiations on the one hand, but it also conversely meant that there was a lack of civilian involvement in the process of creating the new police. This lack of involvement remains a problem for many. *"They did not involve the population in the birth of the new creature from the beginning and in the nurturing. [the population] were finding out things in a very disorganised manner.... So the population ... did not become part of it. They did not become parents of the idea".*[218]

This lack of wider involvement was not the only problem however. A very major criticism of the process has been the way the new institution was allowed to be 'contaminated' by its predecessor. Given that the new police was being created anew, it was agreed to move one of the detective units en masse into the new police. It was argued (particularly by the United States) that the expertise these units had amassed in investigative work could not be denied to the new force, since it would take some time to train the new recruits in investigative measures (Hemisphere Initiatives, 1996). As a result of this pressure, whole units of the old force were incorporated into the new one, including the anti-narcotics unit and the special unit of investigations. In reality, this decision proved disastrous. A UN evaluation later found evidence of serious corruption within the new Criminal Investigation Department

---

[218] Luis Cardenal, Member of Public Security Commission, interviewed February 1997.

units (including involvement in death-squad type murders and organised crime).[219]    It became necessary to reorganise the whole department and screen all members of the criminal investigation unit, purge some, send them all back for retraining and disperse most to other units within the police.

Important lessons from all the above seem to be the need for proper screening; the need for effective training for all officers; the dangers of contamination from introducing whole units from old police into new; the need for proper monitoring and publicly available information on disciplinary problems.

An almost unique element in the Salvador situation, whose significance cannot be over-emphasised, was the vital mediation role which the United Nations played at the request of the two parties to the conflict.  The UN, together with certain interested member states,[220] played a key role in keeping the talks on track. The specially-created UN Mission in El Salvador (ONUSAL) [221] was charged with verification of the Accords. Human rights, civilian police, military observer, and the election components were all included in the UN's oversight activities.   ONUSAL played a vital role in designing the structure, laws, doctrine, and entry criteria for the new police service, the PNC.   After the Accords, the UN monitored National Police officers during the transition, provided field training to the newly deployed PNC, and provided extensive communications and transportation support.  The US Justice Department provided extensive material support and advice.[222]

International involvement was critical in the development of the new police. It helped to ensure that human rights were considered in all aspects of policing, produced a programmed

---

[219] MINUSAL Evaluation 1995.
[220] Spain, Mexico, Colombia, Venezuela plus the USA.
[221] ONUSAL operated from July 1991 until April 1995.
[222] Through their International Criminal Investigations Training Assistance Programme.

calendar of activities (to the day) and ensured that targets and deadlines were met. This involvement also ensured that there was a constant process of monitoring and evaluation with recommendations for improvement being regularly made (Call, 1996: 16). The role of the international community was particularly important in dealing with internal opposition to the reforms, and in ensuring that the old police was effectively disbanded and handed over its weapons. *"There were interests - powerful interests - that did not want the police to work, because they were going to lose power. ... Some were from the armed forces, some were from economic interests, some of them were from political interests."*[223]

Even with external supervision, however, there were problems. The military refused to hand over its sites for the development of police training institutions and there are allegations that the military refused to hand over equipment to the new police. Problems also resulted from the activities of former combatants: thousands of soldiers had been demobilised, and many of them found their way into organised criminal groups (Hemisphere Initiatives, 1996).

Very importantly, the need for speedy deployment of the newly-constituted civilian police service, created inevitable pressures on the training programme. Police officers were deployed halfway through their ten-month training period, and then brought back to the Academy later to finish their training. It is agreed now by all sides that the training period was too short and police were sent out with insufficient experience.

*"The most common manifestations of these shortcomings are a lack of understanding of legal procedures, an inability to handle crowd control without excessive use of force, and poor handling of weapons."(Call, 1996: 34).*

---

[223] Interview Luis Cardenal, San Salvador, February 1997.

A joint report of the Washington Office on Latin America (WOLA) and Hemisphere Initiatives found that the *"quality of training is still weak, particularly in the area of legal procedures and due process."* (Hemisphere Initiatives, 1996: 24). The Human Rights Ombudsoffice has confirmed that the majority of complaints against the PNC have resulted from procedural faults probably due to deficient training. In trying to train so many police in such a short time the Academy were facing a monumental task. However, to have done otherwise would have meant recruiting fewer civilians to the new force or arranging a lengthier period of transition. Neither of these options was politically acceptable to the negotiators.

Furthermore, not all of the problems of transition relate directly to policing, though they have an important impact on policing. The courts, for example, have resisted change quite successfully. The removal of judges known for their appalling human rights records has been very slow, and allegations of impunity within the courts still abound. There is a widespread belief that political corruption taints police investigations, with officers being warned off certain investigations for fear of political embarrassment. The El Salvador experience demonstrates clearly that policing change cannot occur within a vacuum and that it must be part of a broader process which includes change in the legal framework, and in the make up and training of the judiciary.

However, *"while the justice system rarely convicts and sends to prison criminals, there is now a reasonable chance that human rights abuses, corrupt practices and other abuses of authority will be denounced, publicised and investigated"* (Call, 1996: 26).

The Truth Commission in El Salvador played a critical role in ensuring that some of the most notorious human rights abuses (by both sides) were investigated and publicised.[224] It was important in ensuring the credibility of the Commission that some of those responsible for committing atrocities were named in the report. However, despite a purge of over 100 senior armed forces officers for human rights violations, an amnesty, passed by the legislature in 1992, ensured that these persons would never be tried or sentenced for their abuses. FMLN members, implicated in serious but fewer abuses, were also amnestied. As a result, there is a feeling that the perpetrators of brutal acts received impunity.

In conclusion, one can say that the new civilian police are clearly better than their predecessors in respect of human rights. Allegations of torture and disappearances are now almost unheard of. The overall performance of the PNC is perceived by most of the population as being more humane and more courteous than the bodies they replaced.[225] At the same time, however, there are worrying trends which suggest potential problems in the future. Riot control methods (including the use of tear gas and plastic bullets) have led to public concern. Police members are still living in barracks, despite a commitment to civilianisation. Accountability structures are not as strong as they might be, and there is very limited community involvement in developing policing policy. Even more alarming is the trend towards repressive policing. A key lesson from El Salvador is that the implementation of new policing arrangements cannot be seen as the end of the transformation process. Real progress requires that the impact of whatever arrangements are agreed should be continually

---

[224] Report of the Commission on the Truth for El Salvador: From Madness to Hope. UN Doc. 2/25500 (1993). For a discussion of the process of setting up the Truth Commission written by one of the commissioners see "The United Nations Truth Commission for El Salvador", Thomas Buergenthal, Vanderbilt Journal of Transnational Law, Vol 27, October 1994, Number 3.

[225] See Call, 1996: 27 for details of a survey carried out by the University of Central America in December 1995.

monitored, evaluated, and where necessary re-formulated in the post-agreement phase.


## South Africa

The political process which culminated in the election of Nelson Mandela as President of South Africa in 1994 began with a series of top level and community negotiations among parties who had once been sworn enemies. How far discussion about changes to policing resulted from a grassroots dynamic, or how far citizens were excluded from this process because of high level and secret negotiations, is impossible to quantify precisely. However, as in El Salvador, debates about the kind of policing needed for the new South Africa were a crucial part of the overall political negotiations. Many in the liberation movements argued that the apartheid police system be totally disbanded. Yet - in an interesting contrast to the Salvador example - the final decisions about police restructuring involved an agreement to by-and-large keep the existing police personnel intact, while restructuring service provision and ethos in a number of ways.[226]

South Africa undertook a massive task. They amalgamated 11 police forces into one new service; they adopted a South African concept of community policing which attempted to import good practice from other jurisdictions[227]; they changed the name, uniform and rank structure, but essentially retained the same personnel as before the 1994 elections. Furthermore, these changes took place against the backdrop of massive

---

[226] See National Peace Accord 1991; also interview with Andre Coetzee, of the Change Management Team, Pretoria, South Africa, December 1996.

[227] A former British senior police officer now in South Africa acting as adviser said that much in South Africa is "streets ahead" of Britain. Unfortunately, there is no formal mechanism for such lessons to be fed back to the British government. Interview with Peter Stevens, Cape Town, December 1996.

poverty, illiteracy, major political and social upheaval, and deep, understandable, distrust on the part of the vast majority of South Africans for the institutions of the law and its supposed agents.[228]

One of the crucial elements in this massive programme of fundamental change was the attitude of the police itself. They were prepared to admit that past policy and practice, once a source of so much pride in the war against communism and the 'black threat', was fundamentally flawed. They had to admit that the threat of terrorism was no justification for so many of the practices and cover-ups which had once seemed so necessary. They accepted that policing had long belonged to, and defended, the apartheid regime and had been carried out for the benefit of white South Africans only. Gradually, as it became obvious that inexorable changes were underway, certain police officers, particularly within the main South African Police (SAP), gained enough confidence to start agitating for change within the organisation itself. [229]

This internal lobby received encouragement and support from a number of international experts in policing who, in the opinion of Peter Gastrow, in many cases came to South Africa with no agenda other than to offer help and support to colleagues.[230] The South African police had become increasingly isolated from international colleagues as the movement against apartheid grew, and they appreciated this input as important in their own coming to terms with change. This collegial support from international experts, able to speak to the police in their own terms, helped convince the SAP to take control of its own destiny, rather than have change thrust upon it by external forces.[231] The police became aware that they would have to

---

[228] See South African synopsis.
[229] Interview with Peter Gastrow, Special Adviser to Minister for Safety and Security, Pretoria, South Africa, December 1996.
[230] ibid.
[231] ibid.

adapt, and began to explore concepts and structures that would render them more accountable and acceptable to the whole community.[232]

Change was therefore in process long before any final political settlement was achieved. The Interim Constitution, in many ways, merely articulated principles and structures that were already some way to being implemented. Indeed, policing was seen - at least at the level of negotiators and advisers - to be integral to a broader political settlement. As such, progress on this issue eased progress in other domains, since it showed, by example, that change could be credible, consensual and lasting.

In practical terms, a number of specific measures were taken to ensure that change both occurred, and that it occurred in such a way as to secure broad support, within and outside the police. For example, officers were helped to deal with the changes in a number of ways. So as to have as positive effect as possible on the morale of officers, the final settlement produced 'sunset clauses' by which civil servants, including police officers, were assured of their jobs for the next five years. In other cases, packages (with a fixed cut-off date for take up) allowed officers unable to agree with the changes, or with problems in their past, or those who simply wanted to change career and pave the way for new blood, to leave the force under generous terms. Yet these measures, while reassuring the police, could hardly be expected to reassure an abused community to work with and trust the police. To respond to the imperative of creating a climate whereby the community would work with and learn to trust the police, the infamous Internal Security Branch was disbanded, and a number of senior police officers, known to have colluded in widespread human rights abuses, either directly or indirectly, were dismissed or allowed to take early retirement. A more open and transparent process was then put

---

[232] Interview with Andre Coetzee, Change Management Team, South African Police Service, December 1996.

in place to replace these officers with others committed to the creation of a new police service for a new South Africa.[233]

Interestingly, and perhaps somewhat surprisingly given the massive crime problem in South Africa, a moratorium was declared on recruitment after only one new intake of recruits. The reasoning behind this move was that the police needed time to adjust to the sweeping changes both to assess the current and future deployment of officers, and to identify training and other needs. It was argued that it is not necessarily more police officers which reduces crime, but that crime is more effectively tackled by ensuring resources are used most efficiently, training is sufficiently sophisticated, and accountability is greater.[234]

This approach is likely to be closely scrutinised by police services and commentators around the world. For example, training of new recruits was provided by South African and international expertise and was independently evaluated soon after the new officers were deployed. An important finding of the early evaluation was the conclusion that human rights had been successfully integrated into the training as something fundamental to policing, rather than as an add-on. Early results indicated new officers being willing, and having the necessary confidence, to challenge practices or policies which existed at station level but which did not accord with the concept of policing inculcated during their training period. It will obviously be interesting to monitor this finding over time.

It is clear that public discussion of legislative change - and in particular the Interim Constitution - has been effectively used to raise the profile of human rights and to develop greater

---

[233] Interviews with among others Peter Gastrow, Andre Coetzee (December 1996).
[234] Interviews with members of the civilian Secretariat on Safety and Security – December 1996.

community involvement in policing. The development of a National Crime Strategy, with input and co-operation required from a range of different groups in society, has been a particularly useful exercise. Amongst other things, it highlighted that the need the police have of the community is at least, if not more, valuable than the need the community have of a state police.[235]

A civilian secretariat to advise the minister has drawn extensively on human rights activists from non-governmental organisations for its personnel. A range of other accountability mechanisms have also been set up to provide civilian oversight on a number of levels. There is clearly a risk that some police will change their language and style, but not change in any fundamental sense. One concern raised in interviews[236] was that the elite of the notorious security branch, responsible for the most horrific of atrocities, were also the brightest, and the most able to affect the appearance of change. Comfortably conversing about new concepts like 'transparency' and 'transformation', these officers have been able to secure their own position firmly at the heart of a supposedly new service, and often with 'community relations' responsibilities. This does not bode well for the future. Nor does the practice of dividing functions within the new service in such a way that good work done on a community relations level could be seriously undone by a unit of 'outsiders' being brought in to deal with public order disputes.

The new South African police service still faces many problems in terms of restructuring its personnel and deploying limited resources to the greatest benefit. Downsizing is one option being pursued, given that 10% of the 138,000 serving officers are currently based in Pretoria in administrative work.

---

[235] Interview with Deputy Silvester (December 1996).
[236] Interview with Wilfred Scharf, Institute of Criminology, Cape Town, December 1996.

Civilianisation and mentoring are other areas being extended, though a scheme to fast-track appointees from civilian backgrounds has faced difficulties, with non-police personnel being sidelined and excluded from line management responsibilities. The initial fast-tracking scheme has recently been scrapped and, based on extensive re-evaluation, a new affirmative action mechanism has been put in place. Mentoring schemes have been used to allow extremely able civilians to work alongside a senior officer and thereby gain experience of practical policing, support systems etc. This scheme too has had its problems but has had some positive results. The head of affirmative action, until relatively recently a civilian activist in the voluntary sector, is now the most senior black woman police officer within the SAPS - ranking 9th in the hierarchy.

Issues of past human rights abuse still need to be comprehensively dealt with to ensure that abusive policing is stamped out altogether. The Truth and Reconciliation Commission has been one forum for police officers to expunge the record and put the past to rights. A relatively small number of officers have come forward to admit crimes of the past and to seek amnesty. However, despite its failings, the initiative to create such a Commission was a recognition that the future cannot be built on foundations of wrongs done in the past. In Northern Ireland too, the past must be acknowledged and laid to rest to avoid its re-emergence in a way that could destroy any future solution. Whether some form of Truth Commission is the appropriate mechanism for dealing with the past in Northern Ireland needs to be the subject of thoughtful debate.

## Lessons for Northern Ireland

An overview of the process of transition in several jurisdictions reveals patterns which constantly recur and from which Northern Ireland could learn much.

## 1. Crisis and change in policing

In each of the countries visited, and throughout the wider world, policing and police organisations are in a state of crisis and change. Whether because of corruption scandals, too frequent recourse to the use of deadly force, highly politicised, repressive policing or major societal change, many forces have lost credibility or even legitimacy. Given the nature of the institution, some academics have even argued that 'crisis' is the norm in policing: the institution of policing must constantly re-evaluate and adapt to changing circumstances.

## 2. Denial

Yet the stock initial response from the police to criticism or pressure for change is usually to ignore or vilify critics, or deny any wrongdoing. The denial phenomenon generally stems from an instinctive desire to protect colleagues or an established sense of identity. Often loyalty to the force makes criticism and change seem something to fear. In many instances, denial derives from a feeling that because of the difficulties of the job, the police are beyond reproach or should not be criticised.

## 3. Consensus building around the need for change

In many of the jurisdictions studied, there has, sooner or later, been an important process of consensus building around the need for change. In some cases this has been brought about from some wider social change (e.g. Canada, South Africa). In others, a degree of consensus has developed on a more ad-hoc basis around a particular incident or practice (e.g. Netherlands, Australia). In some jurisdictions politicians have spearheaded the process and the need for change becomes a matter of consensus. In others, the impetus towards change has come from public interest groups or major public outcry generated by police/government failure to deal with scandalous behaviour.

## 4.    External push for change

Generally speaking, the impetus for concrete and radical change has come from outside the forces themselves. In countries like South Africa and El Salvador, international pressure and co-operation have also played a part. In other places, public outrage has been sparked by media reporting of controversial incidents or miscarriages of justice. In many cases, it has been continued police denial which has fuelled campaigns by non-governmental organisations or individual victims of police abuse.

## 5.    Internal moves/private acknowledgement

Outside pressure of this kind sometimes leads the police themselves to question their own policy and practice. All too often though, acknowledgement of problems takes place, when and if it does take place, in private or between colleagues. Without a major culture shift, those individuals arguing for change from within the police can quickly become marginalised and isolated. External factors can often give support to such isolated officers helping them articulate views which seem to run contrary to accepted thinking.

## 6.    Public acknowledgement of the problem

Problems in policing are often only publicly acknowledged in a meaningful way when a certain combination of external and internal factors come together. This could be due to political pressure, a recognition of the futility of further denial, a growing public consensus on the need for something to change or a feeling within courageous and strategically-positioned members of the force that there must be a break with the past. Experience from elsewhere shows how public acknowledgement of past wrongs can be cathartic, and release energy hitherto tied up in presenting a united front or a wall of silence. In itself, it can send signals of a willingness to embark on a new process. Much depends on how the public acknowledgement occurs and is handled.

## 7.    Political will

Central to change is the question of political will. Where acknowledgement of a problem is grudging or partial, any changes instituted are likely to be cosmetic. Similarly remedial action might meet with resentment or obstruction which can thwart real improvement. So, Commissions of Inquiry can provide the impetus for major change, or they can prove totally irrelevant.   New legislation can be visionary and creative, ushering in greater transparency and accountability or, on the other hand, prove no more than a piecemeal approach providing only paper safeguards.   Complaints systems can provide an important mechanism for individual redress and a crucial management tool, or they can, by merely providing a façade of accountability, undermine confidence in the whole criminal justice system.   What is needed is genuine and constructive commitment to change – the institutions, legislative and behavioural changes then follow.

## 8.    The legacy of the past and building for the future

Divided societies and those emerging from violent conflict have had to deal with the legacy of the past constructively.   Two issues in particular could usefully be highlighted:

## a.    The right to truth

In both El Salvador and South Africa (and indeed in many other jurisdictions not covered by this report)[237] a Truth Commission was established.    This initiative has come about in many societies where major political change has taken place because an importance has been invested in dealing with the legacy of the past.   A Guatemalan human rights lawyer, Frank LaRue, explained at a human rights conference why the right to truth is seen as a necessary building block for the future:

> *"Peace can only be achieved with justice and where there is no justice, there will be no peace, no matter how many agreements are signed....Truth is the essence of justice......A society can only build its future if it fully acknowledges its past: otherwise that future will always be handicapped by the lack of knowledge of the past....Truth is not only part of our past, truth should also be the basis for our future"* (CAJ, 1995).

There is, furthermore, a key educational element in the search for truth – since people with perhaps totally different experiences of the conflict have to work together to establish what human rights violations are, accept that they occurred, and have those responsible for such abuses recognise this also. The right to truth is of course something which must be equally availed of by all and cannot be selective.    At the same time, implicit in the right to truth is the right to change.   Perpetrators of human rights violations – whatever their motivation – must be allowed to, and indeed helped to, reform and to be rehabilitated into society.

---

[237] See for example "Fifteen Truth Commissions: A Comparative Study", Priscilla B. Hayner, Human Rights Quarterly 16 (1994).

## b. The place of former combatants and (re) integration programmes

The latter point also means that mechanisms and structures must be established which allow former opponents to work together in a new and different society. This is being tried in places like South Africa, El Salvador, and Palestine, by incorporating into the new or existing police institution those who have formerly been in opposition, and reintegrating police officers from the old police force.

In South Africa, many members of the paramilitary wings of resistance movements were integrated into the state security forces. Most of these joined the army, with a small number taking up office in the police through lateral entry and mentorship schemes or otherwise. In El Salvador, it is almost certain that the peace process only succeeded because former opponents of the state were integrated into the new police. Quotas of ex-combatants and ex-security force members were established amidst some concern as to how people who had recently been enemies would take part together in new training courses. By and large this proved not to be problematic and the new recruits quickly took on a police identity.[238] Problems have, however, also been identified. Continuing political divisions and mixed loyalties have been identified in Palestine, and in the Basque Country there was some infiltration of the Basque police by members of the paramilitary group, ETA, to obtain weapons. This has clearly been extremely damaging to attempts by a nascent force to establish itself.

New systems have also been abused by former police officers continuing to serve within the newly constituted or restructured force. In El Salvador, many problems arose from a

---

[238] This was so to the extent that former FMLN members, acting as police officers, broke up demonstrations that they formerly would have been leading. (information from interviewees in El Salvador, February 1997).

failure to screen out corrupt police officers from the criminal investigation department in particular. This led to corruption continuing within the new structure. In South Africa, officers suspected of previous involvement in human rights abuses, managed to manoeuvre themselves into safe positions of authority within the reformed police force. There is also the issue of moving from a quasi-military police structure while at the same time retaining or bringing in people who have been inculcated with a military-style culture. It is clear from these examples that the effective and publicly accountable screening of new recruits is paramount. While all criminal offences might not be a bar to serving as a police officer, some undoubtedly should, and while some previous police misconduct can be corrected by retraining, counselling and early warning systems - steps must be taken to ensure that those who have abused human rights are not dealt with impunity.

The situation in Northern Ireland is obviously different - not least because the conflict has not been on such an enormous scale. Few people have been directly involved in armed action of any sort. There are also serious clashes of political identity to be resolved. Nonetheless, an important lesson in terms of representation and recovery from past conflict seems to be that as political settlements are made, there should be a policy of inclusiveness. There must be attempts to involve within the new or reformed structures, people who were previously opponents or reluctant to join the institutions. Clearly, if this approach were to be taken, and indeed more generally, some screening mechanism would be needed to ensure that 'bad apples' among the existing police force are removed, and that people who are genuine security risks are not recruited.

## 9. Effect on morale

A further issue noted in the course of research into change management generally is that scrutiny of police practice undoubtedly has an effect on the morale of serving officers. Any period of transition breeds very natural uncertainty and fear, making it difficult to embrace change openly. This is all the more reason why change should be inspired by a participative vision and be real rather than tokenistic. Even with this, it must be recognised that any period of transition and restructuring is likely, at some point or other, to lead to the lowering of morale. It should be noted, however, that clinging trenchantly to the past can also take its toll on morale.

## 10.   Holistic and visionary change

Best practice is attested to in those forces which have been creative about the forms change might take, and have been prepared to look beyond traditional boundaries in instituting the process. In many cases, tackling symptoms rather than causes has not improved the situation, and occasionally made it look as if change was not worthwhile. Technical or administrative restructuring has not been sufficient to deal with underlying problems of acceptability and legitimacy. Instead, the best change is effected when the following factors exist:

- openness and transparency
- holistic vision and real commitment from the top of the institution;
- retraining and freeing middle management up to ensure changes are followed through;
- consultation with lower ranks to give some ownership of the process and incentives to implement change;
- working in tandem with the wider community.

## 11.   Constant re-evaluation and monitoring

Coupled with the above, there is a need to build certain flexibility and fluidity into the process to allow for future analysis and re-evaluation. The views of critics or those resistant to change should be factored into the process to allow the value of any change to be measured against their initial concerns and fears.   Perhaps early changes will in practice prove unsuitable.   If so, it is important that those involved in the process are flexible enough to recognise this and adapt. Change cannot be a one-off response.   An institutional commitment to the process of regular change and adaptation is as important as the nature of the specific changes themselves.

## 12.   The role of international support mechanisms

El Salvador and South Africa clearly found it invaluable to draw on international experience and expertise in their move to new police services. This report is one contribution to the debate in Northern Ireland about the relevance of international standards and of international experience, but it is insufficient in isolation.   There are many international and regional bodies which have amassed a great deal of expertise about policing around the world.   Bodies such as the Council of Europe, the Commonwealth Secretariat, the Organisation for Security and Co-operation in Europe, and the United Nations, to mention just a few, all have specialists in policing who might be willing to assist us in this important peace-building project.   As noted at the very outset of this report, there are no single models, or mechanistic analogies, on which we can or should draw. Nevertheless, our problems are not unique, and the contribution of an external perspective could be very beneficial.

# Summary of Conclusions

All over the world, policing is undergoing massive change. The issue is not whether or not policing should change, but how change should be managed to ensure that the desired objectives are achieved.

Northern Ireland is currently witnessing political negotiations which have been described by many as historic. It is inconceivable that if the negotiations succeed in discussing, and agreeing upon, new political or constitutional arrangements for Northern Ireland, policing will not be a central concern. Both unionists and nationalists, and those who consider themselves neither, will want to ensure that the police are able to uphold the rule of law, whatever the new dispensation.

Indeed, one can go further and assert, on the basis of international experience, that policing change can be a critical element in building a sustainable peace. In order to maintain the cease-fires, secure political stability, and achieve social consensus, we must accept that changes to policing are important building-blocks. If policing change in Northern Ireland is managed in a fair and open way, involves the broad community, and brings about a police service which is representative, responsive accountable, and effective (because of greater community support), this will underpin and guarantee the peace.

Certainly one conclusion which can be drawn from the international parallels is that early disinterest and even hostility to proposals for change can change over time. It is in the interests of all within society, including the police, that we develop a police service which can work effectively with the whole community to uphold the rule of law. To engage in constructive criticism of the police is a duty of active citizenship; it is clearly in the interests of the police to act in concert with this approach. International experience of the management of change suggests that:

1. Change is dependent upon a combination of the right planning, a willingness to be open and accountable, good leadership and the right structures in place to manage change.

2. Generally, innovation requires input from outside agencies, but police involvement in the process is vital. Nearly always, the changes once so strongly resisted by the police are eventually welcomed by these same critics since they improve relations with the community and therefore make policing by consent a feasible objective.

3. Commitment to change from within the highest echelons of the police, and government authorities, is vital if any opposition to change is to be countered. Rapid change is normally more effective for the same reason.

4. There must, however, also be involvement in the process by middle management and by regular officers, who will have to implement the change. If change can be seen as beneficial to effective policing it is more likely to secure support, and this realisation will only come about if the process of change is a participative and visionary one.

5. The process of change cannot be seen as one-off; real progress requires that whatever arrangements are agreed are continually monitored, evaluated, and where necessary re-formulated over time.

6.     Change should be based on the principle of
       inclusiveness, the right to change, and the value of
       shared aspirations.

# Summary of Recommendations

1.  There must be a recognition of the current problems with
    policing (regarding its unrepresentative, highly militarised,
    and insufficiently accountable nature) so that change is
    effectively targeted at those problems. Serious
    consideration should be given to what role, if any, a truth
    commission could play in such an analysis, given the value
    it has had in other societies going through political
    transition.

2.  The authorities should pledge themselves publicly to
    ensuring fundamental changes in policing to ensure that the
    police service is accountable, representative and responsive
    to the whole community.

3.  The government should introduce legislation aimed at
    bringing about the necessary structural, legal, and
    disciplinary changes which will bring about such a police
    service. A broad public debate about the philosophy of
    policing needs to be facilitated so that the legislative changes
    secure broad popular support, meet internationally-agreed
    human rights standards, and go beyond policing to have an
    impact on the wider criminal justice system.

4.  Community leaders, political representatives, and civil
    society in general should engage in constructive debate
    about the form of policing they would prefer to see.
    Criticism of current policing should be seen as active
    citizenship, rather than dismissed. To advise effectively,

this broader constituency of interest need to be aware of the international legal and human rights framework within which any police service is expected to act.

5. To facilitate such a broad debate, it would be useful to draw on international support mechanisms. A Commission on Policing should be established, drawing together relevant international experience. It would canvas views as widely as possible within and outside Northern Ireland. Given the enormity of change that is involved (the Chief Constable has talked of a halving in numbers) such a body would provide the support necessary to bring about effective change.

6. Specific measures of change are cited throughout this report. The government, or ideally the Commission on Policing once established, should examine the numerous recommendations made here with regard to recruitment, training, mechanisms of legal and political accountability, and structures with a view to developing an overall action-plan for change.

# Appendix 1 : Acknowledgements

**AUSTRALIA:**

**Special thanks to Dr Colleen Lewis, Professor, Centre for Police and Justice Studies, Monash University, Melbourne.**
Michael Barnes, Chief Officer Complaints, Criminal Justice Commission, Queensland; Michael Barnett, Australian Law Reform Commission, Sydney; Peter A. Boyce, Ombudsman for the Northern Territory of Australia, Darwin; David Brereton, Director, Research and Co-ordination Division, Criminal Justice Commission, Queensland; Ann Carson, Research Director, and research team, Wood Royal Commission, NSW; Justice Bill Carter, Police Education and Advisory Council, Queensland; Jennifer Choat, Police Recruitment Branch, NSW Police; Chief Supt. Patrick Cioccarelli, NSW Police; Chief Supt. Cliff J. Crawford, Metropolitan North Region, Brisbane; G. W. Crooke QC, Senior Counsel Assisting, Royal Commission into the NSW Police Service; Dr Chris Devery, Senior Policy Analyst, NSW Police; ProfessorAndrew Goldsmith, Monash University, Melbourne; Paul Herring, Conflict Assistance Group, NSW Police; Professor Ross Homel, School of Justice Administration, Griffith University, Queensland; Supt. Commander, Steve Ireland, Royal Commission Implementation Unit, NSW Police; Inspector Roger Lewis, Queensland Police Service; Paul Lostroh, Acting Superintendent, Queensland Police & Emergency Services Academy; Irene Moss, NSW Ombudsman, Sydney; Sally Moyle, Australian Law Reform Commission; Terry Neilson, Cadet, Queensland Police Academy; Christine Nixon, Assistant Commissioner, NSW Police; Superintendent George Nolan, Acting Dean, Queensland Police Academy; Peter O'Brien, Australian Law Reform Commission; Terry O'Gorman, Civil Liberties Union, Brisbane; Jim O'Sullivan, Commissioner of Police, Queensland Police Service; Sergeant Ovett, Queensland Police Service; Sue Pidgeon, Senior Assistant Ombudsman, Canberra; Dr. Tim Prenzler, School of Justice Administration, Griffith University, Queensland; Inspector Rand, Professional Services Unit, Queensland Police Service; Ann Scott, Queensland Police Service; Inspector Tony Sgrogi, Queensland Police Service; Clive Small, Assistant Commissioner, NSW Police; Inspector Scott Trappett, Freedom of Information Service, Queensland Police

Service; Superintendent Vic Steer, Queensland Police Academy; Dick Warry, Executive Director, Corporate Services, Queensland Police Service; Sergeant Matt Wilson, Operational Programs and Procedures, Queensland Police Service.


## BELGIUM:

Professor Cyrille Fijnaut, Katholieke Universiteit, Leuven; Frank Vefbruggen, Katholielke Universiteit, Leuven; Staff at Ligue des Droits de l'Homme, Brussels.


## CANADA:

**Special thanks to Dr. Tammy Landau and Dr Willem de Lint, Centre for Criminology, University of Toronto.**
Allan Borovoy and colleagues, Canadian Civil Liberties Union; CACOLE - Canadian Association for Civilian Oversight of Law Enforcement; D. G. Cleveland, Assistant Commissioner, Director of Personnel, Royal Canadian Mounted Police; M.R. Cleveland, Staff Inspector, Internal Affairs, Metropolitan Toronto Police; Bernard Cloutier, Directeur Exécutif, Comité Externe d'Examen de la Gendarmerie Royale du Canada; John. L. Evans, Associé Principal, Le Centre International pour Reforme du Droit Criminel et la Politique en Matiere de Justice Penal, Vancouver; Claude. J. L. Gauthier, Inspecteur-chef Commandant, Division des Affaires Internes, Communauté Urbaine de Montréal; Frances Gordon, Complaints Commissioner, British Columbia Police Commission, Vancouver; Dr Ross Hastings, Chair, National Crime Prevention Council, Ontario; Frum Himelfarb, Officier Responsable, Gendarmerie Royale du Canada; Joseph Hunter, Deputy Chief of Police, Metropolitan Toronto Police; David Lang, Detective, Public Complaints Investigation Bureau, Metropolitan Toronto Police, Ontario; Gerald. S. Lapkin, Commissioner for Police Complaints, Toronto; Barry Leighton, Soliciteur général, Secteur des politiques, Secrétariat du Ministère, Ontario; Chief Inspector Jacques Letendre, Directeur, Professional Ethics Directorate, Montréal; Constable Vic Lochead, Community

Policing Support Unit, Metropolitan Toronto Police; Jennifer Lynch, Q.C., Présidente interimaire, Comité Externe d'Examen de la Gendarmerie Royal du Canada; Brian McGuinnes, Deputy Chief, Vancouver Municipal Police; Professor Maeve McMahon, Carlton University, Ottawa; Vicki Meikle, Montreal; Murray Mollard, Policy Director, British Columbia Civil Liberties Association, Vancouver, B.C.; Louis Monette, Coordonnateur des services techniques, Direction des relations de travail, Fraternité des policiers et policières de la Communauté Urbaine de Montréal; Louis. Gord Norwood, Acting Inspector, Complaints Review, Metropolitan Toronto Police; Stephen Owen, Q.C., Deputy Attorney General, British Columbia; David C. Perrier, Saint Mary's University, Nova Scotia; Maureen Prinsloo, Chair, Metropolitan Toronto Police Services Board; Célyne Riopel, Director General, Complaints, RCMP Public Complaints Commission; Professor Clifford Shearing, Director of Criminology, University of Toronto, Ontario; Jenny Smet, Agente de personnel, Programme d'accès a l'égalité, droits de la personne et qualité de vie au travail, Communauté Urbaine de Montréal; Philip. C. Stenning, Associate Professor, Centre of Criminology, University of Toronto; Hoanh Van Dam, Responsable, Programme d'accès à l'égalité, droits de la personne et qualité de vie au travail, Communauté Urbaine de Montréal; S/Sergeant Dave Wojcik, RCMP headquarters; Scot Wortley, Assistant Professor, Centre of Criminology, University of Toronto; Peter B. Yeomans, Vice Chair, Public Security Commission, Communauté Urbaine de Montréal, Québec.

## EL SALVADOR:

### Special thanks to Chuck Call and Mike Lanchin

Mirna Perla de Anaya, Judge in Juvenile Court, San Salvador; Victoria de Aviles, Human Rights Ombudswoman, San Salvador; Pablo Escobar Banos, Director, Internal Disciplinary Unit, PNC; Dr Jose Mario Bolanos, Director of the National Public Security Academy; Luis Cardenal, Public Security Commission; Ana Maria Castro, Inspector General's Office, Santa Ana; Benjamin Cuellar, Director of Human Rights Institute, Central American University; Francisco Diaz; Jose Jacobo Flores, Subcommissioner; Ayudante to Director of PNC; Juan Faroppa Fontanna, Political Affairs, UN Mission; David Galindo,

Public Security Council member; Sub-Comisionado Garcia, Santa Ana, PNC; the family of Ing. Carmen de García Prieto; Juan Gonzalez, ICITAP: José Granadina Mejía; Jaime Granados, Head of Family Division, PNC; Elisabeth Hayek, Police Development Project, UN Development Programme; Maria Julia Hernandez, Head of Tutela Legal; Dr Luna, Ombudsoffice for Human Rights, Santa Ana; Jaime Martínez Ventura, Director, The Centre for Application of Law, specializing in PNC; David Morales, Director of Investigations, Ombudsoffice for Human Rights, San Salvador; Henry Morris, Oficial Encargado, UN Mission; Rachel Neild, Washington Office on Latin America; Dr Jesús P Rodolfo Majano, Sub Director, Police Academy; Inspector Alberto Rubio, European Community adviser to the PNC; Salvador Samayoa, Public Security Council member; Dr Mario Antonio Solono Ramírez, Magistrate, Supreme Court of Justice; Geoff Thale, Washington Office on Latin America; Victor Valle, Inspector General of the PNC; General Maucicio Vargas; Ruben Zamora, presidential candidate for FMLN.

## NETHERLANDS:

### Special thanks to  Peter Klerks
Anita Hazenberg, European Network for Policewomen, Amersfoort; Dr Oskar Huurdeman, Social Science Research Department, Regional Police Force, The Hague; Robin Lindthorst, Netherlands Police Institute, Department of International Relations; Dr Jan Naeye, Amsterdam; Peter Oudenhoven, Police Selection and Training Centre, Amersfoort; Dr. Kees Van der Kijver, Dutch Police and Foundation Society, Dordrecht; Renate Van der Veen, Commission for Police Complaints, Amsterdam; Frits Vlek, Police Directorate, Ministry of the Interior, the Hague; Dr Sandra Wykjuys, Police Training Centre, Amersfoort; and in the Amsterdam police, Mrs. Winjmalen, R Groenewegen (Complaints Mediator), U Millerson (Complaint Coordinator), Bernard Scholten, (Manager, Public Relations).

**SOUTH AFRICA:**

**Special thanks to Daniel Nina, Programme Manager, Community Peace Foundation, Cape Town, and Peter Gastrow, Special Adviser, Minister of Safety and Security.**
Antony Altbeker, Director, Secretariat for Safety and Security, Pretoria; Professor Kader Asmal, MP; Nico Bezuidenhout, Institute for Democracy in South Africa, Pretoria; Lala Camerer, Crime and Policing Policy Project, Institute for Defence Policy; Chairperson, Community Police Forum, Khayelitsha; John Cloete, Western Cape Community Policing Project, Cape Town; Andre Coetzee, Change Management Team, South African Police Service, Pretoria; Inspector Kat Coetzee, SAPS, Western Cape; Hugh Corder, Professor of Public Law, University of Cape Town; Supt. Ockie Gows, SAPS, Western Cape; Phillip Heymann; Zelda Holtzman, SAPS Change Management Team, Pretoria; Faizel Kader, Anti Corruption Unit, SAPS, Western Cape; Carol Koffman, CCRS Regional Director, Independent Mediation Service of South Africa, Richmond; Marietjie Louw, Station Director, SAPS, Pretoria; Melanie Lue, Co-ordinator, Investigation Task Unit, Civilian Support Component, Pinetown; Neville Melville, Executive Director, Independent Complaints Directorate, Pretoria; Members of IDASA, Pretoria; Duxita Mistry and colleagues, Centre for the Study of Violence and Reconciliation, Institute for Democracy in South Africa, Braamfontein; Joe Mkhise, Ex Community Police Forum and Street Children Project, Pretoria; Mbali Mncadi, Director, Secretariat for Safety and Security, Pretoria; Joey Moses, Lawyer, Cape Town; Jan Munnik, Former Police Reporting Officer, Witwatersrand; Sylvester Rakgoadi, Deputy Director (Policy), Secretariat for Safety and Security, Johannesburg; Janine Rauch, Chief Director, Secretariat for Safety and Security, Pretoria; Research Section, Secretariat, Pretoria; Ricky Rontsch, Regional Co-ordinator, Human Rights Education, Lawyers Committee for Human Rights, Cape Town; Riaz Saloojee, Regional Director, Lawyers Committee for Human Rights, Cape Town; Wilfried Scharf, Associate Professor, Director & Head of Departtment, Institute of Criminology, University of Cape Town; Mark Shaw, Crime and Policing Policy Project Leader, Institute for Defence Policy, South Africa; Stef Snel, UMAC, Cape Town; Roger Southall, Professor Political Studies Department, International Studies Unit, Rhodes University, Grahamstown; Staff and Colleagues at Huis Duveen Van Bothe; Peter Stevens, Community Policing Adviser

(formerly Overseas Development Administration), Cape Town; Wendy Stoffels, Community Peace Foundation, Cape Town; Tom Winslow, The Trauma Centre for Victims of Torture, Cape Town.


## SPAIN – BASQUE COUNTRY AND CATALONIA

**Basque Country: Special thanks to Hans Harms, Citcon, San Sebastían**
Gorka Agirre, Encargado de Relaciones Internacionales PNV; Juan Maria Atutxa, Counsellor of Internal Affairs, Basque Government and Head of Autonomous Police in Basque Country; Xavier Bover I Font, Cabinet Chief, Sindic de Greuges de Catalonia; Beatrix Casares, Faculty of Law, Basque University, San Sebastian; Jesus Conde, Head of Department of Justice, Basque Government, Vitoria; representatives from DENON ARTEAN, San Sebastian; ERNE (police trade union) Castro Inaki (secretary general); Paco Gonzalez Legarreta, (lawyer); Teo Santos (training and studies); Eli Galdos, former Vice Secretary Basque Government, San Sebastian; Juan Gutierrez, Director, Gernika Gogoratuz; staff at the library of the International Institute of Sociology, Onati; J. Gurutz, Faculty of Law, Basque University, San Sebastian; Mikel Korta, Gestoras pro Amnestia, Hernani; Karmelo Landa, member of regional Basque Parliament, Herri Batasuna; representatives from SENIDEAK, Prisoners Families Association, San Sebastian; Enrique Villar Montero, Spanish government representative in Basque Country, Vitoria; staff and students from the Political Science and Sociology Department, German University, Bilbao.


**Catalonia:**
**Special thanks to Francesc Guillen, Police Training Academy**
Angel Abad, Assessor del Conseller de Governacio, Department de Governacio, Barcelona, Bernat Baro Police Training School, Catalonia; Alex Bas Vilafranca, Adviser to the Director, Generalitat de Catalonia; Jordi Bascompte, sots-inspector, Mossos d'Esquadra, Blanes; Josep Canabate, Autonomous University, Bellaterra; J. Dominguez, Police Training School, Catalonia; Isabel Estany, research student, Police Training School, Catalonia; Antonio Gimenez, research student, Police

Training School, Catalonia; Bernat Gondra, Police Training School, Catalonia; Amadeu Recasens, Director, Police Training School, Catalonia.

## OTHER JURISDICTIONS:

**Special thanks to Ralph Crawshaw, Council of Europe; Mustafa Mar'i, Head of Al-Haq Legal Department, West Bank; and Ed Neafsey, Acting Prosecutor of Union County, New Jersey.**
Rogelio Alonso; Christine Bell, Centre for Human Rights, Queens Belfast; Ann Blyberg, Executive Director, International Human Rights Internship Program, Washington D.C; Kevin Boyle, Director, Human Rights Centre, Colcheste; Mike Brogden, Institute for Criminology, Queens Belfast; Keith Bryett, Institute of Criminology, Queens Belfast; Nathalie Caleyron, Queens Belfast; Colm Campbell, University College Galway; Nancy Cardia, Center for Study of Violence, University of São Paulo, Brazil; Donald. L. Casimere, Investigative and Appeals Officer, Police Commission, Richmond, Virginia; Stanley Cohen, Hebrew University, Jerusalem; Christine Collins, Northern Ireland Office; Professor Brice Dickson, University of Ulster; Graham Ellison, Keele University; Michael Farrell, Chairperson, Irish Council for Civil Liberties; Professor Frances, Department of Social Policy and Politics, Goldsmiths University, London; Halya Gowan, UK Researcher, Amnesty International; Gene Guerrero, Citizen Organisation; Steven Greer, University of Bristol; Dr Maurice Hayes; Angela Hegarty, University of Ulster; Phillip B. Heymann, Professsor of Law, Director of Centre for Criminal Justice, Harvard Law School, Boston; Neil Jarman, Centre for Study of Conflict, Coleraine; Professor Colin Knox, University of Ulster Jordanstown; Avraham M. Levi, Identification and Forensic Science, National Police Headquarters, Jerusalem; IACOLE, Eric Lotke, Associate Director, National Criminal Justice Commission, Virginia; Bronwin Manby, Justice, London; Otwin Marenin, Department of Political Science/Criminal Justice Program, Washington State University; Neil McCarthy, Amnesty International, Dublin; Kieran McEvoy, Institute of Criminology, Queens, Belfast; Clodach McGrory, Law Centre, Belfast; National Association of Black Police Officers, USA; Robbie McVeigh, Queens, Belfast; Beverly Milton Edwards,

Queen's Belfast; Timothy Moore; Aogan Mulcahy, Keele University; Jannie Nijwening; Eric S. Nonacs, The Foundation for a Civil Society, New York; Peter Noorlander, Justice, London; Steven Rayner, Amnesty International, London; Nancy K. Rhodes, National Coalition on Police Accountability, Chicago; Sam Walker, University of Nebraska; Simon Rogers; Cristina Soto; Ivan Topping, Senior Lecturer, University of Ulster, Jordanstown; Dermot Walsh, University College, Limerick; Robert Weiner, Co-ordinator, Latin America & the Caribbean, Lawyers Committee for Human Rights, New York; Ron Weitzer, Sociology Department, George Washington University, Washington D.C.; Lynn Welchmann, Al Haq; Jane Winter, British Irish Rights Watchp; Kimberely Wittchow, CAJ intern; and all the CAJ staff and interns, Christine, Emma, Liz, Martin, Paul and Veronica.


**Sincere apologies to anyone unintentionally omitted.**

# Appendix 2: Brief country synopses

## AUSTRALIA – New South Wales (NSW)

**Structure:** New South Wales Police Service: currently 13000 sworn and 3000 non-sworn officers for a vast territory; The trend is towards flattening out the rank structure with more direct reporting relationship to headquarters. Last major reform of structure followed the Lusher inquiry 1981, and new structures are under review.

**Background to Woods Commission (1994-97)** A Royal Commission was set up in 1994 under the auspices of Judge James Wood to look into corruption within the NSW police - its terms of reference extended from employment policy and practice to paedophilia. Parliament decreed that no serving or former NSW police officers were to be involved in the investigation. The Commission initially gave the appearance of being very ineffectual, which disarmed opponents and allowed it to marshal enormous surveillance and hi-tech capabilities to conduct an unprecedented covert operation into police practices and policy, exposing corruption to very senior levels.

An interim report published by the Commission in February 1996 highlighted the fact that a number of watchdog bodies - particularly ICAC (a type of standing Royal Commission) and the Police Board had failed to prevent widespread corruption. The Wood Commission has left a number of legacies, perhaps most importantly a Police Integrity Commission which came into operation on 1ˢᵗ January 1997 and the work of the Ombudsoffice continues as regards complaints. The service itself is struggling with the processes set in train by the Wood inquiry. There has been a fair degree of turmoil and a number of police officers have already left or are in the process of leaving the service. However, the bulk of those interviewed were open to the need to change with a view to drastically rooting out corruption and prevent its occurrence in the future.

**Recruitment:** Trend towards developing a more representative force with a higher level of education. Average class: 50% school leavers, 12% graduates and 38% mature recruits.

**Training:** Training and education is currently undergoing major reform. Despite recommendation from Lusher that training take place on a university campus, the training academy continues to be stand-alone. Presently however there are a significant and increasing number of non-sworn academic staff. As training and specialised programmes develop further up the ranks there is increased input from outside bodies. The initial training for a constable consists of 18 months: 8 units of study; 6 months pre service; and then once attested as a constable, 12 months probation followed by 2 final weeks at academy.

**Civilianisation:** Senior executive positions externally recruited since late 1980s. Senior officers currently looking more to what types of things can be done by non-police officers.

**Representation:** Try to target culturally and linguistically diverse groups - flyers in 19 languages. Anti-discrimination legislation, female recruitment strategy and changes to physical agility testing appear to be effective in that the number of women recruits has increased (by 30.7% in November 1995 and 39.2% in 1996).


## AUSTRALIA – Queensland

**Population:** 3 million inhabitants covering huge land mass.

**Police Organisation: Queensland Police Service:** Around 6500 police.

**Structure:** QPS divided into 8 regions each headed by Assistant Commissioner with budgetary control and much autonomy

**Relevant Legislation:** Criminal Justice Act 1989; Police Services Administration Act 1990; Public Service Ethics Act 1994; Whistleblowers Protection Act 1994; Freedom of Information and anti-discrimination legislation etc.

**Representation:** Currently around 65% of recruits with some third-level qualification; 30% of recruits are women; proactive policies re recruiting from Aboriginal and ethnic backgrounds.

**Training:** Takes place in academy setting. Advisory committee on education consists of former Supreme Court judge, university professors, representatives from Department of Education and wider community. Some interesting training initiatives and models eg Competency Acquisition Programmes. Recently Bingham review made a series of recommendations which highlight some problems remaining.

**Brief Background:** Queensland is widely viewed as a very conservative state. For a period in the recent past, marches were banned altogether, and a huge number of peaceful protesters were arrested for exercising basic civil rights. That situation has now changed and Freedom of Information legislation, equal opportunities and anti-discrimination legislation is now in place. Policing is still very much affected by the legacies of the Fitzgerald Commission (1987-9) which uncovered systemic corruption within the organisation going right to the top. Only around 20 high ranking officers were eventually implicated, but the shock waves are still being felt today.

**Criminal Justice Commission:** The Criminal Justice Commission was set up in 1990. Its remit extends beyond the police, but one of its functions is to monitor that the QPS implement the changes recommended by Fitzgerald. In recognition of its importance it has been very well resourced and combines an Official Misconduct Division, a Research and Co-ordination division and three other organisational units - Intelligence, Corruption Prevention and Witness Protection. Fitzgerald had concluded that these functions were not being fulfilled in any meaningful way and was of the opinion that one organisation should house them all. The CJC is a proactive and independent body which has done extensive and useful work. However, partly due to its effectiveness in exposing some unsavoury dealing between government and the Police Union, it suffered a 10% budget cut and an extremely political public inquiry was set up into the CJC itself .

The inquiry into the CJC came about largely as a result of its remit extending beyond police to people holding office in other areas of public administration and the fact that it has been extremely proactive in a number of ways. Further, the government which regained power in February 1996 and had already been subject itself to investigation following the revelation that, while in opposition, it had entered into a secret "memorandum of understanding" with the police union. The party, in return for political support, is said to have promised to reduce the powers of the CJC on being re-elected. Whatever the truth of this, there are in fact moves underway on the part of government to reduce the CJC's powers. This despite the fact that the Police Commissioner himself has indicated that he would not welcome such a move.

**Transition/Management of Change:** Promotion is no longer based on seniority but merit based. This has encouraged officers to be responsible, motivated and proactive. In the past it was the case that an officer would eventually attain commissioned rank. This is no longer the case.

Many people have left, resigned or gone on long term sick leave. The resistance to change appeared to come most strongly from sergeant/senior sergeant level. This is understandable given that many would feel resistant to being bypassed for promotion. Groups were established to seek views from all ranks before changes were made. Also, the regionalisation of the policing model has meant that authority has been pushed out and down.

## CANADA:

**Structure:** Royal Canadian Mounted Police (the RCMP – commonly called the Mounties) is the federal force with provincial responsibility for all (12) provinces except for Ontario and Quebec which have their own provincial policing. The RCMP also have certain territorial and municipal responsibilities. The RCMP comprises of 20900 members: 15000 regular officers, 2200 civilian support and 3700 public service employees. There are 14 policing divisions each with a commanding officer.

**Main Legislation:** Charter of Rights and Freedoms 1982 and RCMP Act 1986. The Solicitor General is responsible for the RCMP

**Background:** Following three commissions of inquiry, and in the context of the adoption of the Charter of Rights, many changes were instituted in 1980. In due course (in1986) civilian oversight bodies were created – a Public Complaints Commission, to oversee complaints against the police, and an External Review Commission to deal with in-service issues in the non-unionised force.

**Main Issue canvassed for this report:** New training models adopted after wide consultative process.

**Other police forces interviewed:** Surete de Quebec; Montreal Urbain and Toronto Metropolitan.

**Issues discussed -** training, civilian oversight and representation issues; Security Intelligence Review Committee which is of particular interest as model for intelligence oversight.

## EL SALVADOR[239]

The transformation of policing in El Salvador was an essential part of the peace process there.   The 12 year civil war which preceded the negotiations had left over 75,000 people (mostly non-combatants) dead.   Both police and army had been implicated in torture and murder and it was essential that radical changes in policing be made if confidence in the settlement was to be achieved.  Policing, therefore, was a key element in the negotiations which lasted from 1989 to 1992 between the government of President Cristiani and the armed opposition group, the FMLN.   The final Accordwas the result of compromise and negotiation: the police was disbanded and a new force created, drawing its membership from both former guerillas and former security forces.   Recruitment was based on quotas of 20% former FMLN fighters, 20% former security force members and 60% civilians.

The PNC (National Police) is explicitly described as apolitical in the constitution.   Art 211 says "The Armed Forces is a permanent institution at the service of the nation."

The United Nations played a key part in the creation and development of the new police at the request of both parties to the conflict.   UN bodies played a vital role in designing the structure, laws, doctrine and entry criteria for the new police service (the PNC). After the Accords, the UN monitored the training and practice of the new police.

The police in El Salvador are responsible to the Ministry of Public Security, as is the Director and staff of the police training academy. The Inspector General of the PNC reports directly to the Minister and is named by him with the approval of the Attorney General and the Human Rights Ombudswoman.   The Legislative Assembly has three important powers in relation to policing.   First it has the right to remove from office the Director General of the PNC for violations of human rights.   Second, the legislature has control over passage of the budget for public security.   Third it has the power to call the director of the PNC to testify before legislative committees.

The first units of the PNC were deployed in March 1993, and numbers had reached about 9,000 by February 1996.   The aim is to create a force of around 20,000 members. The PNC is the first police

---

[239] Much of the information for this segment comes from a background paper produced for CAJ by Charles Call (Call, 1996).

organisation in El Salvador's history to admit women in any other than an administrative capacity.

The new police is fighting a difficult battle against massive crime waves both in urban and rural areas.

## NETHERLANDS[240]

Policing in the Netherlands underwent a complete overhaul following the passage in April 1994 of a new Police Act. Prior to re-organisation there had been three police forces in the Netherlands:

*Rijkspolitie*: state police for rural areas, responsible to the Minister of Justice. Approximately 13,400 officers. Functions included patrol, traffic enforcement, water traffic, security and policing at airports, crowd-control and criminal investigation.

*Gemeentepolitie* or Municipal Police. 148 municipal forces responsible to local mayors. Around 32,600 personnel.

*Koninklijke Marechaussee* or Royal Military Police, responsible to Ministries of Defence, Justice and Interior. Approx 3,500 strong. This force is responsible for border controls.

The system suffered from a lack of co-ordination and inefficiency. By the 1960s a crisis of policing had arisen, most notably in Amsterdam. A series of government recommendations followed but few were implemented. In the early 1980s there were serious riots over issues such as the eviction of squatters and blockades of nuclear installations. The policing of these protests led to widespread complaints about alleged police brutality. A series of informal Police Complaints Bureaux were organised and run by concerned lawyers and law students to help people file complaints against the police. By the mid to late 1980s, it was clear that change was inevitable, and the entire structure of policing was transformed. A national police force was created with 25 regional forces (ranging in size from 450 - 4,500 officers), and one National Police Service Agency.

Responsibility for policing at a national level lies with the Minister of the Interior. The Minister is responsible for financial matters and for setting minimum standards for the police. On a regional level, accountability is based around a tripartite structure involving the mayor (either the mayor of a provincial capital or the mayor of the

---

[240] Much of the information for this synopsis is taken from Klerks (1993), Benyon et al (1995) and Jones (1995).

largest municipality in the police region) the local chief of police and the chief public prosecutor. The chief of police has responsibility for decision making on day to day policing operations. The mayor is responsible for public order policing. In matters of criminal investigation the police are responsible to the public prosecutor. The triangle meets regularly to discuss policing in the region and important decisions are usually taken together. In each region there is also a regional committee made up of all the mayors together with the public prosecutor. This regional authority has the final say in decisions about the administration of the police force. However, in reality the committees only meet twice a year and have little influence on day to day policing.

Formal structures for dealing with police complaints have been developed through municipal Police Complaints Commissions and the Ombudsman. Affirmative action programmes have been used to increase recruitment and promotion of women and minority groups (including ethnic minorities and gay officers). As a result of pressure from both internal and external sources, the police in the Netherlands have made substantial efforts to improve the representation of women within the service. Key to this process has been the development of the European Network for Policewomen, ENP). The ENP was founded in the Netherlands in 1989 and most of its funds are received from the Dutch government. The Network aims to improve conditions for women within police organisations across Europe and to encourage the recruitment of more women into policing. Its members include police organisations in Catalonia, England (e.g. Hampshire and Essex), Switzerland, USA, Germany.[241]

**NORTHERN IRELAND**

Northern Ireland came into being in 1922 when the six north-eastern counties of the island of Ireland remained part of the wider union of the United Kingdom, and the rest of the island left the union. The latter jurisdiction initially declared itself a Free State and subsequently a Republic. From 1922 until the imposition of Direct Rule by Westminster (the UK seat of parliament) in 1972, Northern Ireland was governed through its own parliament (Stormont). Those in power

---

[241] The European Network for Policewomen is based at Postbus 1102, 3800 BC Amersfoort, Netherlands.

at Stormont from the outset feared the threat inherent in the fact that a substantial section of the population (and indeed the rest of the island) had no allegiance to the new political entity of a Northern Irish state. Nation building therefore involved ensuring the eradication or at least the suppression of this threat, and a strong police force was inherently tied up with defence of the new and disputed jurisdiction.

The police force established for Northern Ireland was the Royal Ulster Constabulary (RUC). Of its proposed 3000 members, a quota system was designed to ensure that a third of its members were Catholic, mainly drawn from the Royal Irish Constabulary (RIC) which had previously policed the whole of Ireland. Another third were to be Protestant, ex-RIC, and the remainder were drawn from *"the Protestant dominated Ulster Special Constabulary, a body established in 1920 as an alternative to the paramilitary Ulster Volunteer Force, though in reality many of its recruits came from the UVF."*(Brewer & Magee, 1991). In practice the Catholic quota was never filled. Representation peaked in 1923 at 21.5% and has since decreased to its present level of 7.5% (the Catholic population of Northern Ireland is approximately 40%).

With the development of the Northern Ireland parliament, moves were quickly made to turn the RUC *into "almost the armed wing of unionism"* (Brewer & Magee, 1991:3). Whereas members of the RIC had been forbidden to join political or religious organisations, the ban on RUC members joining the Orange Order was lifted within 3 months of its inception and a lodge was formed specifically to cater for police membership (Brewer & Magee, 1991; Farrell, 1976). The delegation of a range of highly repressive emergency powers[242] to the police fuelled alienation, given that the powers were used predominantly, although not exclusively, against the nationalist community. These moves quickly led to Catholic/Nationalist communities perceiving the RUC as a partisan force, and a key weapon in Stormont's discriminatory regime (Cameron, 1969). The legitimacy and impartiality of the police were questioned almost from birth.

Much more recently, a pivotal moment for relationships between the police and many within society was the police response to the civil rights movement of the 1960s. There was frequent confrontation between the demonstrators on the one hand, and the RUC and the "B-

---

[242] The Civil Authorities (Special Powers) Act (NI) 1922 provided for internment without trial, sweeping powers of search, arrest and detention; powers to ban demonstrations and newspapers; the outlawing of organisations and many other abrogations of basic rights.

Specials" which assisted them on the other, and a number of well-publicised incidents showed that police were prepared to use unlawful means to quell the rising tide of protest.[243] The Cameron Commission set up by the UK government to examine the reasons for violence since October 1968 found the RUC *"guilty of misconduct which involved assault and battery [and] malicious damage to property"* (Cameron, 1969). In 1970, following the death the previous year of Samuel Devenny from injuries received while beaten by the police, the then Chief Constable Sir Arthur Young admitted that there was *"a conspiracy of silence"* among RUC officers over the identity of police involved in the incident (Bew & Gillespie, 1993: 17).

Pressure was put on the Stormont government to restructure and reform the police force (see the then Prime Minister, James Callaghan's, autobiography and Foster, 1988). Initially, the Hunt Inquiry (Hunt, 1969) led to the passage of the Police Act (NI) 1970, which accepted the principle of a civilianised and unarmed police force and established a Police Authority intended to be representative of the whole community. However, following a short period of disarmament, the RUC was quickly re-armed in the face of continuing unrest. The RUC's role in policing the policy of internment in 1971 gave more cause for alienation from a sizeable proportion of the community. The government established an inquiry under Lord Scarman (Scarman, 1972), but allegations of partisan policing continued.

The prorogation of Stormont and the introduction in 1972 of Direct Rule from Westminster institutionalised a system of QUANGOs[244] which put much of Northern Ireland's affairs into the hands of civil servants, and has served as the basis for the government of Northern Ireland to the present day. *"Northern Irish legislation...previously debated at length...is now largely dealt with by the use of Orders in Council*

---

[243] e.g. see *Fortnight magazine*, October 1988 which commented: *"The [violent] events of October 5th 1968 resulted from inadequate planning and leadership by the organisers of the march, and from stupidity and a breakdown of control on the part of the authorities. But the greater share of the blame lies with those who had the greater power - the Minister for Home Affairs and the Royal Ulster Constabulary"*. Further, *"The media gave widespread coverage to the unrestrained police batoning of demonstrators, including MPs, 'without justification or excuse' according to the Cameron Commission. The perception rapidly developed that something was rotten in the state of Northern Ireland."* (cited in Bew & Gillespie, 1993: 4).
[244] Quasi-Autonomous Non-Governmental Organisations with extensive administrative powers and, being unelected, limited accountability.

*at Westminster which are simply voted through without discussion and often against the wishes of all Northern Irish MPs"*, and the Secretary of State for Northern Ireland (a member of the UK government cabinet) has almost complete control of all major areas of administration affecting the day to day life of the people of Northern Ireland (Bew & Gillespie, 1993:49). This has had profound implications for security forces and citizens alike in terms of accountability structures and legal and political redress for perceived wrongdoing.

Nor did the imposition of Direct Rule resolve many of the criticisms of policing: government reviews have continued into a range of areas concerning policing, but have largely failed to address underlying issues of mistrust and lack of representation within the police (see chapter 3). Presently the RUC draws just under 90% of its regular officers from the male population, and slightly more than this total are from the Protestant community (HMIC, 1996).

Human rights abuses have also continued. These have included:

- allegations of a "shoot to kill" policy in the early 1980s. A major investigation of these allegations by John Stalker of the Greater Manchester Police, completed by the West Yorkshire Chief Contable, Colin Sampson, was dogged by controversy and neither of these reports has ever been made public (Amnesty International, 1994 and annual reports);
- allegations of collusion between the police and paramilitary groupings. Some of these allegations were investigated by yet another police officer, John Stevens (then Deputy Chief Constable of the Cambridgeshire police), but this failed to assuage public concerns in that no officers were held accountable. Again the report's findings have never been made public and calls for an independent public inquiry have been ignored (Amnesty International, 1994; Lawyers Committee on Human Rights, 1993)
- the use of plastic bullets by the security forces, including the police. Plastic and rubber bullets have resulted in the deaths of 17 people (8 of them children) and thousands of injuries (Human Rights Watch/Helsinki 1997);
- the use of stop and search powers which have led to widespread complaints of harassment - largely from the working class nationalist/Catholic communities - but also from loyalist/Protestant areas (McVeigh, 1994);

- powers of arrest and detention for up to seven days without charge or judicial oversight, coupled with the possibility of denial of access to family and legal advice for up to 48 hours.

The paramilitary cease-fires period from 1994-1996 saw some decrease in the application of emergency powers. However, the legislative regime remained essentially unchanged.[245] The fact that during 1995 (the only full year of the cease-fire) the RUC were able to recruit just 35 Catholics to their ranks is an indicator of the extent of the problems faced in developing a truly representative force) (Parliamentary Questions, 12 December 1996).

There have been moves in the RUC towards civilianisation (particularly of administrative and forensic tasks), and recent government consultative documents have emphasised the need for greater professionalisation (NIO, 1996). In an internal review of policing (RUC, 1996), it was also proposed that more power be devolved to divisional level, and that the rank structure be flattened somewhat in the process. It is clear, however, that these proposed changes are minimal. Yet, the Police Federation (the representative body for the majority of RUC officers) has publicly and recently expressed concerns about even this pace of change, and the motivations of those who urge change (19 November 1997). Also, the responsible minister announcing the timetable for new legislation on policing at the annual conference of the Community Police Liaison Committees in October 1997 was at pains to reassure people that *"Contrary to recent speculative press reports 'shock reform' is not on the agenda!"* (punctuation and underlining in original written text). This reaction clearly does not reflect the seriousness of the challenge facing the police service in a society like Northern Ireland. Nothing less than fundamental change will bring about the representative, responsive and accountable police service that is needed.

## SOUTH AFRICA

**Structure:** The South African Police Service is a unitary force resulting from the amalgamation of 11 forces in the early 1990s. There are around 138 000 police officers, 50-60% of whom are black, but black officers form less than 5% of senior management.

---

[245]The Emergency Provisions and Prevention of Terrorism Acts were both renewed during this period.

**Main legislation:** South African (interim and final) Constitution; Police Service Act 1995.

**Background:** In South Africa, blacks form by far the majority population (80%). Apartheid deprived them of the most basic of rights and policing was discriminatory and brutal. Political negotiations began in South Africa following the release of Nelson Mandela from prison in 1989. A political settlement was reached in the 1991 National Peace Accord and this paved the way for a new constitution and South Africa's first democratic election in 1994. In May 1994, Nelson Mandela became President of the Government of National Unity.

By the National Peace Accord, South Africa did not disband the apartheid police but instead, with "sunset clauses", guaranteed all civil servants (including police) their jobs for a number of years.

A number of changes were made to break from the past - including new uniform, rank structure and a new Commissioner who accepted publicly that the apartheid police had been responsible for much brutality and that change was necessary. Changes in senior management resulted from a number of measures - allowing a number of people to leave, retrenching a number of senior officers and bringing in new appointment procedures. Affirmative action schemes were initiated and the concept of community policing embraced as the way forward for South African policing. The government set up new structures and new lines of accountability, while the police brought in civilians to advise and become police themselves. Notorious units within the old forces such as the infamous Security Branch were disbanded and new units renamed.

The process is not without its problems. An unknown number of human rights abusers - including torturers and murderers are still to be found within the ranks of the "new police". Communities understandably find it difficult to work co-operatively with the same people who shot at them and inflicted enormous brutality pre-1994.

A Truth and Reconciliation Commission was set up to try to heal some of the wounds of the past. However, it can only deal with those perpetrators of human rights abuse who choose to come forward. The numbers of perpetrators, particularly police, coming forward has, not surprisingly, been very low.

The constitution guarantees a number of fundamental human rights, and under the interim constitution, each police station was to have a registered community police forum which would discuss areas

of concern and provide guidance for the police. On a political level -
the Minister for Safety and Security is responsible for policing at a
national level. He is advised by a civilian secretariat and also works
closely with senior police management. The ministry is replicated on a
provincial level.  The Human Rights Commission does not have
special responsibility for the police, but its remit does extend to them.
The Independent Complaints Directorate is the body which has
superseded Police Reporting Officers as responsible for complaints.

## SPAIN - Basque Country and Catalonia[246]

Policing in the Basque Country and Catalonia has undergone radical
change since the death of General Franco in 1975.  Historically there
has been a struggle in both regions for autonomy or independence
from Spain, this has taken both peaceful and violent forms.   In
particular, ETA has waged an armed campaign for independence for
the Basque Country and has been responsible for the deaths of over
600 people since 1968.

Franco's dictatorship had been characterised by repression,
including the suppression of the languages of the Basque Country and
Catalonia.  Policing was carried out by the Spanish state forces - the
Guardia Civil (a military force) and the Policia Nacional.  Members
from these forces came from outside the areas they were policing, and
were seen as unwelcome outsiders by local people (particularly in the
Basque Country).  The Guardia Civil lived in military-style barracks,
separate from local communities.

During the late 1970s and early 1980s there were allegations of a
shoot to kill campaign against Basque activists.  Over 50 people were
killed by these groups whose links with the state were strongly
suspected and have recently come under the scrutiny of the Spanish
courts.[247]

Since the 1980s a degree of political autonomy has been won in
both areas.  Local parliaments were created and these had the power
to create their own police organisations.  A local Basque police service,
the Ertzaintza, was officially formed in 1981.  In Catalonia, the Cuerpo

---

[246] Much of the information for this synopsis was provided by Hans Harms in
a background paper for CAJ (Harms, 1996).
[247] See for example, Miralles M and Arques R, 1989, *El Estado contra ETA*.

Mossos d'Escuadra, took responsibility for policing functions from 1994.[248] Both forces are responsible to their respective parliaments.

While policing under Franco had been predominantly military in character, the autonomous police organisations are based on a community/civilian policing model. The researcher was told by numerous respondents that the idea was to create a police service like the 'British bobbies' The process of handing over policing functions from the Spanish state forces to the autonomous police was a gradual process - function by function across the regions. The autonomous forces have grown from a few hundred officers to over 6,000 in the Basque Country and over 2,450 in Catalonia (Benyon et al, 1995:52). The federal forces still retain responsibility for some policing functions. In both regions they still carry out policing in relation to border control, security of Spanish state buildings, and drugs control . In the Basque Country both the Ertzaintza and the Guardia Civil carry out security policing functions, in Catalonia the Guardia Civil have sole responsibility for 'anti-terrorist' policing.

Democratisation, together with the policy of creating and developing autonomous forces, has been quite successful in satisfying the demands of local populations for self-policing and has weakened support for ETA and Herri Batasuna (the political expression of radical Basque nationalism). However, these reforms have ameliorated but not ended the conflict and the ETA campaign continues. This has taken the form of 'Basque against Basque' as not only Spanish crown forces but also members of the Ertzaintza are targeted (sometimes fatally). In turn the Ertzaintza has become increasingly militarised in uniform, and style of policing.

---

[248] The Mossos d'Escuadra has a long history as a local police organisation in Catalonia. See chapter 6 for more details on them and Ertzaintza.

# Appendix Three
## PLASTIC BULLETS & POLICE AUTHORITY SCRUTINY

**July 1996:** In response to CAJ inquiries as to the Authority's role in the matter of contentious marches, PANI wrote that it was: *"mindful that one of its duties is to protect the operational independence of the police and in such circumstances it is for the Chief Constable and his senior officers to exercise their professional judgement in deciding precisely how any particular event might be policed within the law."* In another exchange, the chair wrote: *"The Authority has not considered the use of observers at (marches/protests)... I would have concerns, however, about authorising any action which would result in additional people being in a locality in which disorder is taking place and, thereby, making the task of the police even more problematic"* (CAJ, 1996).These replies suggested that PANI was unwilling to exercise leadership in advance of public order disputes.

**October 1996:** CAJ has a meeting with PANI to convey its concerns about the events of July and August.

**November 1996:** The CAJ publishes The Misrule of Law, a report about policing the summer's events compiled largely from reports of independent observers. Evidence shows that:
- plastic bullets were fired on occasion indiscriminately;
- plastic bullets were fired in contravention of guidelines (above the waist, in non-riot situations, at people not engaged in any public disturbances);
- the number of plastic bullets fired at nationalists (5340) and at unionists (662) raised concerns about the sectarian use of the weapon.

A copy of the report is sent to the Police Authority for comment; no substantive response is forthcoming.

**December 1996:** A PANI discussion of the summer led to the conclusion that - *"Both the Authority and the Chief Constable of the RUC have acknowledged that the events of the past summer have undermined the confidence of people both in the police and the rule of law. The Chief Constable said recently that the damage to relationships with the RUC had been particularly marked within the Catholic community."* (PANI, 1997:8). The Chief Constable gave the Police Authority statistics relating to the number of petrol bomb incidents and refuted charges of sectarian use of plastic bullets in the following terms: *"around 90% (of plastic bullets were) fired at nationalist crowds who were responsible for around 90% of the petrol bombing incidents)"* This contention appears to fly in the face of material collected by CAJ, including that of the RUC Information Office, but *"The Authority accepted the Chief Constable's explanation about the deployment of PBRs (plastic baton rounds/plastic bullets) in July"* (PANI, 1997: 15).

## PLASTIC BULLETS AND
## POLICE AUTHORITY SCRUTINY contd.

**January 1997:** PANI commissioned consultation confirms the serious damage done to confidence in the police in the course of the 1996 marching season and the need for serious action (PANI, 1997).

**January 1997:** Her Majesty's Inspector of Constabulary reports on police use of plastic bullets and confirms many concerns about police training, authority levels for plastic bullet use, and insufficiently rigorous guidelines. A CAJ commentary on HMIC is sent to the Police Authority in February 1997. No response (other than acknowledgements) received until five months later (see July 1997 entry)

**July 1997:** The Police Authority is informed by the RUC of the withdrawal of a batch of defective plastic bullets. The Ministry of Defence apparently knew them to be defective 15 months earlier.

**July 1997:** The Authority responds to CAJ correspondence from November 1996 and February 1997. The reply does not deal substantively with concerns about policing and the use of plastic bullets, but offers a meeting to discuss the review PANI has undertaken into plastic bullet usage. The internal review is apparently nearing completion; CAJ still awaits substantive responses to its many detailed questions.

**August 1997:** The Authority is informed by the RUC that a second batch of defective bullets has been withdrawn, suggesting that pre-testing procedures have not improved. The guidelines for RUC use are finally put into the public domain as a result of a series of Parliamentary Questions in Westminster (as late as 3 April 1997 in correspondence with CAJ, ACPO were describing the guidelines on plastic bullets as a *"document subject to privilege"*, the contents of which could not therefore be described or discussed). Important discrepancies between practice in NI and in England and Wales are highlighted. PANI has not explained why the guidelines were secret, and has not commented publicly on the discrepancies.

**October 1997:** The Authority replies to further correspondence from CAJ to insist that our concerns are being taken seriously, their review of plastic bullets *"has indeed called upon the evidence of those outside the ranks of police officers"*(though no details are given), and that a meeting will be organised in due course.

# Select Bibliography

**Agirrzokvenga, I** (1993) *The Lethal Use of Force by the Security Forces ithe Basque Country*, unpublished paper

**Alderson, J** (1979) *Policing Freedom*, London : Macdonald and Evans

**Alderson J** (1992) *Human Rights and the Police*, Council of Europe Press

**Amnesty International**, *Annual Reports*, 1995, 1996, 1997

**Amnesty International** (1994) *Political Killings in Northern Ireland*, EUR 45/01/94

**Anderson, T P** (1971) *Matanza : El Salvador's Communist Revolt of 1932*, Lincoln NE : University of Nebraska Press

**Ardoyne Association** (1994) *A Neighbourhood Police Service – Ardoyne*, Belfast : Ardoyne Association

**Balbé, M** (1985) *Orden Publico y Militarismo en La Espana Constitucional*, Madrid : Alianza Editorial, 1985

**Bayley, D** (1985) *Patterns of Policing*, Rutgers University Press

**Bayley, D** (1994) *Police for the Future*, New York : OUP

**Baldwin, R & Kinsey, R** (1982) *Police Powers and Politics*, London : Quartet

**Bell, C** (1996) 'Alternative Justice in Ireland' in Dawson, N et al (eds) *One Hundred and Fifty Years of Irish Law*, Belfast : QUB

**Benyon, J, Morris, S, Toye, M, Willis, A & Beck, A** (1995) *Police Forces in the New European Union : A Conspectus*, Leicester : Centre for the Study of Public Order, University of Leicester

**Bew, P & Gillespie, N** (1993) *Northern Ireland: A Chronology of the Troubles 1968-1993*, Gill & Macmillan

**Bew, P, Patterson, H & Teague, P** (1997) *Between War and Peace : The Political Future of Northern Ireland*, London : Lawrence and Wishart

**Bittner, E** (1980) *The Functions of the Police in a Modern Society*, Cambridge, Oeggleschlager, Gunn and Hain

**Boyle, K & Hadden, T** (1994) *Northern Ireland : The Choice*, Penguin

**Braiden, C** (1994) "Policing from the Belly of the Whale" in McLeod & Scheiderman (eds) *Police Powers in Canada: The Evolution and Practice of Authority*, University of Toronto Press

**Breen, R, Devine, P & Robinson, G** (1995) *Social Attitudes in Northern Ireland*, Belfast : Appletree Press

**Brewer, J** (1988) *The Police, Public Order and the State*, London : Macmillan

**Brewer, J** (1990) "Policing in Northern Ireland" in the *The Elusive Search for Peace*, (eds) Giliomee and Gagiano, London: OUP

**Brewer, J & Magee, K** (1991) *Inside the RUC*, London : Clarendon

**Brewer, J** (1992) "The public and the police" in Stringer, P & Robinson, G, *Social Attitudes in Northern Ireland, 2nd report 1991-1992*, Belfast: Blackstaff Press

**Brewer, J** (1993) 'The Policing of Ordinary Crime in a Divided Society' in, *Politics of Crime; Report of NIACRO Conference on Crime Prevention*, Belfast : Northern Ireland Association for the Care and Resettlement of Offenders

**Brewer, J** (1993a) 'The History and Development of Policing in Northern Ireland' in Mathews, N. L, Heyman P. B and Mathews A. S (eds), *Policing the Conflict in South Africa*, University Press of Florida

**British Columbia Civil Liberties Association**, The Democratic Commitment, Vol 27, September 1993, No. 3

**Brodeur, J P** (1983) "High Policing and Low Policing : Remarks about the policing of political activities", *Social Problems*, 30

**Brogden, M** (1982) *The Police: Autonomy and Consent*, New York : Academic Press

**Brogden, M, Jefferson, T & Walklate, S** (1988) *Introducing Policework*, London : Unwin Hyman

**Brogden, M & Shearing, C** (1993*) Policing for a New South Africa*, London : Routledge

**Brown, J** (1993) 'The Costs of Sexual Harassment in the Police' in *How to Combat Sexual Harassment within the European Police Services*: Report of the European Conference 1-4 December 1993, Amersfoort : European Network for Policewomen

**Buckland, P** (1979) *The Factory of Grievances: Devolved Government in Northern Ireland*, New York : Barnes and Noble

**Buergenthal, T** (1994) 'The United Nations Truth Commission for El Salvador', *Vanderbilt Journal of Transactional Law*, Vol 27, No. 3

**Bunyan, T** (1993) (ed.) *Statewatching the New Europe : a Handbook on the European State*, London : Statewatch

**CAJ** (1988) *Police Accountability in Northern Ireland*, CAJ

**CAJ** (1990) *Cause for Complaint: The system for dealing with complaints against the police in Northern Ireland*, CAJ

**CAJ** (1992) *The UK Government's approach to the Irish Language in the light of the European Charter for Regional or Minority Languages*, CAJ

**CAJ** (1992a) *Inquests and Disputed Killings in Northern Ireland*, CAJ

**CAJ** (1993) *A Fresh Look at Complaints against the Police*, CAJ

**CAJ** (1995) *Human Rights : the Agenda for Change*, CAJ

**CAJ** (1995a) *Submission from the Committee on the Administration of Justice to the Police Authority (PANI) Consultation on the Future of policing in Northern Ireland*, August, CAJ

**CAJ** (1996) *The Misrule of Law : A Report on the policing of events during the summer of 1996 in Northern Ireland*, CAJ

**CAJ** (1997) - *Policing the Police: A Report on the policing of events during the summer of 1997 in Northern Ireland*, CAJ

**CAJ** (1997a) - *Commentary on 1996 Primary Inspection report by Her Majesty's Inspectorate of Constabulary with reference to the Royal Ulster Constabulary*, March, CAJ

**Call, C** (1996) *Background Paper on El Salvador's Public Security situation*, written for CAJ

**Cameron Commission** (1969) *Disturbances in Northern Ireland: Report of the Commission appointed by the Governor of Northern Ireland* (Cameron Report) Cmnd 532 Belfast HMSO

**Campbell C** (1996) "A Problematic Peace: International Humanitarian Law and the Israeli-Palestinian Peace Process" in E Schulze.Kirsten *Nationalism, Minorities and Diasporas: Identities and Rights in the Middle East*, London and New York : Tauris Academic Press

**Canadian Civil Liberties Association** (1995), *Summary of Recommendations to Metropolitan Toronto Police Services Board re Police Intelligence Gathering*

**Cashmore, E & McLoughlin, E** (eds) (1991) *Out of Order? Policing Black People*, London : Routledge

**Casteils, J M** (1988) *La Policié Autonómie*, Onati Institute

**Chan, J** (1997) *Changing Police Culture : Policing in a Multicultural Society*, Melbourne : Cambridge University Press

**Chevigny, P** (1996) *Edge of the Knife: Police Violence in the Americas*, New Press : New York

**Cioccarrelli, P** (1996) *Police training - Athens or Sparta: a question of location*

**Cohen, S** (1995) "The Classic Discourse of Official Denial" in *Denial and Acknowledgement: The Impact of Information about Human Rights Violations*, The Hebrew University of Jerusalem : Centre for Human Rights

**Connolly, J** (1997) *Beyond the Politics of 'Law and Order' : Towards Community Policing in Ireland*, Belfast : Centre for Research and Documentation

**Conway, P** (1997) 'A Response to Paramilitary Policing in Northern Ireland' in *Critical Criminology*, vol 8, No 1, Spring

**Costa, G** (1996) *"La Reforma Policial en El Salvador : El Papel de las Naciones Unidas"*, Draft Manuscript

**CPLC - Community and Police Liaison Committees** (1997) *Conference Report*, Belfast : Police Authority for Northern Ireland

**Crawshaw, R** (1995) *Human Rights, the rule of law and policing*, Introductory paper delivered to the Council of Europe seminar "Human Rights and the Police", 6-8 December 1995, Strasbourg

**Criminal Justice Commission** (1995) *Ethical Conduct and Discipline in the Queensland Police Service : The Views of recruits, first year constables and experienced officers*, Queensland, November

**de Lint, W** (1997) *Shaping the Subject of Policing Autonomy, Regulation and the Police Constable*, unpublished PhD thesis, University of Toronto

**Dunhill, C** (ed) 1989 *The Boys in Blue : Women's Challenge to the Police* London : Virago

**Ellison, G** (1997) *Professionalism in the Royal Ulster Constabulary : An examination of the Institutional Discourse*, unpublished D.Phil., University of Ulster

**Ellison, G** (1997a) "Under Fire" in *Fortnight magazine*, June

**European Network for Policewomen** (1993) *How to combat sexual harassment within the European police services*, Amersfoort, ENP

**European Network for Policewomen** (1994, 1995, 1996) *Annual Reports*, Amersfoort: European Network for Policewomen

**European Network for Policewomen** (1995) *Women in European Policing: What's it all about?*, Amersfoort : ENP

**European Network for Policewomen** (undated) *Equal Treatment of Policewomen in the European Community*, Amersfoort, ENP

**Farrell, M** (1976)  *Northern Ireland: The Orange State*, Pluto Press

**Farrell, M** (1983) *Arming the Protestants* London : Pluto

**Field, J** (1995) 'Policing Monitoring : The Sheffield Experience' in Fine, B and Millar, R, *Policing the Miners Strike*, London : Lawrence and Wishart

**Fielding, N** (1995) *Community Policing*, Oxford : Clarendon

**Fine, B & Millar, R** (1985) *Policing the Miners Strike*, Lawrence and Wishart

**Finnane, M** (1990) 'Police Corruption and Police Return : The Fitzgerald Inquiry in Queensland, Australia', in *Policing and Society*

**Fitzgerald Report** (1989) *Report of a Commission of Inquiry Pursuant to Orders in Council : Commission of Inquiry into Possible Illegal Activities and Associated Police Misconduct*, Brisbane : Queensland Government Printer

**Foster, RF** (1988). *Modern Ireland: 1600-1972*, London: Allen Lane

**Giliomee, H & Gagiano, J** (1990) *The Elusive Search for Peace : South Africa, Israel and Northern Ireland*, Capetown : OUP with IDASA

**Goffman, E** (1961) *Asylums: Essays on the social situation of Mental Patients and Other Inmates*, New York: Doubleday & Co.

**Goldsmith, A** (1991) *Complaints Against the Police, The trend to External Review*, Oxford : Clarendon

**Graef, R** (1990) *Talking Blues : The Police in their own Words*, London : Fontana

**Green, P** (1990) *The Enemy without : Policing and Class Consciousness in the Miners Strike*, Buckingham : Open University Press

**Hadden, T & Donnelly, A,** *The Legal Control of Marches in Northern Ireland*, Community Relations Council 1997

**Haines, K** (1997) *Some Principled Objections to a Restorative Justice Approach to working with Juvenile Offenders*, unpublished paper given at National Association of Youth Justice Conference, Shropshire

**Hall, S Critcher, C Jefferson, T, Clarke, T & Roberts, B** (1978) *Policing the Crisis*, London : Macmillan

**Hamilton, A, Moore, L & Trimble, T** (1995) *Policing a Divided Society: Issues and Perceptions in Northern Ireland*, Coleraine : Centre for the Study of Conflict

**Harms, H** (1996), *History and Process of the Creation of the Autonomous Police Forces in Spain*, written for CAJ

**Hayes, M** (1997) *A Police Ombudsman for Northern Ireland?* Stationery Office : Belfast

**Heidensohn, F** (1992) *Women in Control?*, Oxford : Clarendon

**Hemisphere Initiatives/Washington Office on Latin America** (1993) *Risking Failure : The Problems and Promise of the New Civilian Police in El Salvador*, Washington, D.C.

**Hemisphere Initiatives** (1996) *Protectors or Perpetrators? The Institutional Crisis of the Salvadorean Civilian Police.*

**Hillyard, P** (1993) *Suspect Community: People's Experience of the Prevention of Terrorism Acts in Britain,* London : Pluto Press

**Himmelfarb, F** (1991) "A Training Strategy for Policing in a Multicultural Society" in *The Police Chief*, November

**HMIC - Her Majesty's Inspectorate of Constabulary** (1996) *Primary Inspection, RUC : A Report by Her Majesty's Inspectorate of Constabulary*

**Holdaway, S** (1983) *Inside the British Police*, Oxford : Basil Blackwell

**Holiday, D & Stanley, W** (1993) Building the Peace: Preliminary Lessons from El Salvador, *Journal of International Affairs*, Vol 46, No. 2

**Holland, J & Phoenix, S** (1996) *Policing the Shadows,* London : Hodder and Stoughton

**Horgan, G & Sinclair, R** (1997) *Planning for Children in Care in Northern Ireland,* London : National Children's Bureau

**House of Commons,** Home Affairs Committee (1997) *Freemasonry in the Police and Judiciary,* Vol 1, London : HMSO

**Hudson, R C** (1988) 'Democracy and the Spanish Police Forces since 1975', *Police Journal,* vol 61, No 1

**Human Rights Watch/Helsinki** (1991) *Human Rights in Northern Ireland,* New York : HRW

**Human Rights Watch/Helsinki** (1992) *Children in Northern Ireland : Abused by Security Forces and Paramilitaries,* New York : HRW

**Human Rights Watch/Helsinki** (1997) *To Serve Without Favor : Policing, Human Rights, and Accountability in Northern Ireland,* New York : HRW

**Hunt, Lord** (1969), *Report of the Advisory Committee on Police in Northern Ireland* (Hunt Report) Cmnd 535 Belfast : HMSO

**International Commission of Jurists** (1983) *States of Emergency: Their Impact on Human Rights,* ICJ : Geneva

**Johnston, E** (1991) *Royal Commission into Aboriginal Deaths in Custody : National Report : Overview and Recommendations,* Canberra : Australian Government Publishing Service

**Jones, J, Newburn, T & Smith, D J** (1994) *Democracy and Policing,* London : Policy Studies Institute (PSI)

**Jones, T** (1995 ) *Policing in the Netherlands,* London : PSI

**Jones, T & Newburn, T** (1996) 'Policing Disaffected Communities' in *Annual Report of the Standing Advisory Commission on Human Rights,* London : HMSO

**Karl, T L** (1992)"A Negotiated Revolution" *Foreign Affairs,* Spring

**Kennedy, L** (ed) (1995) *Crime and Punishment in West Belfast,* Belfast : The Summer School

**Kleinig, J** (1996) Police Loyalties: A Refuge for Scoundrels? *Police Ethics,* Vol 5 No1

**Klerks, P** (1993) *The State of Europe : A digest of European Police Systems, prison conditions, private security, human rights and civil liberties and the internal security situation in the 1990s,* Amsterdam : Domestic Security Research Foundation

**Klerks, P** (1996) Background paper prepared for CAJ

**Landau, T**(1994) *Public Complaints Against the Police: A view from complainants,* University of Toronto Press
**Lawyers Committee for Human Rights** (1993) Human Rights and Legal Defense in Northern Ireland, New York : LCHR
**Lawyers Committee for Human Rights** (1996) *At the Crossroads : Human Rights and the Northern Ireland Peace Process*, New York : LCHR
**Lea, J & Young, J** (1984) *What is to be done about Law and Order?* Harmondsworth : Penguin
**Lopez Nuila,** Col. Carlos Reynaldo (1993) *"La Seguridad Pública de El Salvador"* Paper delivered at conference sponsored by the Woodrow Wilson Centre of the Smithsonian Institution and Florida International University, October
**Lustgarten, L & Leigh, I** (1994) *In from the Cold : National Security and Parliamentary Democracy*, Oxford : Clarendon
**Manning, P** (1977) *Police Work : The Social Organization of Policing*, Cambridge, Massachusetts Institute of Technology
**Mapstone, R** (1992) 'The Attitudes of Police in Divided Society', *British Journal of Criminology*, Vol 32, No 2, Spring
**Mapstone, R** (1994) *Policing in a Divided Society: A Study of part-time policing in Northern Ireland,* Aldershot: Avebury
**Marais, E & Rauch, J** (1992) Policing South Africa: Reform and Prospects; Centre for the Study of Violence and Reconciliation
**Marenin, O** (1996) *Creating Democratic Police Forces: Goals, Processes and Constraints*, Washington State University
**Marenin, O** (1996a) *Policing Change; Changing Police – International Perspectives*, New York : Garland Press
**Mar'i, M** (1996) *Policing in a Period of Transition: Learning from Palestine,* unpublished paper
**Martin, S** (1980) *Breaking and Entering : Policewoman on Patrol*, Berkeley: University of California Press
**Martin, S E & Jurik, N C** (1996) *Doing Justice, Doing Gender : Women in Law and Criminal Justice Occupations*, California : Sage
**Mathews, Heymann & Mathews** (eds) (1993) *Policing the Conflict in South Africa*, University Press Florida
**Maxwell, G & Morris, A,** (1996) 'Resource on Family Group Conferences with Young Offenders in New Zealand' in Hudson, J et al (eds) *Family Group Conferences : Perspectives on Policy and Practice*, Leidhardt : Federation Press
**McClintock, M** (1985) *The American Connection, Volume One : State Terror and Popoular Resistance in El Salvador* : Zed Books

**McConville, M & Shepherd, D** (1992) *Watching Police, Watching Communities*, London : Routledge

**McVeigh, R** (1994) *Harassment : 'It's Part of Life Here'*, Belfast : CAJ

**McWilliams, M & McKiernan, J** (1993) *Bringing it all out in the open : Domestic Violence in Northern Ireland*, Belfast : HMSO

**Milton–Edwards, B** (1996) 'Policing the Peace : Northern Ireland and the Palestinian Case' in *Contemporary Politics*, Vol 2, No 3, Autumn

**Mitchell, A** (1995) *Revolutionary Government in Ireland : Dáil Éireann 1919-1922*, Dublin : Gill and Macmillan

**Mullan, D** (1997) ed. *Eyewitness Bloody Sunday: The Truth*, Wolfhound Press

**Munck, R** (1988) 'The Lads and the Hoods : Alternative Justice in an Irish Context' in Tomlinson, M et al (eds) *Whose Law and Order : Aspects of Crime and Social Control in an Irish Society*, Sociological Association of Ireland

**NACRO** (1997) Haringey Community and Police Consultative Group, Policing Local Communities: the Tottenham experiment, NACRO

**New South Wales Police Service** (1994) *Working Party Review of Changes to Recruitment Policing and Practice*, New South Wales Police

**Niederhoffer, A** (1967) *Behind the Shield*, New York : Doubleday

**North Report** (1997) *Independent Review of Parades and Marches*, Belfast The Stationery Office

**NIO - Northern Ireland Office** (1996) *Foundations for Policing*

**Northern Ireland Social Research Agency** (1997) Community Attitudes Survey : Fourth Report, Occasional Paper 7, Belfast : NISRA

**Oakley, R** (1995) *Police Training concerning migrants and national minorities*, Paper for Seminar on Human Rights and the Police, 6-8 December 1995, Council of Europe

**Oliver, I** (1997) *Police, Government and Accountability*, Basingstoke : Macmillan

**Oppal Commission Report** (1993), *Closing the Gap: Policing and the Community, volumes I and II*, British Columbia, Canada

**O'Mahony, D, McEvoy, K ,Geary, R, Morison, J & Brogden, M** (1997) *The Northern Ireland Communities Crime Survey*, Institute of Criminology & Criminal Justice/School of Law, Queens, Belfast

**Paisley, I** (1995) "Policing in Northern Ireland" in Kennedy, L (ed) *Crime and Punishment in West Belfast*, Belfast : The Summer School

**PANI – Police Authority for Northern Ireland** (1997) *'A Partnership for Change' : Report on Further Consultation by the Police Authority for Northern Ireland*, December 1996/January 1997, Belfast: PANI

**Pat Finucane Centre** (1997) *For God and Ulster : An Alternative Guide to the Loyal Orders*, Derry : Pat Finucane Centre

**Pollak, A** (ed) (1993) *A Citizens' Inquiry : The Opsahl Report on Northern Ireland*, Dublin : Lilliput Press

**Project Honour** (1996) Draft Report, Queensland Police Service

**Queensland Criminal Justice Commission** (1993) *Recruitment and Education in the Queensland Police Service : A Review*

**Queensland Police Academy** (1993): 'Aborigines and Torres Strait Islanders' *in Australian Society : Race Relations Competency Acquisition Program* CI004, Queensland Police Academy

**RCMP – Royal Canadian Mounted Police** (1992) Basic Recruit Training Review : Report 1 Training Research Section

**Rauch, J** (1992)*"Drill is the Means, Discipline is the End: Basic Training in the South African Police*, unpublished

**Reiner, R** (1992) *The Politics of the Police*, University of Toronto Press, second edition

**Rodes Commission** (1991) *"Informe de la Mision de las Naciones Unidas Sobre la Creación de la Policía Civil"* : Author Files

**Roach, J & Thomaneck, J** (1985) *Police and Public Order in Europe*, Kent : Croom Helm

**Rose, D** (1996) *In the name of the law: The collapse of criminal justice*, Vintage Press

**RUC - Royal Ulster Constabulary** (1996) *A Fundamental Review of Policing : Summary and Key Findings* (undated)

**Ryder, C** (1997) *The RUC, A Force Under Fire*, London : Mandarin, second edition

**Scarman, Lord** (1972) *Violence and Civil Disturbances in Northern Ireland in 1969 : Report of Tribunal of Enquiry* (Scarman Report) Cmnd 566, Belfast : HMSO

**Scarman, Lord** (1981) *The Scarman Report : The Brixton Disorders*, Cmnd 8427, London : HMSO

**Scharf & Van der Spuy** (1996) Final Report of Training Evaluation Group: Pilot Basic Level Training Programme SAP(S) 1995

**Schoonings, K** (1992) *Equal Treatment of Policewomen in the European Community*, Amersfoort : European Network for Policewomen

**Scraton, P** (1985) *The State of the Police*, London : Pluto

**Scraton, P, Jenphrey, A & Coleman, S** (1995) *No Lost Rights : The Denial of Justice and the Promotion of Myth in the Aftermath of the Hillsborough Disaster,* Liverpool City Council/ Centre for Studies in Criminal and Social Justice : Edge Hill College

**SDLP – Social Democratic and Labour Party** (1995) *Policing in Northern Ireland* Belfast : SDLP

**Shearing, C** (1991) *Participatory Policing : Modalities for Lay Participation,* Community Law Centre : University of Western Cape

**Shearing, C & Ericson, R** (1991) "Culture as Figurative Action" in *British Journal of Criminology*

**Simey, M** (1988) *Democracy Rediscovered : A Study in Police Accountability,* London : Pluto

**Skolnick, J** (1966) *Justice Without Trial,* New York : Wiley

**Skolnick, J & Bayley, D H,** *Community Policing : Issues and Practices around the World,* Washington DC : US Department of Justice

**Smith, D J** (1983) *Police and People in London,* London : Policy Studies Institute

**Southgate, P** (1984) *Racism Awareness Training for the Police,* London : Home Office

**Stalker, J** (1988) *Stalker,* London : Harrap

**SACHR - Standing Advisory Committee on Human Rights** (1997) *Employment Equality : Building for the Future,* London : HMSO Cmnd 3687, and annual reports

**Stanley, W** (1996) *The Protection Racket State : Elite Politics, Military Extortion and Civil War in El Salvador,* Philadelphia : Temple University Press

**Stanley, W & Call, C** (1996) "Building a New Police Force in El Salvador", Chapter in Krishna Kumar (ed) *Rebuilding War Torn Societies,* Boulder : Lynne Rienner Press

**Stringer, P & Robinson, G** (eds) (1992) *Social Attitudes in Northern Ireland : 1991-1992,* Belfast : Blackstaff

**Topping, I** (1997) "Public Perceptions and Private Lives - Lessons in Policing, in the *NI Law Quarterly, vol. 48, 2, Summer*

**Ulster Peoples College/ Ultach Trust** (1994) *The Irish Language and the Unionist Tradition,* Belfast: UPC

**United Nations** (1995) "Report of the Commission on the Truth of El Salvador (March 15, 1993)" in *The United Nations and El Salvador 1990-1995,* The United Nations Blue Book Series, Volume IV : New York

**United Nations** (1995) Report of the Secretary General to the Security Council on the Situation in El Salvador S/1995/220

**United Nations/Government of El Salvador (**1994) *Report of the Joint Group on Illegal Armed Groups in El Salvador*
**Waddington, D** (1992) *Contemporary Issues in Public Disorder*, London : Routledge
**Walker, C** (1990) 'Police and Community in Northern Ireland' Northern Ireland Legal Quartely, Vol 41, No 1
**Walker, S** (1977) *A critical history of police reform*, Lexington, Mass: DC Heath
**Walsh, D** (1997) *The Bloody Sunday Tribunal of Inquiry: A Resounding Defeat for Truth, Justice and the Rule of Law*, University of Limerick
**Weatehritt, M** (1986) *Innovations in Policing*, London : Croom Helm
**Weitzer, R** (1992) 'Northern Ireland's Police Liaison Committees' in *Policing and Society*, Vol 2
**Weitzer, R** (1993) 'Transforming the South African Police' in *Studies*, Vol. 16, No. 1
**Weitzer, R** (1995) *Policing Under Fire, Ethnic Conflict and Police Community Relations in Northern Ireland*, State University of New York Press
**Wiley, Manning, P & Van Maanen, J** (eds) (1978*) Policing : a view from the street*, California : Goodyear
**Winston, T** (1997) "Alternatives to Punishment Beatings and Shootings in a Loyalist Community in Belfast" in *Critical Criminology*, vol 8, no 1, Spring
**Wintle, M** (1993) *The History of the Development of Democratic and Policing Institutions in the Netherlands*, University of Hull : unpublished
**WOLA -Washington Office on Latin America** (1995*), Demilitarizing Public Order, The International community, Police Reform and Human Rights in Central America and Haiti*, WOLA.
**Wood JRT** (1996) Royal Commission into the New South Wales Police Service, Interim Report (February)
**Wood, JRT** (1996a) Royal Commission into the New South Wales Police Service: Immediate Measures for the Reform of the Police Service in New South Wales (October)
**Wood, JRT** (1997), Royal Commisson into the New South Wales Police Service: Final Report

# CAJ Publications list

No. 1    **The Administration of Justice in Northern Ireland:** the proceedings of a conference held in Belfast on June 13th, 1981 (no longer in print)

No. 2    **Emergency Laws in Northern Ireland:** a conference report, 1982 (no longer in print)

No. 3    **Complaints Against the Police in Northern Ireland**, 1982, £2.50

No. 4    **Procedures for Handling Complaints Against the Police,** 1983 (updated by pamphlet No.16)

No. 5    **Emergency Laws: suggestions for reform in Northern Ireland**, 1983 (price £1.50)

No. 6    **Consultation between the Police and the Public**, 1985 (price £3.00)

No. 7    **Ways of Protecting Minority Rights in Northern Ireland**, 1985 (price £4.00)

No. 8    **Plastic Bullets and the Law**, 1985  (updated by pamphlet No. 15)

No. 9    **"The Blessings of Liberty":** An American Perspective on a Bill of Rights for Northern Ireland, 1986 (price £2.50)

No. 10   **The Stalker Affair: More questions than answers**, 1988 (price £3.00)

No. 11   **Police Accountability in Northern Ireland,** 1988 (price £2.00)

No. 12   **Life Sentence and SOSP Prisoners in Northern Ireland,** 1989, £1.50

No. 13   **Debt - An Emergency Situation?** A history of the Payments for Debt Act in Northern Ireland and its effects on public employees and people on state benefits, 1989 (price £2.00)

No. 14   **Lay Visitors to Police Stations in Northern Ireland**, 1990, £2.00

No. 15   **Plastic Bullets and the Law**, 1990 (price £2.00)

No. 16   **Cause for Complaint:** The system for dealing with complaints against the police in Northern Ireland, 1990 (price £2.00)

No. 17   **Making Rights Count.** Includes a proposed Bill of Rights for Northern Ireland, 1990 (price £3.00)

No. 18   **Inquests and Disputed Killings in Northern Ireland**, 1992, £3.50

No. 19   **The Casement Trials:** A Case Study on the Right to a Fair Trial in Northern Ireland, 1992  (price £3.00)

No. 20   **Racism in Northern Ireland:** The need for legislation to combat racial discrimination in Northern Ireland, the proceedings of a CAJ conference held on 30th November 1992, (price £3.00)

No. 21   **A Bill of Rights for Northern Ireland**, 1993 (price £2.00)

No. 22   **Staid agus Stadas Gaeilge i dTuaisceart na hEireann** - The Irish Language in Northern Ireland: The UK Government's approach to the Irish Language in light of the European Charter for Regional or Minority Languages, 1993 (price £3.50/IR£3.50)

No. 23   **A Fresh look at Complaints against the Police**, 1993 (price £3.50)

No. 24   **Adding Insult to Injury?** Allegations of Harassment and the use of Lethal Force by the Security Forces in Northern Ireland, 1994 (price £3.50/IR£3.50)

No. 25    **The States We are In:  Civil Rights in Ireland, North and South -** proceedings of a conference held in Dublin by the Irish Council of Civil Liberties and the CAJ, 1993 (price £3.50)

No. 26    **Civil Liberties in Northern Ireland: The CAJ Handbook** (2nd edition), June 1993 (price £6.00)

No. 27    **"Harassment:  It's part of life here..."** Survey of young people's attitudes to and experience of harassment by the security forces, December 1994 (price £5.00)

No. 28    **No Emergency, No Emergency Law: Emergency Legislation related to Northern Ireland the case for repeal**, March 1995 (price £4.00)

No. 29    **Right to Silence debate**, the Northern Ireland Experience (May 1994) (price £3.00)

No. 30    **Human Rights: The Agenda for Change - Human Rights, the Northern Ireland Conflict and The peace Process** (includes proceedings of a conference held in Belfast on 11th & 12th March 1995), December 1995 (price £3.50)

No. 31    **Fair Employment For All**:  Submission to the Standing Advisory Commission on Human Rights on Fair Employment, February 1996 (price £4.00)

No. 32    **The Misrule of Law:** A report on the policing of events during the Summer of 1996 in Northern Ireland, October 1996 (price £5.00)

No. 33    **Mainstreaming Fairness?**: A discussion paper by Dr. Christopher McCrudden, on "Policy Appraisal and Fair Treatment", November 1996 (price £3.00)

No. 34    Mainstreaming Fairness, **"Policy appraisal and Fair Treatment",** A summary of a consultation process around "Policy Appraisal & Fair Treatment", June 1997

No. 35    **Making a Bill of Rights Stick: Options for implementation in Northern Ireland**, A discussion paper, September 1997 (price £2.50)

No. 36    **Policing the Police:** A report on the policing of events during the summer of 1997 in Northern Ireland, November 1997 (£2.00)

No. 37    **Civil Liberties in Northern Ireland: The CAJ Handbook** (3rd edition) November 1997 (price £7.00)

## Submissions

S1    **Submission to the UN Human Rights Committee "Human Rights in Northern Ireland"**, 1991, (price £1.00)

S2    **Submission to the United Nations Committee Against Torture,** November 1991 (price £1.50)

S3    **Submission to the Royal Commission on Criminal Justice,** November 1991 (price £1.00)

S4    **Submission to United Nations Sub-Commission on the Prevention of Discrimination and the Protection of Minorities**, August 1992 (price £1.00)

S5     **Submission to United Nations Sub-Commission on the Prevention of Discrimination and the Protection of Minorities,** August 1993 (price £1.00)

S6     **Submission to United Nations Sub-Commission on the Prevention of Discrimination and the Protection of Minorities,** August 1994 (price £1.00)

S7     **Submission to Initiative '92,** January 1993 (price £1.00)

S8     **Allegations of Psychological Ill-treatment of Detainees held under Emergency Legislation in Northern Ireland,** February 1993, ( £2.00)

S9     **Combating Racism in NI - Submission to the Central Community Relations Unit,** March 1993, (price £3.00)

S10    **Submission to the United Nations Committee on the Elimination of Racial Discrimination,** August 1993 (price £2.00)

S11    **Combating Racist Harassment in Northern Ireland:** A joint submission by the Chinese Welfare Association, CAJ and the Northern Ireland Council for Travelling People to the Home Affairs Committee Inquiry into Racial Attacks and Harassment, June 1993 (price £3.00).

S12    **Response to the Draft Children (Northern Ireland) Order 1993,** December 1993 (price £1.00)

S13    **Submission to President Clinton "Civil Liberties in Northern Ireland",** 1993 (price £1.00)

S14    **Submission to President Clinton "Civil Liberties in Northern Ireland",** 1994 (price £1.00)

S15    **Response to the NIO Consultation Document "Policing in the Community",** May 1994 (£1.00)

S16    **Response to the Draft Prison and Young Offender Centre Rules (Northern Ireland) 1994,** June 1994 (price £2.00)

S17    **Comments on the Proposal for Draft Local Government (Miscellaneous Provisions) (NI) Order** (Irish Language Street Signs), June 1994 (price £1.00)

S18    **Submission to the United Nations Committee on the Rights of the Child,** August 1994 (price £3.00)

S19    **Comments on the Criminal Cases Review Authority** August 1994 (price £1.50)

S20    **A Major Miscarriage of Justice: The Casement Trials,** September 1994 (free leaflet)

S21    **Selected Examples of Foreign Experience in the investigation of complaints against police personnel,** March 1991 (price £1.00)

S22    **Submission to United Nations Commission on Human Rights,** 1993 (price £1.00)

S23    **Submission on the killings of Pearse Jordan, Gerard Maginn & Patrick Finucane, to the UN Special Rapporteur,** 1993 (price £2.50)

S24    **Submission to United Nations Commission on Human Rights,** 1994 (price £1.00)

S25     **Submission to Joint Oireachtas Foreign Affairs Committee,** 1994 (price £1.00)

S26     **Submission to the Committee on Economic, Social and Cultural Rights,** November 1994, (price £1.00)

S27     **Response to "Learning for LIfe: the Education Service in NI",** 1994 (price £1.00)

S28     **Killings by the Security Forces - an information Pack for Families of Victims,** 1994 (free)

S29     **Proposal for a Draft Police (Amendment) (N.I.) Order,** 1995, (£1.00)

S30     **Submission to the United Nations Human Rights Committee,** June 1995 (price £4.00)

S31     **Submission to the Police Authority for Northern Ireland (PANI) Consultation on the future of policing in Northern Ireland,** August 1995 (price £2.00)

S32     **Submission to the United Nations Committee Against Torture,** Oct. 1995 (price £3.00)

S33     **Submission to the International Body,** Dec. 1995 (price £1.50)

S34     **Response to "On the Record";** the Home Secretary's Criminal Records proposals, Sept. 1996., (price £1.00)

S35     **Submission to the United Nations Committee on the Elimination of Racial Discrimination,** March 1996. (price £1.00)

S36     **Submission to the United Nations Commission on Human Rights,** March 1996. (price £1.00)

S37     **Submission to the United Nations Sub-Commission on the prevention of Discrimination and the protection of Minorities,** 1996 (price £1.00)

S38     **Response to the Draft Race Relations (NI) Order 1996,** August 1996. (price £1.00).

S39     **Fair Employment For All; Commentary on research commissioned by the Standing Advisory Commission on Human Rights** (SACHR) for the Employment Equality Review, October 1996, (price £2.00)

S40     **Presentation to the Organisation for Security and Co-operation in Europe (OSCE) Review Conference, Vienna 1996 on the implementation of OSCE commitments in the human dimension,** October 1996 (price £1.50)

S41     **Submission to the Independent Review of Parades and Marches,** October 1996 (price £1.00)

S42     The **Case for Repeal of the Emergency Law** in Northern Ireland, January 1996 (price £1.50)

S43     The **response to the discussion paper on Committal proceedings in Northern Ireland,** 1996, (price £1.00)

S44     **Response to the Northern Ireland Office (NIO) Consultation paper on Disclosure in Criminal Cases,** August 1995 (price £1.00)

S45     Response to the **Consultative Draft on the Equal Opportunities Commission for Northern Ireland** (EOCNI) recommendations for change to the Sex Discrimination legislation, October 1996 (price £1.00)

S46 **Submission to the United Nations Committee on the Elimination of Racial Dsicrimination,** March 1997 (price £1.00)

S47 **A response to the draft Northern Ireland (Emergency provisions) Act, Code of Practice,** February 1997 (price £1.00)

S48 **Commentary on 1996 Primary Inspection report by her Majesty's Inspectorate of Constabulary with reference to the Royal Ulster Constabulary,** March 1997 (price £1.00)

S49 **Submission to the United Nations Commission on Human Rights,** March 1997 (price £1.00)

S50 **CAJ response to the Draft Criminal Justice (Children) (Northern Ireland) Order 1997,** March 1997, (price £1.50)

S51 **A joint submission by British Irish Rights Watch, CAJ and Irish Commission for Prisoners Overseas on the Situation of Irish Republican Prisoners in the United Kingdom,** March 1997 (£3.00)

S52 **Submission to the United Nations Committee on Economic, Social and Cultural Rights for consideration during the Committee's listing of issues relevant to the UK government report,** May 1997 (price £2.00)

S53 **Submission to the Department of the Environment (NI) on the Draft Local Government (Northern Ireland) Order,** May 1997 (price £1.00)

S54 **Comments on the Drat Criminal Justice (Northern Ireland) Order 1996,** June 1996, (price £1.50)

S55 **Submission to the Forum for Peace and Reconciliation,** 1995( £1.50)

S56 **Submission on the killing of Patrick Shanaghan to the Special Rapporteur on Summary or Arbitrary Executions,** August 1997 (price £2.00)

S57 **United States Congressional Hearings on Human Rights in Northern Ireland – testimony from Martin O'Brien on behalf of CAJ,** June 1997 (price £1.50)

CAJ is a membership organisation. Requests for information and/or Publication orders should be addressed to: **C.A.J.**
**45/47 Donegall St**
**Belfast**
**BT1 2FG**

• **Please note these publication prices do not include the cost of posting**